AT THE FIFTH ATTEMPT

AT THE FIFTH ATTEMPT

JOHN ELWYN

Leo Cooper

First published by Leo Cooper Ltd
Leo Cooper is an indepedent imprint of
the Heinemann Group of Publishers,
10 Upper Grosvenor Street,
London W1X 9PA.
LONDON MELBOURNE JOHANNESBURG AUCKLAND

ISBN: 0-85052-3613

Printed by Redwood Burn Ltd
Trowbridge, Wiltshire

Rhagair

Hogyn cydnerth bochgoch o Gymro oedd yr Awdur yn 1939 yr oedd gyda'i fataliwn yn Ffrainc a phan ddechreuodd lluoedd Hitler rowlio fel caseg eira enfawr tua gogledd Frainc yn Haf 1940 chwalwyd a lladdwyd miloedd o filwyr Prydeining ac yn y gyflafan diddymwyd catrawd yr Awdur.

Dechreuir y stori ymysg hwrlibwrli yr wythnos cyn Dunkirk a gorffena yn dawel ar hen Bont Fawr, Dolgellau yn 1944 gyda'r Awdur yn ymfalchio ym mhrydferthwch bro hardd a rhamanthus yr Wnion a Chadair Idris.

Rhwng y ddau ben byrlyma llanc ifanc nwyfus oedd yn ymfalchio yn ei aelodaeth o'r Gatrawd Gymreig. Gwerinwr i'r carn yw – ef a'i deulu wedi'u naddu o graig mor gadarn a chreigiau Cadair Idris. Mae pob gair a ysgrifennodd yn yr hanes yn adlais o'r weriniaeth syml hon ac o'r cadernid cynhenid sydd yn deillo ohoni. Ar wahan i'r ochr anturiaethus – mae y dull y datblygodd ei alluoedd meddyliol yn y cyfnod tywyll yn batrwm a symbyliad i ieuenctid Cymru – mynnodd hogi ei feddwl trwy ddysgu ieithoed y gwledydd y bu ynddynt – Ffrangeg, Almaeneg, Rwseg a Phwyleg.

Mae cof gennyf am Haf 1936 – mynd am dro heibio Esgeiriau a chartref yr Awdur, Bryn Mawr, Dolgellau a dod ar draws hogyn boch-goch o'r Ysgol Ramadeg wedi gwthio fforch drwy ei droed wrth godi tatws nes roedd hi allan trwy wadn yr esgid. John Elwyn oedd yr hogyn as yr oedd mor dawel a digyffro ynghylch y peth ag yr oedd, fel y tybiaf, ym munudau tywyllaf ei brofiadau yn ystod y bedair blynedd a dreuliodd fel carcharor rhyfel. Un fel yna oedd John Elwyn erioed – ac am fy mod yn ei adnabod fel y cyfryw mi gredaf mai dyma'r unig hawl sydd gennyf i gynnig yr ychydig eiriau hyn.

Mae'r hanes yn ddeniadol i bron bob cenedl yn Ewrop a braint mawr i mi yw cael darllen yn ein iaith ein hunan. Braint fawr i mi hefyd, yw cael ysgrifennu'r Rhagair yma!

(Richard Oliver Jones, "Wenallt", Dolgellau)

BALTIC SEA
DANZIG BAY
Danzig
GERMANY
Stettin
Bydgoszcz
GERMANY
BERLIN
Frankfurt-am-Oder
WARSAW
POLAND
Oder
Neisse
Lublin
Dresden
Goerlitz
Breslau
Lelow
Kielce
Elbe
Münsterberg
Brieg
Czestochowa
Oppeln
Vistula
Sosnowiec
Glatz
Gleiwitz
Katowice
Ratibor
Krakow
Tarnow
Pilch
Moravska-Ostrava
Teschen
Olmutz
CZECHOSLOVAKIA
0 20 100 miles
20 100 km
International frontiers September 1939

Every Man for Himself

'Every man for himself! Every man for himself!'

'What's that? Who is that shouting?'

'The Platoon Commander! "Every man for himself." Let's get out of it, sharp!'

Every man for himself? I had never expected to hear such a cry of despair. Had our Platoon Commander lost his nerve?

A dozen of us had set off at dawn to clear the Germans out of the small hamlet some five hundred yards in front of our defensive position astride the main Boulogne – Montreuil road, about six miles from the former. Apart from a skirmish the evening before and an exchange of fire with a German patrol which alerted us all at about two o'clock in the morning, the night had been reasonably quiet with a most welcome absence of artillery activity, so most of us had managed to get a little sleep.

We were 9 Platoon, 3 Company, 2nd Battalion, Welsh Guards, forming part of the 20th Guards Brigade, which, together with other units, had been given the task of holding back the advancing German columns so as to enable the evacuation of the BEF to continue. Our morale was excellent. We were literally spoiling for a fight and believed we could knock the Germans over like ninepins. In fact some of the lads were saying that they preferred to hold their fire until they could get stuck in with a bayonet. We had been told so many times by our officers that we were much better than the Germans that we really believed it. In one memorable lecture, Colonel the Lord Glanusk, a veteran of the First World War, said that were he to be asked to compare the relative fighting qualities of the average German soldier and a Guardsman he would without hesitation say that a Guardsman was equivalent to six Germans! Is it, therefore, to be wondered that we had such overwhelming arrogance and such misplaced self-confidence?

What did Lord Glanusk mean by such nonsense? Did he believe it himself?

Our fighting patrol, all volunteers, twelve strong and led by the Platoon Commander, set off at dawn towards the cluster of houses occupied by the enemy during the night, but before we had gone a hundred yards several tanks trundled out of the hamlet and sent a hail of machine-gun fire in our direction. This caused us to beat a hasty retreat to our prepared positions. From behind the tanks appeared the German infantry and the battle began.

Fortunately we had a two-pounder anti-tank gun, a mere pea-shooter compared to the guns that came into service later in the war, but, nevertheless, quite effective against the tanks then in use by the Germans. In a short time two of the tanks had been knocked out and the others had beaten a hasty retreat. It was then infantry against infantry, we having the advantage of being behind cover. Before long the enemy were scuttling back whence they came, leaving several dead and wounded behind on the open field.

After a short lull the battle started again, with our 7 and 8 Platoons, who were dug in on either side of us, being heavily engaged. From the increasing intensity of the enemy fire, which now included machine-guns and mortars, it was clear that a major battle was developing. However, we were giving as good as we got and managed to keep both infantry and tanks at bay. The greatest menace were the mortars, which, once they had got our range, started to wreak considerable havoc. However, after several hours of desperate fighting, it was the tanks that finally overwhelmed us. Our anti-tank gun had received a direct hit from a shell; the three men who served it were either killed or badly wounded. As soon as the Germans realized what had happened they drove their tanks right up to our positions and opened up with all they had. I certainly thought my end had come and experienced a few moments of cold, paralysing fear.

It was then that our Platoon Commander shouted:

'Every man for himself!'

This resulted in a panicky dash to the rear across an open field literally swept with machine-gun fire. I and a friend were about to join this panic-stricken flight when we realized that it meant certain death, for we could see those who were dashing towards the cover of a hedge a hundred yards away falling like ninepins.

Behind our trench was a hedge surrounding a garden, at the far end of which stood a house. My friend and I squeezed through the hedge and ran into the house where we were very surprised to find our Platoon Commander, a couple of corporals and six guardsmen. The family, consisting of father, mother and two young children, was also there. The eleven of us in that house were all that was left of a platoon of thirty-six.

The Platoon Commander told us that he hoped we would be able to stay in the house until dark and then make our way through the German lines towards Boulogne where we might join up with the rest of the Battalion.

The firing outside continued unabated, the crump of mortar shells exploding all around. The French family was in a state of panic and wanted to be allowed to leave. Our officer, however, was afraid that the Germans might get hold of them and so discover that we were in the house, so a sentry was posted in front of the door to prevent their escape.

It was then about midday so there was some time ahead before it would be dark enough for us to make our getaway. Since we had had very little sleep in the previous twenty-four hours many of us were soon making up for the loss, myself included.

I don't know how long I slept but I was rudely awakened when a shell hit the upper storey of the house, setting it alight and showering us all with debris. There was no longer any possibility of preventing the departure of the French family. The door was opened and they were allowed to make their escape. That was the last I saw of them until 1960 when, visiting the area, I called at the house which I noticed had been re-roofed. In answer to my knock at the door an elderly man and a young woman with a child in her arms appeared. I explained to them that I had taken shelter in their house in 1940 and I wondered whether any of them were related to the people who lived there then.

'I lived here then,' said the elderly man, 'and I remember the occasion very well.'

'You had two children,' I said, 'a boy and a girl. Did they survive the war all right?'

'Yes,' he said, 'this is the girl,' and pointed to the young woman with the child!

The fire in the upper storey soon drove us out of the house as well. We went out into the garden where there was a small shed and we crept into it. I, being the last to enter, had to be content with sitting across the entrance, where, with my rifle laid across my knees, I soon resumed my interrupted sleep. But I was doomed to get very little sleep that day, for not long after I was awakened by a hand across my mouth and a voice whispering in my ear: 'Hush!

Germans!' Opening my eyes I saw three Germans some five or six yards in front of me in the garden. They appeared to be setting up a mortar. I lifted my rifle to my shoulder and took aim, but just as I was about to call on the Germans to put their hands up the rifle was knocked down by the Platoon Commander who called out, '*Kamerad! Kamerad!*'

The Germans turned towards us. I have seldom seen such a look of fright and surprise on anyone's face. They bolted as one man but our Platoon Commander ran after them, calling, '*Kamerad! Kamerad!*'

The Germans got the message. They stopped in their tracks, whipped out their pistols and came back shouting, '*Raus! Raus! Schnell!*'

We simply gave ourselves up. We, eleven proud Guardsmen, gave ourselves up to three frightened Germans! But they were not frightened for long. They made unmistakable signs to us to throw down our rifles, to put our hands up and to move at the double along the road towards the crossroads which it had been our duty to deny to them and where a large party of them was now assembled. I wonder if they got a medal for it!

Here an officer took over. Having ordered us to throw our equipment and steel helmets into the ditch, he spoke those words which so many British prisoners were to hear in 1940:

'For you Tommies ze var ist over!'

Having then told our Platoon Commander that he would be held responsible if any one escaped, he pointed inland and told us to start marching. No escort! He just pointed the way to captivity and we took it. We had changed masters and the change-over could hardly have been smoother! It was incredible but true.

Off we went in file, the Platoon Commander leading, the Corporals bringing up the rear, and, being Guardsmen, we naturally marched in step, our arms swinging and our heads held high. The road was full of advancing Germans who stared at us, whether with respect or not I am not sure. Did our proud bearing indicate to them defiance or gladness that 'for us ze var vas over'? I wondered.

It had all happened so quickly, so unceremoniously, so lacking in drama and so different from what I had ever imagined that I felt stunned. I was a prisoner and the war had hardly started! Never for one moment had I imagined that I would ever be a prisoner. Wounded? Yes! Killed? Yes! Prisoner? Never! Wasn't there something shameful in being a prisoner, something singularly unheroic? To be killed facing the enemy and to have one's name on the village war memorial above the words: 'Their name liveth for ever more' was no disgrace; on the contrary; not to be desired, of course, but nevertheless quite romantic. To be wounded, but not too severely – a couple of bullets through the fleshy part of a limb, preferably a leg – there is something quite attractive about a slight limp and a walking stick – and a nice long convalescent leave had a very decided appeal. What a figure one could cut with the women. And with what understatement one could describe the action in which one received one's wound.

But to be taken prisoner, and in such circumstances, in a garden shed! It was more than I could bear. All the more so when, having marched a few miles, we found ourselves in open country surrounded by cornfields stretching as far as the eye could see on both sides of the road and not a German in sight.

I ventured to ask the Platoon Commander why we were marching into captivity instead of escaping across the fields but was told to put the idea out of my mind. We were prisoners, we had been counted and he had been made responsible for us, and that was that. I remonstrated with him but was told to shut up and reminded that I was still subject to military discipline and had better look out. I tried to appeal to the other men, but without success. As far as they were concerned what the Platoon Commander said was law and my behaviour was a serious breach of discipline. I asked to be allowed to escape on my own but not only was that refused but I was told that any attempt would be forcibly prevented. The men were under the impression that, in the event of anybody escaping, the Platoon Commander would be shot. How naive we all were in those days and how abysmally unprepared for war, not to mention how ignorant we were of what the war was all about and what kind of enemy we were fighting. How foolish I was to allow myself to be persuaded to march voluntarily to a German prison camp. I should have just run off across the fields. It would have been child's play to reach Boulogne where the rest of the Brigade was still fighting.

In the early evening we arrived in a small town. Stopping in the square, not knowing which of several roads to take, for not one of them was sign-posted 'To the German Prison Camp', we looked around. The place was crowded with French people and not a German in sight. There was an air of great excitement. France was undoubtedly collapsing but it had all happened so suddenly that the enormity of it all had not yet sunk in.

In front of us was an *estaminet* and in we went. It was packed with people and I decided there and then that I would take leave of my comrades and lose myself among the French clientele. I sat down on a bench next to a young woman and began talking to her. Although my French at that time was not brilliant, I could make myself understood. It transpired that my companion was a married woman whose husband was somewhere on the Maginot Line. She had not heard from him for a couple of weeks and was very worried about him. She had two children and they lived with her parents in the town in which we were.

It all sounded very promising. I didn't tell her that we were prisoners, merely that we had become separated from our unit in the general confusion and that we might well be taken prisoner if we could not hide up somewhere until the position stabilized. I tried to encourage her and the other people with whom we sat by saying that a mighty Allied counter-attack was in progress and that the advance German columns would soon find themselves cut off. Like a dying man clutching at a straw, they appeared to be only too glad to believe me. We clinked glasses to our imminent victory.

It did not prove very difficult to persuade the young woman to take me home with her and to give me some of her husband's civilian clothes. However, instead of pressing her to leave at once, I allowed myself to be persuaded to accept another drink from my newly-found friends. We drank another toast to victory! This was followed by another and another. After that I didn't much care when we left. With every drink my confidence grew. My few hours as a prisoner of the Germans already appeared to be a bad dream. To walk home with the sympathetic and attractive young woman was an adventure well worth anticipating.

My dreams came to an abrupt end when a bunch of German Military Policemen came into the *estaminet* and ejected everyone in uniform. There was no arguing with the machine-pistols they carried. We were lined up outside, counted and, under an escort of motor-cyclists, were literally run out of town, our hands on our heads. If the French laughed at us, they could not be blamed. That we, members of the Brigade of Guards, would submit to that I would never have believed.

Being drunk, I fully appreciated the comedy of the situation. I told the Platoon Commander what I thought of him and made myself very unpopular, not only with my friends but also with the Germans who did not take kindly to my *maleesh* attitude and made some rather threatening gestures. I remember not being at all over-awed and saying out loud, 'To hell with you! I'm not afraid of you and never shall be!' I believe that a change came over me that day; I was never quite the same afterwards and from that time on I tended to rely entirely on myself.

That night we were locked in a church with a number of French prisoners. At dawn we were turfed out and given a huge pig, live, for breakfast. Several Frenchmen soon had the animal dead and disembowelled; a fire of straw removed the bristles and after the carcass had been cut up a devil-take-the-hindmost scramble saw to its distribution. I didn't come away empty-handed but neither the means nor the time was given for cooking. I wrapped the warm pig-meat in leaves and stuck it inside my battle-dress blouse.

Breakfast over, we were herded on to the road and marched away.

That afternoon we arrived in Montreuil where the large town square had been turned into a makeshift POW cage by the simple expedient of surrounding it with barbed wire and posting a few armed sentries here and there. There were probably a couple of thousand prisoners milling about inside the wire; the vast majority were French, but there were a few score British. Among the latter were a few Welsh Guardsmen from our No 2 Company, including my old friend Ted Coope from Denbigh, who, being on the Reserve and a policeman in Salford, had been recalled to the Colours soon after the outbreak of war. We were very pleased to find each other still among the living and teamed up straight away. We were both ravenously hungry and on the look-out for whatever might come our way.

Our chance came that evening. An enterprising French farmer had managed to persuade the Germans to allow him to bring his milk-float into the compound, not to give the milk away to the half-starving prisoners but to sell it to them at an exorbitant price. Ted and I didn't think much of that on principle, so when the extortioner was standing on the back of the float doling out the milk from a large churn I grabbed the pony's bridle, then, suddenly, gave it a hefty smack under the belly which caused it to leap forward. The farmer lost his balance and fell out of the back of the float. Ted immediately jumped in and, grabbing the ladle, filled the mess-tins of everyone wearing a British Army battle-dress, not forgetting his own and mine!

That night we slept on the cobbled square with our boots as a pillow.

The next day, hanging around the main entrance to see what was afoot, I heard a German Underofficer ask for a working party and immediately volunteered, together with some half-dozen French sailors. We were taken out of the compound to a building which until recently had been a British NAAFI store. Outside was a lorry; we were given the task of loading it with the contents of the store.

As an advance of payment for the work to be done the Underofficer stuck his bayonet into a tin of condensed milk and graciously allowed us to share its contents. This we did gulp for gulp and it didn't take us long. We then carried cases of tinned meat, tinned fish, sugar, tea, even cases of Guinness, on to the lorry. Most of the cases were unopened. We were closely watched but I did manage to slip half-a-dozen bottles of Guinness down my trouser-legs and about the same number of tins of sardines inside my battle-dress blouse.

When we finished loading the Underofficer gave us a twenty-eight pound tin of British Army hard-tack biscuit to share between us. We were then taken back to the compound and what a sight we must have presented. I was firmly grasping the tin with both hands while each of the French sailors continuously offered to relieve me of it, which offer I politely but firmly declined. My mind was working overtime trying to devise some scheme whereby I could cheat our gallant Allies of their share.

It didn't prove to be too difficult for who was standing by the entrance but Ted. With a '*Dal hwn, Ted!*' (Catch this, Ted), I threw him the tin. Not being slow on the uptake, he caught it and fled. I was not far behind him. Our gallant Allies let out a howl of rage, but little did it avail them for Ted and I were soon safe in that corner of the compound which the British prisoners had made their own and where it would be very unsafe for a foreigner to trespass!

We thought very little of foreigners of any nationality. Weren't they all a scruffy, idle, treacherous and cowardly lot? Weren't we far better off without them? Hadn't they let us down in two wars? Hadn't the Dutch capitulated in three days and had not my own regiment gone to Holland to evacuate their Queen and suffered many casualties in the process? And didn't Leopold of the Belgians accept an armistice from the Germans without giving us any warning and thus open up a gap on our left flank through which the German armoured columns poured? And the French? Whole armies had given themselves up! Didn't we all know someone who had actually seen French civilians firing on our troops or signalling their positions to the enemy? A treacherous lot, not to be trusted on any account! Were we not perhaps fighting on the wrong side? The Jerries were better people than the Frogs, of that we had no doubt. They were good soldiers too, almost as good as us! We should have learnt our lesson after the First World War. The ordinary people had; it was only our stupid politicians who had dragged us into a war against Germany on behalf of Poland, a country about which we knew nothing and cared even less.

That was what I thought at the time and I doubt whether a single soldier in the BEF thought differently.

That night I had a horrible experience. I was awakened in the early hours of the morning by piercing screams coming from only a few yards away. I sat up in a cold sweat. The screams came from a Senegalese soldier and several of his fellow Senegalese were bending over him and shaking him, but with no effect. An armed sentry walked over to him, whipped his machine-pistol off his shoulder and called out an unmistakable warning. In a matter of seconds the people who had been trying to silence the poor wretch had scrambled out of the way. Now the sentry stood over him. Sensing what was coming, I started to tremble. I trembled so violently that my body literally rattled on the cobbles. The sentry pointed his weapon. I saw him squeeze the trigger. There was a burst of fire at point-blank range. I heard the bullets tear through the unfortunate creature and strike the cobbles underneath him. His last scream choked in a horrible gurgle in his throat. The sentry ordered the body to be dragged away. I slept no more that night.

The following day the prisoners were assembled in a column ready to march off on the long, long trail to Germany. It was raining; all that Ted and I had on was our battle-dress; we had neither coat nor headgear, while only a few yards away a couple of Dutchmen were sharing a British Army gas-cape – a long and voluminous article completely waterproof. There were something wrong somewhere! We were British, the gas-cape was British, *ipso facto* it was ours. We went to the Dutchmen and explained the simple fact to them, expecting them to hand it over without demur. An apology for giving us the trouble of asking for it would not be out of place either. Imagine our surprise when neither gas-cape nor apology was forthcoming! The situation obviously called for other and more direct measures. We grabbed the cape. The Dutchmen had the temerity to hold on to it and indulge in a tug-of-war. Did they imagine for one moment that Ted and I would lower ourselves to such an extent as to play such a silly game with a couple of foreigners? They found how mistaken they were when we really set about them. And weren't we surprised when they dared to defend themselves and even to fight back? A couple of foreigners standing up to a couple of Guardsmen! They didn't stand up for very long, although we had to admit, albeit grudgingly, that they showed more pluck than we expected. Anyway the cape was now ours and we marched under it, side by side, all that day and kept dry.

Towards early evening we reached the outskirts of the town of Hesdin and were 'laagered' in a low-lying meadow by the river. The downpour which had continued non-stop all day had caused the river to overflow its banks and to turn the meadow into a soggy marsh. There were thousands of us in the field and the prospect of having to stay there until dawn the following day was appalling. The side of the meadow furthest from the river sloped upwards towards the road along which ran a wall. That was the place to be and it was the place everyone made for. But, of course, there wasn't room for everyone there, so a struggle developed, a struggle which only the strongest and most determined won. Among those were Ted and I and our fellow guardsmen, Welsh and Coldstream.

Food was the next thing. The Germans issued no rations. That is quite understandable. The German Army had no commissariat to feed hundreds of thousands of prisoners. No army has. Had the rations been available the administrative task of issuing them would be beyond the ability of any army.

Because of my modest knowledge of French I undertook the duties of quartermaster; Ted and the others undertook rather more direct duties of a protective nature!

Between us we still disposed of a few Francs. These were handed over to me. What I needed now was someone to run an errand for us. There were several French civilians on the road beyond the wall. I scanned their faces looking for someone I could trust. A middle-aged woman with a shopping basket over her arm caught my eye. I thought she looked the least untrustworthy. I managed to attract her attention and to give her a twenty-Franc note with a request that she buy us some food, preferably bread. She agreed and disappeared in the direction of the town. There then followed a long and anxious wait.

Eventually we saw her returning. She carried a bottle and two parcels. She was obviously looking for us but by now the wall was lined with hundreds of prisoners all appealing for food, scores of them imploring the woman to hand to them her bottle and parcels. I was desperate. I shouted repeatedly at the top of my voice, '*Par ici madame! Par ici! Je vous ai donné l'argent! C'est moi, Madame! C'est moi!'*

It was probably not as grammatically correct as the above but it proved effective. The lady came towards me but was terrified of the scores of out-stretched arms and the imploring and insistent entreaties of their owners. She threw her bottle and the parcels over the wall. There then followed a desperate scramble as scores of men struggled and fought for them. Ted managed to wrest one of the parcels from a Frenchman and I managed to do the same with the bottle. It proved to be red wine, while Ted's parcel contained a whole, round cheese weighing about a pound. I believe they just about saved our lives that night. We stood close together under our water-proof cape with our backs resting against the wall till dawn, alternatively munching a morsel of cheese and swallowing a gulp of wine. We made it last for hours. We could feel every tiny bite and every trickle of wine doing us good, keeping the spark of life alight. We were lucky. We were very lucky. We were relatively dry, we had a wall to lean against. We had life-giving sustenance and when our teeth started to chatter with the cold that preceded the dawn we clasped each other round the waist and shared what warmth our bodies still had. The unfortunate weaklings down on the flat meadow standing in inches of water must have had a terrible time. Those who were too weak to remain on their feet must have either perished or have seriously endangered their health. Throughout the night the struggle to gain the higher ground had continued, those above strenuously resisting the attempts of those below to dispossess them. The evolutionary clock had been put back to the era of the survival of the fittest. Man's primitive instincts had taken over. How thin is the veneer of civilization!

How we welcomed the dawn. What a relief to drag our tired and numbed limbs from that meadow and assemble on the road prior to marching off once more.

I had done a lot of thinking during the night. Initially after having been taken prisoner I had consoled myself with the thought that the German armoured columns had over-reached themselves and had created a salient which presented the Allies with a glorious opportunity for a counter-offensive which would result in us being freed. My faith, however, in that eventuality had by now waned. Moreover, I realized that the further we marched from the front and the weaker we became the more difficult it would be to escape and, since I had no intention whatsoever of marching to Germany, the sooner I made the attempt the better. I discussed the matter with Ted and was most surprised and disappointed when he flatly refused to accompany me.

That morning, as we assembled on the road, we had all been given an International Red Cross Card and told to write on it our number, rank and name. This we had done. The cards had then been collected and would be dispatched to Geneva and from there to the War Office in London. Our next of kin would in turn be notified that we were prisoners of war.

Ted was married and his wife was soon expecting her first child. He knew how desperately worried she would be following the news from France, so the most important thing for him was that she should know that he was still alive. Nothing else mattered to him. He also wanted news that she was all right and if he attempted to escape that would be impossible. Despite my most vehement insistence that our attempt together must surely succeed he was quite adamant.

I therefore had to look for someone else. I didn't think of escaping on my own for the simple reason that I thought a danger shared is a danger less daunting. Time was to prove this theory to be fallacious. Unfortunately it took me far too long to learn that this is so.

The First Attempt

I considered each of my companions in turn before deciding whom I would choose to join me and finally decided on Corporal Price, Welsh Guards. He was about twenty-two or twenty-three, athletic, powerfully built, intelligent, pleasant, in fact an apparently suitable young man who looked as if nothing would daunt him. I broached the subject to him. He said, 'I've been thinking about the same thing for quite some time and I've been wondering whom to ask to come with me.'

His words were sweet music! We discussed the practicalities and, having ruled out an attempt from the night-laager because of the added vigilance of the sentries and of the unpleasant habit the Germans had of mounting a machine gun at each corner of the laager, we decided that an attempt from the line of march would be the most likely to succeed. Having agreed on that, we then discussed when the attempt should be made. Here there was not quite so much unanimity, for, while I favoured an attempt that very day, Price was inclined to stress a wait-and-see policy, that is to say, until a combination of favourable circumstances occurred such as something on the line of march that might attract the attention of the guards, perhaps a low-flying aircraft – a fairly frequent occurrence – plus the existence in the vicinity of suitable terrain, such as a forest or dead ground in hilly country.

I agreed that what Price said made a lot of sense. On the other hand I did not believe that there was much difficulty in making the attempt provided we both remained ready at a moment's notice at all times and were a hundred percent alert so that we could take advantage of any opportunity that presented itself. In addition I stressed that the longer we waited the weaker we would become and that we should hold ourselves absolutely ready from that moment and make a dash for it as soon as we got a chance. We eventually agreed on that.

We were marching in a long straggling column uphill, completely filling the road. Hardly anyone spoke, every ounce of strength was needed to drag one weary leg in front of the other. We presented a picture of utter dejection. The more I looked around me the more determined I was that the sooner I left that demoralized remnant of what once had been the French Army the better. On each side of the column marched the German guards, one every twenty yards or so. Each carried a rifle slung over his shoulder, a knap-sack on his back containing his rations and small kit; hanging from his belt were his mess-tins and water-bottle. Not one of them looked as if he were relishing his extremely boring task. They were mostly middle-aged men, obviously not front-line troops, and if they had once been alert they were no longer so; the need for alertness had long since passed. The prisoners were far too weary and demoralized to think of escaping.

Price and I walked side by side on the edge of the road. We were absolutely keyed up and ready at the first opportunity. The terrain was such as Price had described as being suitable. Below the road on our side was a steep slope leading to scattered copses beyond which was a narrow ravine, the land rising again steeply beyond the small river that flowed through it.

'This is it, Dai!' I said, nodding towards the ravine.

'It looks all right,' he said, 'but what about the guards?'

'You watch the one in front and I'll watch the one behind.'

Both guards were trudging along facing their front, which meant that the one behind would see us were we to make a dash down the slope. We had to wait until he looked back while the one in front continued to look straight ahead. I was convinced the occasion would arise and I was determined that I would not miss it when it did. Sure enough it did. The attention of the guard behind was drawn towards some commotion to his rear, probably a prisoner falling from fatigue, a not infrequent occurrence. With a 'Now for it!' to Price, I jumped from the road and, without looking back, was running down the sloping field. Having reached the copse, I squatted behind a tree and looked towards the road. Price was almost immediately by my side. We had not been seen! I looked triumphantly at my companion and my heart sank. His face was white, his lips trembling, his eyes were full of funk. He was trying to say something but couldn't get the words out. There was no need. The look on his face was far more eloquent than any words could be. I said to him, 'It's all right. You go back. I'll go on on my own.'

Without a word he got up and, without looking, he ran up the slope and rejoined the column. Had he been able to think, he would have realized that he was running a far greater risk of being shot than if he had remained with me. But he wasn't seen and joined the column without a backward glance at the place where I was crouching, feeling lonely and betrayed!

I felt very sorry for myself but never for a moment did I feel like re-joining the column. I kept telling myself that I was far better off on my own, but I didn't find it easy to be convincing for a long time. To give myself something practical to think about I moved very carefully down to the bottom of the ravine, crossed the stream and climbed to the top of the bank opposite, choosing a good position where I could see without being seen. The long, straggling column was still shuffling wearily along the road opposite, the guards moving unconcernedly alongside it. I looked beyond the bank to see what lay ahead – an unending vista of cornfields, not a hedge in sight, no building anywhere, merely the limitless French *campagne*, ending in an indistinct blur of bluish haze on the horizon.

I resolved not to move until dark and that was the worst part of it as I had many hours to wait and was far too keyed up to think of going to sleep. I waited and thought of what lay in front of me.

I watched the sun slowly go past its zenith and sink gradually down towards the western horizon. What shadows it threw, and they were very few on that treeless plain, grew ever more elongated. Eventually the first star appeared in the western sky. This was Venus, the Evening Star, the first and brightest herald of the coming night.

I had a fairly good picture in my mind of the geography of northern France and a reasonable idea of my position. I was some sixty miles from the channel coast south of Calais, so Paris was a good hundred miles to the south-west. That is where I was heading, for I believed that the French Army would fall back to cover the capital. It followed therefore that if I were to go in that direction I would be surely going towards the French lines. I should cover a hundred miles comfortably in six days, or rather six nights, for I intended to move only by night and to take no risks whatsoever. I didn't expect to have to travel a hundred miles; within fifty miles at the outside I should come across our gallant Allies. Keeping direction would present no problem; all I had to do was to keep the Evening Star on my shoulder and press firmly on.

With this simple plan clearly in mind, I set off. In the cool night air I felt full of confidence. I was free, master of my own destiny once more. Instead of dragging my feet wearily towards captivity, I was stepping forth boldly towards freedom. I felt neither weariness nor hunger and was truly amazed at my fitness. Very soon I had broken into an easy trot which I kept up for miles without effort. The corn was knee-high and presented no obstacle. There were no hedges, only an occasional ditch across which I leapt easily. Although I had no means of measuring distance I knew I was eating up the miles. I continued non-stop for hour after hour until I saw the first grey streaks of dawn over the eastern horizon. My star had long since faded from sight but I believed that I had held to my course.

There was no sign of life anywhere, the same unending vista of limitless cornfields lay ahead, no human habitation, no sound, no cock-crow to herald the dawn, no sound of a barking dog. I seemed to have the whole world to myself. I continued for another hour or so, but, although it seemed perfectly safe, I decided I would take no risk. Lying down in the green corn, I composed myself to sleep; I was out of sight and would have to remain so for about seventeen hours!

I awoke about midday. The sun was more or less directly overhead. Sitting up I saw black spots in front of my eyes. My head thumped and I ached in every limb. The sun was scorching hot and I realized that it was the cause of my aches and pains. I tore up bunches of green corn till I had a stack of it; then I lay on my stomach with my head underneath to shelter from the burning rays. I decided that the following morning I would ensure that I had a more effective shelter before laying up for the day.

I had many hours ahead of me and nothing to do but lie and wait and think. Before reaching the French positions I would have to go through the German lines. I wondered how far ahead they were. How many miles had I covered during the night? Twenty perhaps? Probably. I would have to be extremely vigilant from now on.

I lay and waited. Eventually the sun started its downward crawl towards the distant horizon. Its rays slanted and lengthened and became less fierce. Not long afterwards I could see the dim outline of my long-awaited star. As the shadows fell it filled out until at last it shone like a beacon low in the western sky.

I got up and resumed my trek. It was warm but not sultry and, had I not been ravenously hungry, I might have enjoyed my forced march. It was forty-eight hours since I had last eaten and I had only had half a pound of cheese then. It must have been over a week since I had eaten anything approaching what might be called a decent meal. Food was to be the number one priority. I had to find something to eat before lying-up the following morning. Where? A lonely farm-house? A hen coop? Anything would do, provided it was food.

I kept going, walking and running alternately and never stopping for a rest. But I could not keep my hunger out of my mind but kept thinking of food all the time. This brought about a kind of delirium. I imagined that an old woman with a basket of apples was walking by my side and from time to time giving me an apple which I munched as I went. The old woman was no stranger, I had seen her before when I was nine or ten years old. She had appeared to me in an abandoned orchard after I had eaten at least twenty, I believe more, unripe apples one hot August afternoon. When I went home and told my parents they looked rather strangely at me and asked me to describe her. I did so and they laughed and said, 'You must have dreamt it! Did you have a little sleep in that orchard? That old woman has been dead for years and years. You must have heard someone talk about her and dreamt that you saw her!'

The ghostly apples must have sustained me well for I kept going until the first grey streaks appeared. Even then I did not stop so determined was I to get some food before hiding-up for the day. I moved forward with the utmost caution, scanning the country ahead for the slightest sign of movement. The first sign of human habitation was the barking of a dog about half-a-mile or so ahead. A very welcome sound; dog meant man and man meant food and I did not intend to be lightly denied.

I marched towards the sound and came upon a farm track which led to a small hamlet of half-a-dozen houses. I stopped and watched for some ten minutes but saw no sign of life. Carefully I approached the first house, a delapidated-looking single-storey affair. I went to one of the windows and looked in. It still wasn't properly light in the room into which I peered so it was difficult to see inside but gradually I was able to discern a bed alongside a wall, a couple of pillows and what looked like a pair of heads. I knocked gently on the window pane. No response. I knocked again a little louder and a head was raised, then an old man sat up in bed. He looked towards the window. I gave another gentle knock. The old man got out of bed and came towards the window. He saw me and stopped dead. I made signs to him to open the window. He did so and I immediately thrust my arm into the room and grabbed him by the wrist, saying, '*Silence, monsieur! Je suis Anglais, prisonnier de guerre. J'ai faim. Donnez-moi du pain s'il vous plait!*'

The poor old man was petrified. His wife woke up and sat bolt upright in bed mumbling incoherently.

'*Les Boches!*' said the old man, '*Les Boches sont ici. Allez-vous-en! Vite! Vite!*'

I told him I would go as soon as he gave me some bread and made to get in through the window.

'*Non! Non!*' he said. '*N'entrez pas. Je vous donnerai du pain. N'entrez pas. N'entrez pas.*'

By now the old woman had joined him and was looking at me in terror, and probably no wonder, for I must have presented a fierce sight. I let go of the old man and both disappeared into an adjoining room, presumably to get the bread.

I waited with great expectations, hoping to be given at least half a loaf and congratulating myself on my great good fortune. I was going to be all right for another day at least!

I waited in vain. There was no sign of the old couple and no sound whatsoever within the house. I moved towards the door. I tried to open it, but it was locked. I knocked but received no reply. Reluctantly I went back to the window, it had been fastened again. Nobody was to be seen in the room. Going round to the other side of the house I found what might have been the back door. It was ajar! The old couple had fled to warn the Germans! The treacherous swine! There was no time to lose. I fled back to the farm track and made for the cornfields, calling down every curse I could think of on the heads of all the French. Never would I trust them again and wouldn't I punish them at the first opportunity! What a sweet thought that was; it almost compensated for the betrayal I had suffered!

Walking along the track pre-occupied with my disappointment I was very soon brought back to reality when, passing a gap in the hedge, I saw, not more than about ten yards into the field, a group of German soldiers cooking their breakfast over a spirit-stove. I tip-toed like a wraith across the gap and broke into a trot, taking the greatest care not to make the slightest sound. Looking for a suitable place to cross the hedge on the right-hand side, I continued on my way. To my horror I saw a couple of German soldiers just coming into sight around the bend some hundred yards in front. Without further ado I pushed through the hedge and sprinted like a hare through the cornfield, hoping that I had not been seen. I carried on non-stop for a good half-mile. Then, having put another two or three miles between me and the scene of my discomfiture, I holed up for the day.

Although the excitement had made me forget my hunger momentarily, its pangs returned, gnawing at my vitals, and that is not a figment of the imagination but something very real, as those who have really hungered can testify. However, I did manage to sleep. Had I not, the seventeen hours wait till dark would have been almost unendurable.

It was mid-afternoon when I awoke. The first thing I was aware of was my hunger. So I swore that come what may I would eat before retiring the following day.

On examining my surroundings I saw a line of tall electric pylons a couple of miles away; they ran exactly NE to SW and quite likely carried electricity to Paris. Keeping direction was going to be no problem from now on. All I had to do was to walk parallel to the line of pylons.

I didn't wait until dark but set off in the early evening, very much on the look-out for something to eat. By now I had realized that there were no solitary farmsteads in France, all the farms were congregated in the villages. I had not gone a couple of miles when I saw a herd of cows in a pasture. Having been brought up on a farm, I could see immediately that they were milk cows, so I hurried towards them. To milk one of them into my mouth would be mere child's play provided the animal could be persuaded to stand still. As I approached them, however, I could see that they were in the process of being milked. A man and a woman sat under a cow each milking into a pail while nearby stood a large container. Without even a '*Bon jour*' or a '*Ca va?*' I walked to the container. It was about three-quarters full of frothy milk. Kneeling on the grass I lowered my head into it and drank and drank. I came up for air a couple of times, the froth dripping off the end of my nose, then carried on drinking until I could literally drink no more. I was almost breathless and my belly was distended. The level of the milk in the container must have dropped nearly a foot. Staggering to my feet I walked away without deigning to give the staring, round-eyed peasantry even a '*merci*' or '*au revoir*'. To hell with them, treacherous French! Perhaps I should have kicked over the remainder of the milk as a parting gesture of contempt!

The belly-full of milk slowed me down but I knew it was going to do me a lot of good in the long run.

Pressing on I came to the edge of a village lying in the low ground to my right and through it ran a road, busy with German military transport. On a path a couple of hundred yards short of the first house I came across a man lying on his back on the grass verge. I examined him – a peasant without doubt, shortish, stoutish, middle-aged, rather unkempt. I addressed him. He opened his eyes and looked at me. I said, '*Je suis soldat anglais. J'ai faim. Avez-vous du pain?*'

He jumped to his feet, balled his fists and rushed at me. I grabbed both his wrists and held him so that he couldn't move and was quite prepared to exert more pressure if he didn't behave himself. I repeated my '*Je suis soldat anglais*,' etc. A complete change came over him. He started to shout:

'*Soldat anglais! Vive l'Angleterre! A bas les Boches!*' and a few other choice slogans. He was as drunk as a newt and I regretted having bothered myself with him at all.

When I let him go he took my hand and tried to drag me along with him saying, '*Venez, camarade! Venez!*'

He wanted me to go with him to his house where he would give me a meal. I asked him to point out the house in which he lived. He did so. It was about a quarter of the way down the street leading towards the crossroads where a German soldier was directing traffic. Feeling that it was most unsafe to go any further with my drunken '*camarade*' I shook him loose and told him that I would wait where I was while he brought me some bread. He took a lot of persuading but when he finally realized that I wasn't going to go with him he started off down the street, turning back every few yards to wave and shout '*Camarade anglais!*' I watched his erratic progress with considerable trepidation. He passed the house he had indicated to me as his home and continued right down to the crossroads, where he went up to the German soldier, caught him by the arm and pointed to where I stood!

At that I was away as quickly as my legs could carry me. That was the last straw! Never again would I ask a Frenchman for help.

I kept going parallel to the line of pylons. Dusk was now falling. Suddenly three aircraft appeared flying very low and at great speed. They were Hurricanes! What a cheering sight! At least the RAF was still fighting! But what a fright I had when machine guns opened up all round, some of them not more than a few hundred yards away. The area was obviously swarming with Germans. As far as I could judge the aircraft were not hit and soon disappeared over the horizon. In the meantime I had thrown myself to the ground and there I stayed until it became quite dark, after which I continued with the utmost caution. It seemed to me that I was approaching the German forward positions and that it was imperative that I go through them before dawn. I therefore quickened my pace.

Not long after that I heard a sound which reminded me of home, the sound of jingling harness and iron-shod wheels moving on a country road. Going very carefully, I arrived at a bank overlooking a sunken lane. The horses and carts appeared – German horse-drawn artillery, big guns drawn by two large draught horses, ammunition tenders, water carts, forage wagons, officers on horse-back, the usual paraphernalia of a horse-battery. I lay on the bank and watched them go past, a mere few feet below me. What damage I could have wreaked with a few hand-grenades!

About a quarter of a mile further on I saw the battery turn off the road and into the cornfields. I followed cautiously and realized from the barking of orders that the horses were being unharnessed and the guns placed in position. Unfortunately for me they were right across the line of pylons. I did not let that deter me, however. Moving forward with great caution, crawling in places, I passed through the gun positions. So near was I to them that I could see the soldiers and the horses. What I saw cheered me; it was a further indication that the French army could not be very far away. Ahead must be the German infantry and beyond them the French infantry. I had to reach them before dawn.

As soon as I was well clear of the guns I got to my feet and ran. I felt better than I had felt since the beginning of my escape and quite confident that I would be with the French by dawn.

Suddenly all hell was let loose and I fell flat to the ground. The guns had opened up and shells were whizzing over my head. Looking around I could see the flash of the guns and hear the report which followed almost immediately and ahead I heard the detonation of the shells. Their target was straight ahead but several miles away. I got up, realizing I was quite safe unless I was unlucky enough to have a 'short' drop near me. That was a risk I had to take. Time was now of the essence. I sprinted on. The next thing was the flash of guns ahead and shells whizzing in my direction. The French were firing back. I could see the flashes in the distance, a little to the right and probably a few miles away. I was caught between a counter-battery bombardment and in much greater danger of a 'short'. The further I moved ahead the safer I would be, so I put on an extra spurt.

The counter-bombardment lasted about half-an-hour, then a

deathly silence fell. Where was the German infantry? They couldn't possibly be much further away. It behoved me now to proceed with the greatest possible caution and to ensure that I located the enemy before stumbling into their midst.

The further I went the more jittery I became. I stopped frequently to listen. Nothing stirred. If there were no German infantry, what about the French? Surely they ought to be somewhere ahead defending their guns and the danger from them was much greater as I was coming from the direction of the enemy. Would they challenge me or would they shoot me out of hand before giving me the opportunity to call out?

The uncertainty was agonizing. Should I hide up and wait for the dawn or should I press on? I couldn't face the prospect of another long day so near the German lines so I decided to continue.

Soon it was obvious that the dawn was not far off. Still no sign of anybody. I seemed to be alone in the world and began to feel that that was indeed the case.

It was getting light rapidly. Peering ahead, I imagined I could see strange shapes and shadows. I went forward in a crouching position ready to drop sideways to the ground and roll away at the first sign of danger. Eventually I could see what appeared to be buildings. Surely they were occupied by someone? I dropped to the ground and crawled forward ready to put up my hands if challenged and to call out '*Camarade*', which would have served for either friend or foe.

But I was not challenged. I stopped and looked ahead. I was approaching a large town. Getting up, I walked forward clinging to the sides of the buildings. I went through street after deserted street without encountering a soul until I came to a large square where I learnt that I was in the city of Amiens. I saw the direction signs – one pointed towards Paris. The shop windows were all boarded up; there was no sign of war damage, so it was unlikely that Amiens was the target of the shelling during the night.

As I was pondering what to do I heard the sound of an approaching motor-cycle. Friend or foe, I wondered. Hiding in a doorway, I waited. A motor-cycle combination drove into the square and stopped by the direction signs. Two steel-helmeted Germans sat on the motor-cycle and another sat in the side-car. Having examined the signs they drove off in the direction of Paris. So Amiens and beyond was in German hands. The Allied front must have been torn wide open. My heart sank. Would I ever reach the French lines? Were there such things?

Whatever the answer was, Amiens was no place in which to linger. I set off in the direction of Paris.

On the outskirts of the town I found myself in a long, straight street bordered on the left-hand side by a row of large, bay-windowed houses standing in their own grounds and on the other by a high stone wall. I walked into the garden of one of the houses and peered through a ground-floor window. Although fairly light outside it was relatively dark in the room into which I looked and it was only with difficulty that I could distinguish what was inside. The room looked to be in disarray and there appeared to be packages piled against one wall and it seemed that there were people lying on the floor. The inmates are about to evacuate, I thought; they have put everything away except the packages they intend to take with them and that is why they are sleeping on the floor. I was about to knock on the window when I caught sight of something in the garden while looking round to ensure that I was not being observed. I went to investigate. It was a German BMW motor-cycle combination. Peering through the window again, it was quite plain that the figures lying on the floor were German soldiers. Another narrow escape! I tip-toed back to the road and hurried from the scene.

Soon I was clear of the houses but the high wall on the left carried on. My thoughts must have been on my recent experience because when a convoy of trucks approached from the rear I was caught completely unawares. The first vehicle was almost upon me and there was nothing for it but to stand my ground and bluff it out. Whipping off my battle-dress blouse I put it over my arm. Then, sticking both hands deep into my trouser pockets, I strolled on as I thought a French peasant might on his way to his daily work in the fields.

The convoy rolled past, each open truck full of German soldiers – lorry-borne infantry most probably and as they went each wooden-faced, bleary-eyed soldier seemed to be looking at me, but without evincing the slightest interest, not even when I waved at them. What a relief!

Soon I was clear of the town. Open fields again surrounded me on both sides. I chose the right-hand side and stepped into the young corn. It was high time that I found a lair in which to lie up for the day.

Some hundred yards or so into the field I stopped dead. Twenty or thirty yards in front I saw a row of about a dozen steel-helmeted heads. Their owners were squatting in the corn. I stopped, scratched my head, turned half-left and continued slowly, only to come across another row of heads across my line of advance, and each one was looking in my direction. I stopped again, had another scratch, started to whistle and made another half-incline in to left. Three hundred yards away was a copse. I walked slowly and, as I thought, nonchalantly, as if I did not have a care in the world towards the copse. About a hundred yards from it I saw several German soldiers emerge, stop and look towards me. I was now completely surrounded. There was only one way I could go and that was back towards the road. This I did, but slowly, as if it were of little consequence, when I heard a shout:

'*Hallo da!*'

I looked and saw a soldier aiming a rifle at me. The game was obviously up. I strolled towards the caller and saw next to him someone examining me through a pair of binoculars. It was the end of the road!

Doullens Prison

When I got to the copse I found it to be full of Germans. An officer who spoke English fairly well gave me a cursory interrogation – name, rank, number, my unit and its present whereabouts. I answered him truthfully, but gave my unit as the Light Brigade which as far as I knew had faded from the military scene since its famous charge at Balaclava and when I told the German that I had no idea of its whereabouts I was telling nothing but the truth, explaining that I had become separated from the main body a couple of nights previously and had wandered about aimlessly. The officer took it all down conscientiously. I naturally did not mention anything about having been taken prisoner but tried to take the attitude that it was all a game in which we were involved, that there was no evil intent on either side and that it didn't really matter who won provided we still remained friends. The German no doubt thought that I was a typical sporting English gent. Little did he know!

When he had finished with me he sportingly handed me over to the care of two young soldiers, both my age, who spoke very good English and who shook my hand and told me how sorry they were that I was a prisoner, adding, however, that I had nothing to fear as I would be very well treated and would be sure to survive the war and return to my loved-ones! Very re-assuring! Then one said, 'Hev you honger?'

When I said that indeed I had they cut several slices of bread from a dark-brown loaf and added to them the contents of a tin of corned-beef, saying that the bread was German but the '*Konserv*' was *englisch* and that they had captured a British Army Supply Column.

If I had to be caught I could not have been caught by nicer people. I would gladly have gone with them in the hope that I could make a get-away on arrival at the front. It was not to be. I was loaded into a half-track, driven to a nearby village and lodged in the school which had been turned into a temporary prison-camp. In it were about twenty young Frenchmen, most of whom seemed to be postal workers and of military age. I must say that they were very kind to me and shared their rations and cigarettes freely. They were well provided for as their relations and friends were allowed to visit them daily and to keep them supplied.

After two or three days there, what with the good food and rest, I was fully recovered and ready for any opportunity that might present itself.

One morning, however, without any warning we were made to assemble on the road outside, provided with an escort of two young soldiers on horseback and told that we were to be taken to Doullens, some thirty kilometres away. As we marched through the village there was a tremendous hullabaloo as the friends and relatives of the young Frenchmen took their last farewells from their dear ones. Some of them accompanied us for several miles before taking their final tearful leave.

My French companions were loaded like pack-horses. The sun was hot and the road long and dusty and they were not used to marching. They demanded frequent halts but that was something our escort was reluctant to allow, explaining that they were charged with delivering us to Doullens before dark. The march was nothing to me particularly since I was travelling light, having nothing to carry but what I stood up in. That state of affairs didn't last for long for I was constrained to shoulder some of the baggage of my heavily-laden companions, something I could not very well refuse to do, since I shared freely in their contents. The escort also lent a hand and long before we reached Doullens their horses looked more like pack-mules than cavalry chargers.

Eventually at a crawling pace we arrived in Doullens and were marched through the forbidding-looking portals of a large civilian prison. Before leaving us the two young soldiers of the escort shook my hand warmly and assured me that I would be well looked after in the prison camp in Germany!

The prison was full of prisoners-of-war, mostly French, although there were some British there as well. I decided to ignore them completely and cling to my new friends. The germ of an idea was fermenting in my mind. The young Frenchmen were convinced they would not be detained very long. They believed the war would very soon be over when they would be released to carry on with their very essential duties. Why shouldn't I be released with them? A shirt from one, a pair of trousers from another and a jacket from a third would soon make me a civilian and surely some sort of papers could be cobbled together? I knew quite a bit of French, what with the bit I had learnt in school and what I had picked up in France. A few weeks' constant practice with my companions and I would be fluent. I spoke Welsh and anyone who can speak Welsh can learn any language! I broached the subject and got an encouraging response. I looked forward to the future with confidence and avoided all contact with the British.

But one Sunday, standing by the huge gates and watching a column of British prisoners arriving, I suddenly leapt forward, for there, with a bandage round his head and supported by two companions, was my old friend from recruit days at the Guards Depot, Caterham, 'Butch' Harris. Harris was in our First Battalion and I had not seen him for six months. He was as surprised to see me as I was to see him. With him were several others from the First Battalion, many of whom had been recruits with me.

That was it. I left my French friends and threw in my lot with my Regimental comrades, blood, after all, being thicker than water. Whether it was a wise move I shall never know. I did at least survive the war. Had I stayed in France I might have landed in the Maquis and shared the fate of many of its members.

The following day I marched out of the prison with my friends in a long column of British and French prisoners. Destination – Germany.

It proved to be a particularly miserable experience. Days and days of marching from dawn to dusk without food, of sleeping in fields whatever the weather, of hunger and weariness. As we went through the villages of northern France and Belgium the women would line the street with their aprons full of pieces of bread and buckets of water in front of them on the ground. Since there could not possibly be enough for us all there was a fierce rush to reach the women. Greedy hands grabbed at them, almost tearing their aprons off and even knocking them over. It was a most unedifying sight and I would be very surprised if the women ventured to repeat the experience with the next column that came along.

The kitchen gardens suffered too. The prisoners went through them like a swarm of locusts and, like the followers of Genghis Khan, they left nothing but devastation behind them.

One evening we were going through a large town, I believe it was Cambrai. I was ravenous. It was raining and there was not a soul in the streets apart from us and our guards. I was walking on the edge of the column, which I always did for obvious reasons. Not more than a couple of yards away were houses. It was evening and I imagined in each of those houses the family sitting down to their evening meal. Food on the table not a few yards away – bread, butter, meat perhaps, cheese, vegetables – food! And so near!

Without really thinking, in one involuntary leap I had left the column, had opened a door, had vanished through it and had closed it behind me. I was in a hallway. To the left was a closed door. I opened it. I was looking into a room in which was a large table. Around it sat five or six people. On it was food. In front of each person was a boiled egg on a plate. I ran round the table, removing each egg and putting it inside my battle-dress blouse. Returning to the door I took another look. In the centre of the table was a dish of tomatoes. I thrust the lot inside my battle-dress and returned to the door. Another look at the table revealed a large loaf in front of what appeared to be Grannie. I laid violent hands on it and siezed it. Then I saw that Grannie had a large knife in her hand – she was probably about to cut the bread. I grabbed that as well. At that the family, who had up till then stared at me in silent amazement, rose as one man and uttered a cry in unison. I released my grip on the knife to which Grannie was clinging like grim death and fled through the door and from thence into the street and rejoined the column.

That evening our group had the best supper for many a day!

On another occasion we were marching through Belgium. It was a Saturday afternoon. I was so hungry my jaws kept champing on nothing and the skin of my belly felt as if it were stuck to my backbone, there being nothing to separate the two. I felt like a wolf ready to tear at anything. Marching along the right-hand edge of the column, I was ready to take any opportunity that presented itself to lay my hands on something to eat. My chance came as we marched past an opening leading to a farm. I had my eyes fixed on the guard marching some fifteen yards behind me. He turned around momentarily. It was enough. I was through the opening and in the farmyard. The first thing I saw was the low wall of a pig-sty. Running to it I looked over and saw a litter of little pigs. I jumped over and grabbed one by the hind legs. Before I had time to jump back again the largest sow I had ever seen came rushing out of the sty in answer to the frantic squeals of her offspring. I jumped onto the wall but before I had time to pull my legs up the sow had seized one of them. To prevent myself being pulled down into the pen I had to let go of the struggling, squealing piglet and then to kick its mother on the snout with my free boot. That, together with the sight of its offspring dashing into the safety of the sty, induced the mother to let go. I retired vanquished.

Looking round the yard I saw a hen-coop. Dashing inside I found two hens, each on the nest. Grabbing them both simultaneously I screwed their heads off and put them inside my battle-dress blouse. Under them were several eggs. They were soon in my pocket and I was running back towards the road. As I did so I passed a guard running into the farmyard, his *schmeisser* at the ready. Before he could point it at me I had plunged into the marching column. The guard fired a burst but whether into the air I don't know for I never bothered to look. Instead I was knocking people over in my hurry to catch up with my companions to let them know what a profitable sortie it had been.

That evening we were turned into a large brick-yard on the outskirts of Bastogne. We found a bucket in which we boiled the fowls and had hard-boiled eggs and chicken broth without salt for supper. No one complained.

The following evening we were marched to the station and loaded on to open trucks. Our party, all British, shared a long low-sided wagon. We were lucky as we all had room to sit down, but just before the train left the Germans shoved about twenty Frenchmen in. There was no room for them to sit. Every attempt they made to do so was resolutely resisted with kicks and threats.

Off went the train. It was soon night and for the poor Frenchmen standing up it was very cold. They renewed their attempts to sit down, this time more strenuously. A general mêlée broke out which ended with several Frenchmen being thrown over the side, '*pour encourager les autres*' as their compatriots might have said. The remainder learnt that discretion was the better part of valour and resigned themselves to a cold and uncomfortable ride. As for us, we thought it was great fun. Didn't they deserve it? Hadn't they let us down?

That was how we thought of things in those days. I wonder if the young people of today see things differently. To a certain extent I believe many of them do. But again when I recall some of the scenes during the Falklands War I'm not quite sure, particularly when I think of the line the popular Press took. We had also suffered from the popular Press and from the rubbishy history we had learnt at school with its overtones of chauvinism and jingoism, and were not the villains in the books we read invariably foreigners? We reap what we sow!

The following morning early we de-trained at Trier in Germany, the old Roman town where the robe for which the Roman soldiers played dice at the foot of the Cross hangs in the cathedral.

Although it was early it was not too early for just about the whole population to have got up to welcome us. We marched through streets lined with people and festooned with flags and slogans. It was as if Trier were still a Roman town reliving one of its triumphs – the return of the Legion, driving before it thousands of captives, among them some of the descendants of Caradog, Caractacus as they would have called him. Among the crowds there might have been a few who pitied us and who were aware of the fickleness of the wheel of fortune, but to all appearance they were in the minority. The majority of the people seemed to be drunk with victory. Any doubts they may have had about Hitler's boasts must have been completely allayed. He was indeed the modern Caesar against whom no one could prevail. In nine months he had conquered Poland, Denmark, Norway, Holland, Belgium and now mighty France and sent the British Army scuttling back to its island refuge, never again to interfere in the affairs of Europe. France, the country which for centuries had been the scourge of Germany, now lay helpless and entirely at Hitler's mercy, and all this achieved at minimal loss. Europe had not experienced anything like it since the days of Napoleon. Was it any wonder that the people of Trier were elated? It was perfectly natural and I cannot blame them for it one bit. I remember how we all cheered when, on the newsreel at the cinema, we saw the German prisoners from the *Altmark* being marched through the streets under naval escort. What a petty triumph that was compared to the one witnessed by the people of Trier.

We were taken to the barracks on the hill and told to form a queue; we were going to be fed! The queue formed early in the morning. It was some ten men wide but as to its length I have no idea for I could see neither its beginning nor its end. All I know is that it did not move all day. We sat on the sandy ground under the scorching sun and just waited, our eager expectation of the morning having worn very thin, the voices of the pessimists drowning those of the optimists.

Some time in the early evening things started to happen. The queue was moving, but very slowly. We dragged our bottoms forward along the ground, by now almost too weak to stand and wanting to preserve what little strength we had for the moment when we would have to stand up to receive our portion.

About two or three hours later we had advanced sufficiently actually to see people who had received their ration, and who, although they had already eaten it, were able to tell us that the expected feast consisted of a mass of boiled barley – very filling they said! Boiled barley was food, wasn't it? We had not expected meat and two veg. or steak, egg and chips!

About midnight we could actually see the cook-house door, guarded by a dozen or so armed soldiers. Just then a rumour spread that the supply of boiled barley was nearly exhausted and that there would not be enough for everyone. After waiting some sixteen hours in the queue this was too much. Primitive instinct took over and in a simultaneous but uncoordinated flood we rushed the cook-house door. But the guards had not been posted there for nothing; with rifle butts flailing they sent us scattering in all directions, leaving some where they lay, no longer having any immediate need of boiled barley.

When the queue re-formed I was some fifty yards further away from the cook-house door than I had been before our ill-disciplined rush. About two o'clock in the morning I reached the door and tried to hand the cardboard token I had been given to the guard who demanded it. Unfortunately, however, it was by now only a sodden mess in my hot and sweaty palm. The guard pushed me away with the words: '*Weg*, Chamberlain! *Gibs nicht!*'

But I rushed back at him and, holding the sodden mess under his nose, shouted, 'Here! Here it is! My ticket!'

At that he put a powerful hand at the back of my neck and gave me such a shove that I landed against the big, fat cook who was ladling out the barley. He, in turn, gave me a crack over the head with his metal ladle until I saw stars. He then smiled at me and filled my mess-tin to overflowing!

Was it worth waiting for? Certainly!

Lamsdorf to Laband

The following day we were marched back to the station where we were issued with a ration of bread of about a pound per man and told to store as much water as possible, for none would be available for a long time. We were then loaded into closed railway wagons, the usual '40 men or 8 horses' type. Unfortunately our captors didn't keep to that scale but squeezed nearer sixty into each wagon.

There then followed three or four days during which the conditions that I imagine obtained in the Black Hole of Calcutta were very nearly reproduced. There was no room for all to sit; there was no question of lying except for those who were very ill and there were a number of them. The only opening for air was a small rectangular hole in the top corner of one side. There were no toilet facilities and the doors, securely fastened from outside, were not once opened. Many of the men suffered from dysentery. The stench was indescribable.

Although we only travelled rather less than five hundred miles, the journey took at least three days. Quite often we were aware that the train was being shunted off the main line; each time this happened our hopes were raised that we had arrived at our destination, only to be later dashed as we felt the process being repeated in reverse before the train was off again. This was probably to clear the main line for traffic which merited a higher priority.

Eventually the train did stop and the doors were opened. Loud shouts of '*Raus! Raus! Schnell!*' left us in no doubt that we were to de-train. However, that was easier said than done, so stiff and weak had we become. We could not step down, let alone jump from the trucks. We had to lie on our bellies and lower our feet gradually on to the platform. It took us a very long time to forgive the Germans for that train journey.

When I eventually got on to the platform I tried to stand up, but I had to sit down quickly, otherwise I would have fallen, for I could see nothing except black spots dancing in front of my eyes and I had that light-headed feeling which accompanies a bout of dizziness. I was not the only one; everyone was sitting down and it took the German guards a long time to get us on our feet. I will admit that they did not use force.

The legend on the platform informed us that we were on Annahof station, which served the very large prison camp of Lamsdorf, later known to thousands of British prisoners. For some it was almost a home from home, for others a grim place. For some it meant the Racket Compound and a full belly, for others the Strafe Compound and a régime of solitary confinement and very short commons.

At last we were got to our feet and set off on the long climb to Lamsdorf camp, stopping very frequently to rest. I was too weak to take much interest in our surroundings but I did notice that we were in the depths of the country surrounded by farmland and forest.

At the top of the long hill we came to what we were to learn was the *Vorlager*, where the main guardroom was located, together with the de-lousing rooms, the search rooms, the security check room, the court-martial room, the hospital, the card-index section and other administrative buildings. Beyond were the big gates which led to the camp proper above which might well have appeared the words 'Abandon hope all ye who enter!'

A wide road ran through the middle of the main camp, on each side of which were large compounds containing three wooden barrack blocks, each containing anything up to five hundred men.

Along this road we marched, or rather were driven, a shambling, dispirited and demoralized rabble, nothing like Caradog and his men marching through Rome proud and defiant with their heads held high. We did not present a picture to inspire confidence in the hundreds of Polish prisoners who lined the wire inside their compound bordering the road. But that did not prevent them from raising a defiant cheer which they kept up despite the shouts and threats of the Germans. Nor did it prevent them from showering on us all their possessions – their bread, their tobacco, their knives, their cigarette lighters, their all!

We were turned into a compound opposite the Poles and issued with a ration of some potatoes boiled in their skin and a slice of bread with a dab of jam on it. Little as it was, it was too much for me; having wolfed it greedily, I afterwards suffered acute stomach pains.

The barrack blocks did not contain beds but there was straw on the floor and a roof overhead. What more could we ask for after what we had been used to during the previous three weeks and more?

That evening the Poles gave us a concert. They lined the wire opposite and sang for us, and how they could sing! They sang folk-songs and patriotic songs, many in four parts, harmonizing beautifully. The Germans didn't try to prevent them; they too, probably enjoyed the magnificent singing. When they had finished we sang for them, one song – 'Just a song at twilight'. How I winced! The parody on Colonel Bogey would have been far more appropriate!

The following day we were photographed and registered. Each was given a POW number; mine was 9982. We also had our hair shaved off. Now our humiliation was indeed complete; we no longer looked like soldiers, more like convicts. People who have never suffered this humiliation cannot know what it does for one's ego.

That evening we were bombastically harangued by an English-speaking officer who informed us that news had just been received of the capitulation of France and that we might all be home by Christmas. This was received by prolonged and tumultuous cheering. I asked a man standing next to me why he was cheering. He replied, 'Didn't you hear him say we'll be home by Christmas?'

'But don't you realize that the fall of France means that Germany has won the war?'

'What the hell do I care who's won the war? All I want is to go home.'

Flag-waving jingoism is clearly not a sound basis for patriotism!

The officer also told us that we would be sent to working-camps where our conditions of work would be the same as those obtaining for civilians and where we would be well fed. Everyone as far as possible would be employed in his trade. This latter bit of information resulted in hundreds of men hopefully registering as cooks or long-distance lorry drivers! That, however, did not prevent the majority from finding themselves down a coal mine.

Soon after that – I remember that it was a Sunday, probably the last Sunday of June, 1940 – I and some five hundred others marched down the long hill to Annahof station where we entrained in cattle trucks. Some two hours later we de-trained at the small town of

Laband, Upper Silesia, and marched to a hutted camp directly opposite the station.

First impressions were very good. The huts were divided into rooms in which stood a dozen double-tiered wooden beds, each containing a straw-filled palliasse and a straw-filled pillow. On the palliasse were a couple of clean, folded blankets. In the middle of the room was a long, strong wooden table and there was a wooden stool for each man. We were each provided with an enamel bowl and a spoon, which we took as a sign that we were going to be fed – always the uppermost thing in our minds. The huts were adequately provided with showers and lavatories.

We were the objects of keen curiosity to the locals as we paraded in the compound prior to filing into the cook-house to receive our rations. I was quite surprised to see how tidy and well-dressed the people looked, not to mention well-fed. It seemed to give the lie to the propaganda we had read in our newspapers back in Britain about Germany's imminent collapse as the result of our blockade. We had heard so much about 'Guns before butter' but it seemed that Germany had plenty of both. What I also particularly noticed about the people was the absence of frowns and scowls on their faces and the absence of jeers and cat-calls. If I read their faces right, it seemed to me that pity was the prevailing feeling they expressed.

We were greatly encouraged by our first meal at Laband: a full bowl of boiled potatoes – peeled, not in their skins, a large slice of roast pork, the lot floating in thick gravy. That was only what we received in one hand. In the other we were given half a loaf of bread, probably weighing half a kilo, and on top of the bread a goodish pat of butter and a piece of smoked sausage two inches in length and an inch and a half in diameter! We were handed our rations by women who, if they did not exactly smile at us, did at least look kindly.

It was in a very optimistic mood that we carried our rations carefully back to our rooms where we placed them on the table prior to sitting down on our stools like civilized human beings. The bad times were over. Hadn't the officer in Lamsdorf told us that we would be well fed and had not those young soldiers back in France told me that once I got to Germany my troubles would be over? It seemed that under Hitler's New Order there was justice for all, including prisoners of war.

As we ate our meal we were loud in our praises of all things German and equally loud in our condemnation of our government who had recklessly declared war on Germany in a cause which concerned us not in the slightest. Was it all due to the machinations of the Jews, we wondered, or international financiers perhaps? Of one thing we were certain – the war was not in the interests of the ordinary people of Britain, so many of whom had been unemployed for years, lived in disgraceful slums and who were the non-participating partners in 'England, their England'.

What did all this prove? I think it proved that the majority of us believed in nothing, that we had no ideals, no philosophy, no set of values to cling to, that we were not much better than a dog and were prepared to follow anyone who would feed and house us. But we were not to blame for that. Most of us had been very poorly educated, in fact had hardly been educated at all apart from the little that was required to read our popular, trashy press, whose standard then was much the same as it is now – as illustrated by such headlines as 'Knickers to you, Galtieri!'

The government had not told us what the war was about; they hadn't told us about the magnitude of the evil we were supposed to be fighting. I wonder why not. Was it perhaps because they did not want to offend the Germans or to arouse our passions too much? Perhaps they did not want to jeopardize the possibility of a deal with Germany when she attacked Russia, something that they knew for certain would happen because they intended to use every means possible to make it happen.

We had been given some vague propaganda about 'fighting for democracy'. The slogan of the National Savings movement was 'Lend to defend the right to be free!' Those things meant nothing to the average soldier, but had he been told that he was fighting against the most evil system that the world had ever known, no amount of thick slices of pork would have seduced him!

The next morning we were told off into working platoons, each in charge of a guard. Ours was a short, dandified, cocky little man who introduced himself as Posten Schmidt. He didn't bother with our names but wrote down our numbers in his little book. From now on he was to be our guardian and mentor.

At about eleven o'clock our good impression was further reinforced when we were given another splendid meal.

Half-an-hour later we assembled in three ranks and marched out of the camp, all in step and looking almost like soldiers, Posten Schmidt strutting proudly behind, his rifle slung over his shoulder and his very high-set peaked cap at a jaunty angle.

Through the town we marched, stared at by the inhabitants who stopped whatever they were doing to gaze at us. Apart from two slogans which spanned the street above our heads we encountered no sign of hostility. One slogan read:

'Wir danken unseren tapferen Soldaten'
(We thank our brave soldiers)

The other:

'Niderlage Englands – ewiger Frieden'
(The defeat of England – eternal peace)

They had obviously been hung up by Party Activists for our benefit, but since I doubt if any of us understood them in those early days they had laboured largely in vain.

After a march of some two miles we reached the place of work. It turned out to be a really huge building site in its very early stages. Several bulldozers, which the Germans called *Bagger*, were busily digging out foundations. Around the site were stacked building materials, including large steel girders. A railway siding had been laid from the main line, at which a train was unloading more building material. We were to learn that on this site were to be built the largest steel works in Europe to be called the *Hermann Goering Stahlwerke*.

Our platoon was split up into small parties, each given into the charge of a civilian worker. The one I was with was under the charge of two civilians, one a veritable giant of a man, the other a puny weasel-faced little runt with a mouthful of gold teeth.

The giant immediately bawled at us and, pointing to several pairs of outsize metal tongs, told us to pick them up and follow him. The tongs were so heavy that to lift them was almost more than we could manage in our weakened state. We were led to the railway siding from where we had to drag a huge girder by means of these tongs under the direction of the giant who called out in a mighty voice *'Ho! Ruck!'*. At the *'Ho!'*, having grabbed the girder with the tongs, we steadied ourselves; at the *'Ruck!'* we strained and moved it forward about a foot. Foot by foot: *Ho! Ruck! Ho! Ruck!* It reminded one of galley slaves. We were pitiably weak; our efforts were puny, which called forth the derision of weasel-face and louder shouting of the giant.

This went on for about half-an-hour by which time we were brought to a state of near-impotence. The giant called a halt. Weasel-face sidled away, ostensibly to answer a call of nature but most likely to scrounge.

As soon as he was out of sight the giant squatted on his haunches and made a sign for us to do likewise. He nevertheless continued to shout and to curse for some time. Then, having got up and had a good look around, he again squatted and blinked at us several times with both eyes. Pointing to himself he said: '*Ich Polonais*'. Pointing to us, he said '*Kameraden!*' He then brought out his tobacco-tin and papers and handed them round. Pointing in the direction in which Weasel-face had disappeared he said '*Deutsche!*'. The giant was a Pole, Weasel-face a German and the former's shouting and bawling had been a mere charade. He now looked at us with eyes full of pity. Pointing again to himself he said '*Lis*'. Obviously his name. Then drawing the outlines of a fox on the sandy ground he pointed to it and said '*lis*'. That seemed to afford him considerable amusement. In the circumstances very understandably too.

I managed somehow to ask what time we would finish work. He pointed at the sun overhead, then brought his hand gradually downwards until it pointed to the western horizon and said '*Halb Zehn*'. My heart sank – half past ten! I didn't know until later that half past ten was half past nine.

When Weasel-face returned the charade re-started and went on until half past nine, but since he took every possible opportunity of absenting himself Lis did not fail to see that we profited too. Long before knocking-off time his tobacco tin was empty, a fact for which he was not responsible.

This was our first working day in Germany. So they continued, but not exactly; the eight-hour shifts became twelve-hour shifts. The boiled potatoes and thick slices of pork gave way to watery soup, the butter to margarine and the sausage to jam. What we received we ate at one go and were still hungry, but that was our lot for twenty-four hours. We became thinner and thinner as the days went by. Our shoes wore out. We were given wooden clogs of the Dutch variety. We could no longer march, had we had the strength to, only shuffle along like Orientals. Our battle-dress wore out; we were in rags. Our one and only shirt became an apology for what it once was. We were like scarecrows; we were lousy, so lousy that I once saw a young man who had once been a proud soldier in the King's Royal Rifle Corps catch and count sixty lice inside his shirt.

Before the summer was over many young men looked like middle-aged men while middle-aged men looked like septuagenarians, so low had they been brought. Many of them were Territorials, some of very poor physique, obviously signed-on just to make the numbers up. They would never have been accepted into the Regular Army and had been sent to France with little or no training. Apart from their physical deterioration their morale was at rock bottom. Their optimism of the first few days had turned into bitter disillusion, resulting in sullen hatred of the Germans. But their real anger was reserved for the British Government whom they held responsible for their plight.

In the course of time I was moved from Lis's gang to work as a blacksmith's striker in the forge. I had a partner, a young man called Fletcher of the Gloucestershire Regiment and a fine young chap he was.

There were two smiths in the forge, both old men who had retired and been brought back to help in the war effort; they worked a six-hour shift. One, whose name was Sobota, was short, fat and jolly. The other, Neumann, was tall, thin and miserable. Sobota brought a can of soup each day to share between Fletcher and me; Neumann gave us nothing. Sobota gave us frequent breaks; Neumann kept us at it all the time. He always had two pieces of iron in the fire simultaneously. One was the piece – it might be cold chisel – that he was supposed to be working at, the other was always a section of some eight inches of rail, i.e. a piece of railway line which he was fashioning into a sledge-hammer head. While the cold chisel was being heated the white-hot rail was laid on the anvil and while he, Neumann, kept time with his hand-hammer by steadily tapping it on the anvil, Fletcher and I struck the rail with our sledge-hammers, ding-dong, ding-dong, alternately. What was worse, the old devil kept us at it long after the iron was cold. Then, when the chisel was ready, out that came and we hammered at that.

One day, in a temper, I struck a piece of iron he was holding with his tongs in the anvil with such force that both it and the tongs flew out of his hand. He immediately screamed *'schweinerei'* at me. Thinking that it meant swine, which, of course, it does not, I took great umbrage. Throwing my sledge-hammer down, I shouted back at him: *'Was? Ich Schwein?'* (What? I'm a pig?) He picked up his hand-hammer and threw it at me, whereupon I grabbed a shovelful of hot cinders from the fire and threatened him with them. He rushed out of the forge shouting *'Posten! Posten!'*. Dandy Schmidt, between whom and me was bad blood, happened to be just passing. Acting on information received he chased me out of the forge with his rifle butt. That evening I was punished by having my bread, margarine and jam ration withheld.

I was in Schmidt's bad books because one day I saw him standing by a puddle of water while a British soldier knelt washing his jack-boots with his hands. The temptation was irresistible. I kicked the soldier in the backside which landed him in the puddle. Schmidt unslung his rifle and threatened me, but I stood my ground and managed to make him understand how he would feel were he to see a German soldier washing the boots of a British guard. He contented himself with giving me a violent push and uttering dire threats.

I was lucky in my next job. I shared it with two young Poles, both ex-students of the Jagiellonski University in Cracow. Although they spoke fluent German, our *lingua franca* initially was Latin which they knew extremely well and which I knew very imperfectly but sufficiently well to enable them to give me the basics of German grammar. The vocabulary very soon followed, after I had learnt how to frame questions in German. In a matter of weeks I knew the essentials of German grammar and had acquired a wide vocabulary. They had obtained for me a primer and a little reader entitled *Paul and Purifax*, which gave me endless pleasure, so naive and sentimental it was. Never will I forget one little sentence in which Anne-Marie says to Paul on the eve of his departure to America to become a vacuum-cleaner salesman – Purifax being the make of the vacuum-cleaner:

'Wann werden wir uns wieder unter dem Mond sehen, Paul?'

(When will we see each other again under the moon, Paul?)

The winter came to Laband at the beginning of November. Temperatures of twenty degrees below zero centigrade were common, so was a foot or more of snow. But, fortunately for us and just in time to prevent us from succumbing to the intense cold, Santa Claus came early that year in the shape of the camp authorities who kitted us out in captured uniforms – French, Polish, Belgian and Czechoslovakian, including boots. Although we didn't all receive a pair, we each got two! For instance, I got one boot about two sizes too big which reached half-way up my calf and one which pinched painfully and barely came up to my ankle. The most serviceable article I had was a Polish Cavalry greatcoat which fitted like a glove down to the waist and then opened out like a ballerina skirt and reached to the floor. It was obviously meant to cover the horse when the rider was in the saddle. I also got a red-topped French kepi which I spurned. Nothing would have induced me to wear it, not even the Silesian frost.

The spring of 1941 saw the arrival of Red Cross parcels and what a metamorphosis they brought about. They contained some seven pounds of good food like corned beef, meat and veg, tinned herring, condensed milk, sardines, biscuits, raisins, cheese, chocolate, butter, sugar and tea – a full parcel for each man plus a tin of fifty cigarettes per week. All of a sudden we were rich. Young men became young men once more, the years fell off the apparent septuagenarians, backs straightened, drooping shoulders were raised, heads were lifted again and hollow cheeks filled out. With the return of health and strength pride returned and morale was raised and faith renewed. All this was achieved in a few short weeks. To complete our re-birth came a consignment of brand new British battle-dress, boots, shirts and underclothing.

People who had hardly washed themselves during the winter were now queueing impatiently for the showers and were shaving every day and soon lines of washing were seen stretching across the compounds. We now sang and whistled as we marched in step, arms swinging, to and from work. We even waved at the girls and some even waved back! We looked something like soldiers once more. What is more important some of us started to feel like soldiers.

With good food, the improved conditions and the daily work which had by now been reduced to seven hours a day owing to piece-work arrangements, I was soon fit again – fit enough to start harbouring thoughts of escape. But where to? Switzerland was over four hundred miles away across Germany. Out of the question. My Polish friends had told me that a well-organized Polish Resistance movement had been formed.The pre-war frontier was only some ten miles away which meant that a few hours march would take me among people I knew would help me. The more I thought of the idea the more attractive it became and I began to think very seriously about it. However, something happened that caused me to change my mind.

I met Celinka!

Celinka

It was Saturday, 22 November. By now I was working on a site on which hundreds of houses were being built for the people who were to work in the *Hermann Goering Stahlwerke* which had risen like a phoenix and was about to start production. Whenever the opportunity arose I would slope off from my place of work and wander around the site to glean what news I could from the German and Polish civilians. Neither source was reliable as the Germans told me nothing favourable to us, while the Poles invented British victories at sea or in the sky, just to cheer me up.

While on my round on this particular day, I came face to face with two young Polish girls.

'*Dzien dobry, Panienki!*'

'*Dzien dobry, Panie!*' they replied with a charming smile.

I then spoke to them in German, which they understood, and I learnt that the taller of the two was called Celinka, the other Stasia. I had not spoken to a girl for a year and a half. It was a delightful experience. To me their voices sounded like silver bells. They were pretty girls and I complimented them graciously. They laughed with pleasure.

'You seem to be extremely happy today,' I said. 'Is there any particular reason?'

'Yes,' said Stasia. 'Today is Celinka's birthday; she is nineteen.'

'Congratulations!' I said. 'What a pity I haven't a bar of chocolate with me to give to you, but don't worry I shall bring one on Monday.'

'Oh,' they said, 'we are not working on Monday because next week we start on permanent night-shift, from ten until six in the morning.'

'Will you be working on Monday night?'

'Yes.'

'Here?'

'Yes.'

'In that case I shall bring you your chocolate on Monday night.'

'What? Are you allowed out at night?'

'No,' I said, 'but that will not prevent me from bringing you your birthday present.'

They laughed. That was the kind of answer they admired, the sort of answer that any Pole worth his salt would have given without a second thought. It was a typical example of '*bravura Polska*'. My heart swelled under their admiring gaze.

'So,' I said, '*dowiedzenia* until we meet on Monday night.'

'*Dowiedzenia!*' they said and I felt quite sure they meant it. I was over the moon, for Celinka's laughing eyes had sent an arrow right into my heart.

When I got back to camp and began to think about the enormity of the promise to which I had committed myself I began to quail inwardly, for up to that time no one at Laband had ever broken out. That in itself was not such a daunting task but I would have to break in as well and that was a far more risky business. Had there been an opportunity of conveying a message to the girls suggesting some other means of giving Celinka her birthday present I might have taken it. Yet the truth was that the present was only an excuse, both for me and for her. What we really wanted was to see each other. How could I possibly disappoint her? To one brought up on ancient Welsh history, on the tales of the *Mabinogion*, the chivalry of King Arthur and his knights and on the tradition of the young warriors who, before going to battle, swore a solemn oath not to return unless victorious – *â'r darian neu ar y darian* (with the shield or on the shield) – to disappoint Celinka was unthinkable. To be a hero in her eyes was what I most desired. What was there to prevent me from seeing her on Monday night? Nothing but lack of courage.

My inward struggle over, I got down to the practicalities. I studied the perimeter fence and the movements of the sentry. The fence was of barbed wire ten feet high. At night it was lit by electric lamps on high posts along its entire length. The lamps were twenty feet apart. During the hours of darkness an armed sentry patrolled inside the perimeter. I watched and timed the sentry several times as he made his round. Not once did he take less than ten minutes. The situation of the latrines meant that anyone standing behind them might be out of sight of the sentry for as much as five minutes and would be certain to be out of his sight for at least two minutes.

Thirty seconds should be quite enough for an agile young man to climb the wire, jump down the other side and sprint far enough into the field to be beyond the range of the lights. Beyond that field and about six hundred yards away was a small, white church, beyond that a wood about half a mile across and then an open space leading to the building site.

Each night in the camp we were paraded at about half-past eight, counted, then dismissed to our huts. The doors were then locked and were not unlocked until about half-past five the following morning.

My plan was to place myself in the rear rank of the parade and as near as possible to the latrines. As soon as we were counted I would dash there. If seen, I could plead urgent need. If not I would hide there until the doors were locked. Then I would watch the sentry. As soon as the coast was clear I could shin over the wire, sprint about a hundred yards into the field, lie flat and look back to see whether I had been observed. Should that be the case I would have to consider my position. It might still be possible to break back in before morning. If not I would have to do a bunk to Poland. Celinka might come with me! She would at least be able to advise me.

Having gone over the plan in my mind, I couldn't wait for Monday night. I didn't breathe a word to anyone.

Monday night came at last, after a day of eager anticipation. In the inside pocket of my battle-dress blouse was a bar of chocolate neatly wrapped. On the wrapper I had written the words '*dla mojej kochanej Celinki*' (to my dear Celinka).

At about half past eight the whistle went for the counting parade. The Germans always paraded us in five ranks. I was the left-hand man in the fifth rank. All the Gefreite (corporal) had to do was to count the number of men in the front rank and multiply by five. It was a mere formality, something that happened every night and the Gefreite had never any reason to be suspicious.

We were counted. Being all present, we were dismissed. I legged it immediately to the latrines. I heard the Gefreite going from hut to hut to lock up and then return towards his own quarters. Then, peering around the corner of the latrine entrance, I waited until the sentry made his appearance. Presently he came from the right-hand side, slowly, ponderously, his rifle slung over his shoulder, his two hands deep in the pockets of his greatcoat, the collar of which was turned up to his ears, although it was not a particularly cold night. His thoughts were probably far away for I doubt whether he had ever seen a prisoner in the compound after the counting parade. Had he suddenly come face to face with me he would, I was sure, be far more frightened than I.

Slowly he came abreast of the latrines. I drew back out of sight as he continued on his way and watched him until he finally disappeared beyond the hut in the opposite corner. I waited another minute or so before running to the fence and climbing over. Perched on top as the wire swayed under my weight, I felt uncomfortably exposed. Steadying the wire with one hand, I jumped clear and landed on hands and feet in the field. Springing up immediately, I dashed into the field until I was well beyond the range of the lights. Looking back, I saw no sign of the sentry or anyone else. Getting to my feet, I hurried towards the church. There was a road there, so I stopped, watched and listened. No sign of life being evident, I carried on and was soon in the wood. About five minutes later I was out of it and approaching the building site. I then realized that there was a major flaw in my plan – I had not agreed on a definite place or time at which to meet the girls. Knowing the lay-out of the site well, I made for the street where I had met them on the Saturday morning. After waiting there for about half-an-hour I realized I was much too early and decided to find a more suitable hiding place. I knew of a tool-shed some hundred yards away and went to it. It was open so I went inside, expecting to be perfectly safe. I never stopped to think that the fact that the shed door was unlocked was very suspicious. I soon paid for my lack of thought. Before I had been there long I heard voices approach. Their owners opened the door and came in. One of them tried to light a cigarette lighter. It sparked several times but failed to light which called forth some lurid curses. Had the men only known, they might have been grateful, for as I crouched in the corner my hand had closed around a pick-helve which I would not have hesitated to use had the need arisen.

With a final curse the men went out muttering something about fetching a lantern. I soon followed them, moving very cautiously around the site, keeping close to the walls of the houses. Finding a partially-built house with an exit at both sides I went in and waited.

Having no watch, I had to guess the time. When I was certain beyond all doubt that it was well after ten o'clock I came out and walked around the site, returning frequently to the place where I had met the girls.

After what seemed an endless wait I saw a lantern moving along the dark street. Tip-toeing towards it, I saw that it was being carried by a man and that behind him walked a girl. She was a Pole whom I had previously seen but had never spoken to. Later I got to know her well. Her name was Fredka and she was very beautiful.

I followed the pair. They entered the middle house of a long row. Slipping in after them, I saw a flight of stairs leading to a passage below ground level. I could see the glow of the lantern, so down the steps I went. I was now in a long passage from which openings led on one side to cellars – I later learnt that they were intended to serve as wash-rooms. The man and girl had gone into one of these cellars. I slipped into the entrance of an adjoining cellar and waited. Soon they came out and continued along the passage and entered another cellar. In addition to the lantern the man carried a large iron poker. In each cellar was a coke-burning brazier and it was obvious that my quarry were attending to the fires. The purpose of these fires was to prevent the concrete walls of the cellars, which were probably not entirely dried out, from cracking in the very low temperatures.

The two continued along the passage, attending to the fires in each cellar as they went. I followed them from cellar to cellar, hoping to be able to attract the attention of Fredka so that she could tell Celinka and Stasia that I was there.

Eventually they reached the end of the passage and, having attended to the last fire, they started to come back. I immediately hid myself until they had gone past. The man was leading. Slipping out of my hiding place I tip-toed behind Fredka and tapped her on the shoulder. She looked around and lifted her hand to her mouth in obvious alarm and would probably have screamed had I not held out a warning hand. I retreated to the entrance of the cellar and watched her. She stood stock-still for a few seconds, clearly very frightened and perhaps scarcely believing what she had seen. The man was quite a few paces ahead, but, becoming aware that he was not being followed, he turned around and asked the girl what she was doing. She went to him and I could see her tell him what she had seen and point in my direction. She obviously had no idea who I was. The man came slowly towards me, the lantern held high in one hand and the poker in the other. I retreated into the cellar. In the middle near the brazier was a large iron tub half-full of coke. I bent down behind it and waited. The man came to the cellar entrance, stood there and called out, '*Wer ist da?*' (Who is there?)

There being no escape I stood up. The man said, '*Was machst du hier?*' (What are you doing here?) He then called to the girl,

'*Polizei holen!*' (Fetch the police), and came towards me brandishing the poker.

It was time to act! I rushed right at him and pushed him headlong against the iron tub. Sprinting past Fredka, I pressed the bar of chocolate into her hand with the words: '*Dla Celinka!*' Then, despite the darkness, I ran along the passage until I reached the exit. I could hear the man bellowing '*Polizei! Polizei!*' There was no time to lose, I had to be back in camp before the alarm was raised and before a reception party could be arranged for me. I made the half-mile back in record time. Lying in the field sixty yards from the wire, I waited for the sentry to come past on his round. He soon came, strolling quite unconcernedly, his hands in his pockets, a sure sign that the alarm had not been raised. As soon as he was safely out of sight I sprinted for the fence and climbed over it. Nipping into the latrines I hid until the huts were unlocked at about five-thirty.

The others in my hut had noticed my absence and thought I had escaped. I told them that having had to go to the latrines immediately after parade the previous evening I had found myself locked out and had been forced to shelter there all night. They accepted my story without question. What other possible explanation could there have been for my absence? Had I told them the truth they most certainly would not have believed me!

However, in a moment of folly I did tell the man who slept in the next bed to me. Being from Birmingham he was known as Brummie. I never knew him by any other name. He was quite a game lad and I thought he might be an asset. He thought I'd had a most marvellous adventure and when he learnt that I was going out again that night he asked whether he might come with me. I agreed, although I knew inwardly that I was not taking him for his own sake but because I still thought that danger shared is danger minimized.

That night Brummie and I stood side by side in the rear rank on the counting-parade. As soon as the whistle went for dismissal we bolted into the latrines. Repeating the drill of the previous night we found ourselves safely over the wire and en route for the building site where we hid until it was time to go and look for the girls. When we judged that time to have arrived I set off on a reconnaissance. Almost immediately I saw a lantern moving along one of the streets and stalked it. It was being carried by a girl, another was by her side. They were Celinka and Stasia. Going to within a few yards of them without being seen, I greeted them in what I thought was the most nonchalant and matter of fact way: '*Moje uszanowanie, Panienki!*' (My respects, young ladies!)

They turned around and held the lantern up with an involuntary '*Mój Boze!*' (Good God!) But when they recognized me they burst into peals of laughter, then came and hugged me. They took me into one of the empty houses which they used as their staff-room – No 24 Poststrasse. I visited it again in July, 1984, and recognized it immediately, although the name of the street had by now been changed and the fields then surrounding the building site are now a wooded park. There were several other girls in the house, among them Fredka of the previous night, who was most apologetic about her behaviour. She explained that she had no idea who I was and that her action had been due to the shock she had received when a sudden apparition had so unceremoniously tapped her on the shoulder. She said that the German had not for one moment suspected that I was a prisoner, believing me to be a Pole.

Having fetched Brummie from his hiding place, the girls took us up a couple of flights of stairs from which we emerged into a long passage corresponding to the one that ran under the row of houses. Off this passage were openings leading to what were to serve as drying-rooms. The Germans obviously used their wits when they built houses!

We smoked and talked, the girls eating the chocolate we had given them and all thoroughly enjoyed themselves. Fredka spoke very little German but Celinka and Stasia spoke the language fluently. Brummie spoke nothing but 'Brummagem', nevertheless he too enjoyed himself. Stasia was short and pert and a regular chatterbox. Celinka was taller and prettier and, although by no means taciturn, wasn't quite as garrulous. She had that peculiar Polish combination of dark hair and deep-blue eyes, a bewitching smile and quicksilver animation, a combination of charms that I found quite irresistible. There was no question about it, I had fallen completely in love with her and judging by the look in her eyes I felt that my suit was not entirely hopeless.

We must have made a lot of noise as we chatted and laughed, for suddenly a lantern was seen approaching from the direction of the top of the stairs. As the light approached we realized it was the German of the previous night.

My reaction was to charge straight into him and knock him over but Celinka held my arm and said, 'You two stay here. He hasn't seen you. We'll go and perhaps everything will be alright!'

The girls went towards the German. Brummie and I backed to

the end of the passage where it opened out into a room. We heard the German shout at the girls to return to their work, then we saw the lantern moving towards us. We stood behind the entrance and waited. As soon as he entered the room we gave him a push which sent the lantern flying out of his hand and caused it to go out. We then ran along the passage towards the door leading to the stairs. It was pitch dark. I ran past the door. Then I heard the sounds of a struggle behind me with Brummie calling for help. The German had caught hold of him. He was a big powerful man and more than a match for Brummie. I tip-toed towards the struggling figures, felt for the door and, having found it, tried to discover which was Brummie and which was the German, which was absolutely vital in view of what I intended to do. Having located Brummie, I grabbed him by the arm and, yanking him free, I pushed him through the open door. I then put my hand in the German's face and gave it a shove which sent him flying backwards. Brummie and I went tumbling down two flights of stairs. At the bottom the girls were waiting for us. I just had time to give Celinka half-a-dozen kisses before dashing after Brummie who was making record time in the direction of the camp. I felt confident, however, that we would reach it before the German could possibly raise the alarm. And so it turned out. We got over the wire safely and hid in the latrines until the huts were opened in the morning.

Brummie never offered to come out with me again but promised not to tell a soul about the incident.

The Wedding

Celinka was everything to me; she filled my thoughts to the exclusion of everything else. Escape was forgotten, for that would mean leaving her and that was the very last thing in the world I wanted to do.

She had sent me a letter via an old Polish woman who worked on the day shift in which she warned me not to come out again until I heard from her that it was safe. She said that her German boss was not such a bad chap and that she might be able to square him.

I had also thought of the possibility of squaring him, and some of the guards as well. With the advent of Red Cross parcels a considerable black market had come into being. Both the guards and the civilians with whom we worked were keen to have such luxuries as soap, coffee and chocolate, not only for themselves but for re-sale at considerable profit. They paid for them in bread, eggs or smoked sausage, even a bottle of wine or schnapps. Since I spoke German I was often used as go-between in the transactions.

The chief dealer among the guards was a man to whom we had given, for obvious reasons, the name of Johnnie Pedlar. His real name was Haase, he was a Bavarian, a most inoffensive character and by no stretch of the imagination a typical example of Prussian soldiery. Without being unkind one could have described him in the words of the contemporary German saying as having: '*Mehr Angst als Vaterlandsliebe*' (More fear than love of the Fatherland). All Johnnie wanted was a quiet life, no fighting, no risk and be loved by all.

I had a chat with him one day and told him that I had a Polish girlfriend. I showed him the ring I was wearing, one that Celinka had sent me via the old lady who carried our messages. Johnnie didn't mind at all; on the contrary, he showed considerable interest, asking me what she was like and congratulating me after I had waxed long and eloquently about her beauty and virtues. However, when I told him that with his help I intended to visit her at night he nearly passed away. '*Kommt gar nicht in Frage*' were his words (completely out of the question). He made to move off, signifying that the subject was closed, but I detained him, saying that I was quite determined to break out of camp during his spell of sentry-duty in the early evening and break in again during his second spell in the early morning. He would not have to take any active part. The only assurance I wanted was that, in the event of him seeing me, he would not fire. Nothing else. Poor Johnnie didn't want to know anything about it. But I had to have the assurance I wanted so I put the question to him bluntly: 'If you saw me breaking out or into camp, would you shoot me?'

He looked at me with hurt filled eyes and asked, '*Bist du verrückt*?' (Are you mad?)

I had the answer I wanted.

In the meantime we had been moved into another camp immediately adjoining a camp housing civilian workers which was split into two parts, one for Germans and one for Poles. In the latter lived the girls. Celinka and I were now next-door neighbours and were able to wave to each other across the wire, but the Poles had been warned not to come anywhere near the dividing wire, the warnings being accompanied by dire threats. From my point of view the main attribute of the new camp was the fact that only some three hundred yards of field separated it from the building site. The future looked promising.

In due course I had a message from Celinka saying that she had convinced her boss that I was her Polish fiancé and that, provided she did not neglect her work, he did not object to our meeting. I could therefore come to 24 Poststrasse whenever I had arranged things at my end.

I went out that very night during Johnnie Pedlar's sentry-go and was welcomed with open arms by Celinka and Stasia. There was a cheerful coal fire burning in the grate, the window of the room was covered by a blanket to conform with black-out regulations and a number of empty boxes had been arranged and neatly covered to serve as stools and a table. The girls heated some soup over the fire and we had a cosy little supper together.

Knowing that Johnnie would be on duty between four and six, I returned to camp at about five a.m. and hid in the latrines until the usual time.

I had become very friendly with a Scot from Inverness by the name of Robert Stewart, a corporal in the Cameron Highlanders. Jock was over six feet tall, athletic, strong and full of courage. He was a few years older than I, a reservist who had completed seven years a few months before the war broke out. He was recalled to the colours and served with the First Battalion of his regiment in France. He had been taken prisoner at St Valery along with many others from the Highland Division.

I told Jock about Celinka and about my frequent *rendez-vous* with her at night. He was fascinated and asked me straightaway whether one of the girls might be interested in a visit from him. That being exactly what I wanted to hear, I invited him to join me in my next sortie when he could meet Stasia. What happened after would be up to them.

That night we went out together, taking with us several 'goodies' from the Red Cross parcels. The first words Stasia uttered after the formal introductions were: '*Mój Boze! Taki olbrzym, dwa metry!*' (My God! What a giant, two metres!)

She was rather on the short side. But despite his height, Jock had a kindly, smiling face and a cheerful disposition which more than compensated and very soon it was clear to me that the experiment was going to be a success.

After a most enjoyable evening we both returned safely to camp.

Soon we found an even easier way of breaking out and of meeting the girls in the early evening before they started work and which was much less risky for them. It was now December and dark by about half-past four. At about five every evening we were all marched into the cook-house of the neighbouring civilian camp to draw our rations. On the way back Jock and I would hand our rations to a couple of friends, then, watching the nearest guard closely, we would slip into the shadows at the first opportunity and remain hidden until the coast was clear. Then we quite simply climbed the unguarded fence of the civilian camp into the field and made our way to Poststrasse. After a couple of hours with the girls we would break back into the camp before roll-call.

By this time Celinka and I were engaged. She had told her mother about me and one day, returning from a visit to her home in Bedzin some forty miles away, she brought back a letter which she read out to me and in which her mother gave us her blessing.

In view of the circumstances in which we lived and the danger that one or other might be sent away without even getting the opportunity of saying goodbye or of ever contacting each other again, we decided that we would get married. As a proper church wedding was out of the question we agreed to have an improvised ceremony which both of us would recognize as valid and binding. It would take place on Christmas Eve. Stasia would take the part of the officiating priest and would read out the marriage service and we would make the responses. It was to be no mockery but as near to the real thing as possible and was to be celebrated with due solemnity. Afterwards there would be a banquet!

Jock and I plunged into the Black Market and days before Christmas Eve we had collected sufficient delicacies, not to mention wine and Schnapps, to make the banquet one not to be soon forgotten.

On Christmas Eve we broke out of camp. We had bathed and shaved ourselves with great care, arranged our hair neatly and dressed in our best battle-dress, trousers beautifully pressed, khaki shirts to which we had sewn collars made from the tail, and woollen khaki pullovers. Nor had we forgotten our boots which shone as only soldiers from crack regiments could make them shine. Even so they scarcely matched the shine which must have been in my eyes as I thought of the joy awaiting me.

Never shall I forget that night. As I think of it now I am reminded of that line by Wordsworth, written about something quite different: 'Bliss was it in that dawn to be alive, but to be young was very heaven'.

The frozen field across which we walked sparkled with a million diamonds and above, the clear, cold sky was hung with countless stars. Half way up the eastern sky hung a crescent moon. From the houses on the site, many of which were already occupied, came the strains of carols, while below us in the village we could see the top of the very tall Christmas tree which stood in the square and whose one silver star was plainly visible. It must have been just such a night that inspired that most famous of all carols, Silent Night.

Jock and I were on top form, fit, young, strong and fearless. We were on our way to meet two very special young women between whom and us was an unbreakable bond and to take part in a ceremony which meant very much to both of us. To prevent us would have been no easy task.

Having arrived at No 24 Poststrasse we gave the agreed signal. The door was opened by an excited Stasia. The room was decorated with greenery and Christmas cards and lit with coloured candles. A huge fire burnt in the grate and the improvised table was laid for the coming feast; there were even glasses to drink from instead of the usual mugs. But there was no sign of Celinka. When I asked where she was Stasia told me she was in the next room where Fredka was helping her to get ready for the ceremony and I was forbidden absolutely to go near her. I was also forbidden a glass of schnapps, although she poured one out for Jock.

Soon there was a knock on the door, and when Stasia opened it Fredka led Celinka in. She was wearing a long, white dress and veil and long white gloves. Fredka lifted her veil for us to have one short look at her before lowering it again. Stasia then placed me by the side of my bride-to-be and told Jock and Fredka to take up their positions on either side. Then with a cross in her hand she went through the marriage service in Polish and put the prescribed questions to us to which we made the proper responses. It was as near to the real thing as it could possibly have been in the circumstances and both Celinka and I took it absolutely in earnest. We exchanged rings. The ceremony ended by Stasia breaking a consecrated wafer and sharing it between us. She then lifted Celinka's veil and told me to kiss my bride. Our lips met in reverence and love in full realization of the promise we had made to each other.

But then everyone wanted to kiss her. There followed a veritable orgy of kissing!

The wine bottle was then opened and toasts drunk to our eternal happiness! So naively happy were we, we did not appreciate the bitter irony of the situation. The girls were prisoners just as much as we were; in fact their situation was very much worse as members of a race who the Germans wished to exterminate. We had the International Red Cross to represent us. The girls had no one, they and their families were at the mercy of a country where the very word mercy was regarded as a weakness and had been expunged from the vocabulary.

Naively, happily, light-heartedly we enjoyed the wedding breakfast. We ate and drank, toasted each other and kissed, oblivious of the war and the dangers that surrounded us and I don't mean the danger of being caught.

What a pleasure it was to see the girls enjoying food and drink they hadn't tasted for over two years.

Having eaten as much as we possibly could we sat in front of the fire and sang carols. The girls were good singers. They sang Polish carols and plaintive folk and patriotic songs. I was able to join them in the Polish national anthem, all four verses of it, which was one more than any of them knew. For that I was rewarded with kisses all round. Sitting there in front of the fire on Christmas Eve was a most touching experience, heightened and intensified by the circumstances in which we found ourselves. Quite apart from the personal relationship which existed between us and them, the girls looked upon us as friends and allies to whom they were entitled to look for comfort and succour. They certainly stood in need of that with their country occupied by a ruthless enemy and they and their families and compatriots reduced to a state of near-slavery. They had been torn from their homes and conscripted to work for the enemy, forced to wear the letter 'P' on their lapels as a sign that they belonged to a conquered people towards whom the ordinary German civilians could behave in any manner they pleased and against which there could be no redress.

We sat up very late singing and talking but eventually went to sleep on blankets laid on the floor in front of the fire. Jock and I had intended to return to camp between four and six when our tame Johnnie would be on sentry-go but we overslept and did not wake until we heard persistent knocking on the door.

What to do? Open the door suddenly and fall upon whomever was there? But the girls were much quicker-witted. They opened the window and told us to get out and hide. When we suggested they do the same they pooh-poohed the idea and told us not to worry. After we had gone they opened the door. Our visitor turned out to be the old woman who carried messages between Celinka and me. We were called back. The old woman apparently had become worried at not seeing the girls in their rooms and had come to see whether everything was all right. But she had not come empty-handed. She had with her a can of soup!

Having given her a mug of real coffee with sugar and condensed milk, something she hardly dreamt still existed, we asked her to go out and find a small flat stone. When she returned with it we wrapped a note around it addressed to a mutual friend. We then requested the old dear to throw the stone into the camp when the guard was not looking and where an inmate would see it and wait for an answer. The note asked whether we had been missed and whether in the event of a snap check-parade someone could cover up for us.

In due course we received a reply. We had not been missed and should it prove necessary all that could be done would be done to cover up for us!

I looked forward to another glorious twelve hours or so with Celinka. My happiness was complete!

Things Go Wrong

We went out regularly throughout January, 1942, but early in February Jock was caught by the Police.

Johnny Pedlar had been posted, so going out was a much more chancy operation. We went back to the old method of hiding in the ablutions after roll-call and climbing over the wire when the coast was clear, returning in the early hours in the same way.

But one night when going to the ablutions we found a guard there who turned us back unceremoniously, although we both pleaded urgent need. It was obvious from the way he behaved that he was very suspicious. When we found him there again the following night we came to the conclusion that the authorities were up to something. We then thought of another plan. We would rush off the counting-parade, but, instead of returning to our barrack-room, climb on to the flat roof and wait till all was quiet before climbing down and shinning over the wire.

We managed this a few times but one night we were caught by one of the guards in the very act of climbing the wire. He rushed at us from behind the barrack-block.

'Down! or I'll shoot!'

We jumped down and confronted him. It was Ling, known to us as Linkie, a particularly two-faced unpleasant and treacherous-looking individual whom no one trusted. In summing up a guard a prisoner of war's instinct is almost infallible. It is almost like the instinct of a dog who sums up a stranger and rarely makes a mistake.

Linkie stood in front of us clutching his rifle very tightly, itching to shoot us but lacking the courage. We had placed ourselves some six feet apart and no more than about a yard in front of him, ready to spring upon him at the first sign of danger. He looked from one to the other and what he saw convinced him that, were he to attempt to fire, his number would be up. He had made the fatal mistake of coming too near. Had he stayed some ten paces away we would have been completely at his mercy. Physically he was a poor specimen, a near-miss from either Jock or I would have been enough to lay him low. His face was taut, his eyes staring, his voice was breaking. He tried to shout '*Zurück! Zurück!*' (Back! Back!). I told him in a quiet voice to keep silent and added, 'Open the door of the barrack-room and we'll go in and you'll get twenty cigarettes'.

He kept looking from one to the other, torn with fear and indecision but knowing that he was a beaten man. He had no doubt of what would happen to him were he to make the wrong move.

'*Das letze mal! Das allerletze mal*,' (The last time, the very last time!) he said.

As he was returning, his rifle on his shoulder, Jock snatched it from his shaking hands. '*Soldat!*' he said, '*Scheisse!*' (Soldier! Rubbish!) and thrust it back into his hands. In the meantime I had jumped behind him. He was now our prisoner and knew it.

'Open the barrack-door!' I said and gave him the number.

With a trembling hand he took out his bunch of keys and led us to the door which he opened. In we went but Linkie waited in vain for his cigarettes.

We knew that from then on Linkie would be a very dangerous person. The next time he would fire from a safe distance. We had to find another way of breaking out.

We went back to the method previously used of slipping away while fetching our rations from the Civilian Camp. That was all right as far as going was concerned but we had to return via the perimeter fence and before the 8.30 roll-call. Since the days were lengthening – it being now February or March – we were left with very little time with the girls.

One evening I returned from work about half-an-hour later than usual. Jock's working platoon had already drawn rations and he had gone out. As my gang went for its rations I slipped away and hurried to Poststrasse. Having knocked in the agreed manner on the door I waited for the response. None. I knocked again. Still no answer. I knew immediately that something was wrong. The girls had never once let us down. And where was Jock?

I went back towards the camp. Before I had gone far along the street two men came towards me. When they were some ten yards away one of the men turned off to the left. I heard him say to the other in German in a conversational voice, 'Here is one, but there is another one somewhere.'

The second man stopped where he was. I walked straight past him. He didn't say a word but fell into step behind me. Presently he said, '*Guten Abend, Kamerad! Wohin so schnell?*' (Good evening friend! Where are you off to in such a hurry?)

I didn't reply, just kept going at a fairly fast pace. He continued to follow a few paces behind. Ignoring him, I started off over the field in the direction of the camp. I was on a path which led to a shed half-way across. My shadow was still following and looked as if he were going to continue right up to the wire, when he would no doubt shout to warn the guard. I had to get rid of him. I stopped and turned to face him. He stopped. I walked towards him. He backed away. Suddenly I sprang forward and rushed at him. He turned and fled like a frightened hare. So did I and rushed towards the wire. Without bothering to look if there was a guard nearby I climbed over, tearing my hands in the process as I had no time to place them between the barbs; I jumped into the compound. Dashing into my room I kicked off my shoes and plunged into bed.

I hadn't been there a few minutes when a frantic whistling was heard and guards were rusing about shouting, '*Appell! Appell! Alle mann antreten! Schnell! Schnell!*' (Roll-call! Roll-call! Everybody on parade! Quickly! Quickly!)

I fell in with the rest of the room. The next thing I saw was the *Feldwebel* (sergeant) walking from the direction of the guard-room with two policemen behind him and Jock handcuffed to one of them.

We were counted and re-counted several times. Everyone was present. There followed long discussions between the *Feldwebel*, the *Gefreite* and the policemen. We were counted again several times. All present. They obviously had not expected that, but eventually they had to accept the fact that Jock was the only one not on parade. He was taken away.

We were then treated to a long harangue on the dangers of breaking camp and associating with Polish women whom the *Feldwebel* referred to as '*Polnische Weiber*' but made it sound like '*Polnische Viper!*' That did not endear him very much to me. I thought to myself: If I had you on your own in a quiet spot for a few minutes, my lad, I would shove a viper down your throat! He went on to say that any such conduct would be dealt with not by the military authorities but by others and there was no doubt that he meant the Gestapo. There was also no doubt that the military authorities were averse to handing prisoners of war over to the tender mercies of the Gestapo. However much I resented his

'Viper', I felt that he was genuinely concerned that we avoid anything that might result in allowing the Gestapo to poke their noses into the affairs of the camp.

Jock was placed in the camp guard-room to await transport to Lamsdorf where he would appear before the *Gerichtsoffizier* – Justice Officer. I managed to have a few words with him before he left. He told me that he had gone to No 24 Poststrasse and made the agreed signal. It was answered from inside but before the girls had time to open the door two men had rushed upon him from doorways on either side. He had struggled but his arms had been pinioned and when he felt the muzzle of a pistol pressed against the nape of his neck he knew that further resistance was useless. He did, however, make enough noise to warn the girls.

The two men hand-cuffed him and took him to the Police Station in Laband where all they got out of him was '*Nicht verstehen Deutsch, Kriegsgefangene!*' (Don't understand German, prisoner of war!)

It would have taken wild horses to drag anything more out of Jock.

The girls later told me that they had heard the fracas outside, had heard Jock's voice and, realizing what had happened, had escaped through the downstairs window.

Tragedy

As can be imagined the régime in the camp changed. Extra guards were brought in and security increased. Going out at night was no longer possible. But kindly fate intervened. My working platoon was moved from the building site to a sand pit near the Adolf Hitler Kanal. I was still able to communicate with Celinka through the good, old Polish woman and we soon formulated a plan to continue our meetings.

She was still on night work so in the afternoons she would walk to a spot on the far side of the Canal. When I judged that the time had arrived I would watch for an opportunity to slip away from the sand pit, swim across the canal and go to her. There was a risk of course, but I was well used to risks.

It was now summer 1942 and the news from the war-fronts was particularly distressing. The Germans had resumed their offensive in Russia and were carrying all before them, approaching the Volga in the east and sweeping down to the Caucasus in the south. Russia appeared to be collapsing. In North Africa Rommel was running rings round the 8th Army. Tobruk had fallen and the Afrika Korps was in Egypt. Would it continue across the Suez Canal and link up with the Germans debouching from the passes of the Caucasus? Was Turkey on the point of joining the Axis? In the Far East there was no holding the Japanese. Everywhere our enemies were in the ascendant.

Celinka was very depressed. Poland was suffering as never before. The number of reprisal executions resulting from the activities of the Underground Movement was increasing from day to day and the civil population was being transported by scores of thousands to Germany for forced labour. The people were facing annihilation and there was no sign of deliverance from any quarter. The stoutest-hearted were beginning to quail and to give up all hope. As for her, her position was a truly unenviable one. Although she, her brother and sister were Polish, her parents had been forced to put their names down on the so-called '*Volksliste*', the list containing the names of people who had been born in that part of Poland that had belonged to either Germany or Austria prior to 1918 when Poland became an independent state after nearly 150 years of foreign occupation.

As a consequence of being on the '*Volksliste*' her father had been conscripted into the '*Feldgendarmerie*', a force specifically raised to keep the Polish people down and to combat what the Germans called 'dissident elements'.

Celinka was fanatically Polish and would have willingly died before betraying her country. Although she still cherished the hope of living to see a free Poland once more, the prospect brought her little comfort. What would happen to the father whom she loved if Poland were to regain its independence? Would he not be regarded as a traitor and be required to pay the supreme penalty? And what would be the fate of Poland should Germany prove triumphant? The future held nothing but dread for Celinka. And what was going to happen to us two? Jock Stewart had been removed and Stasia had no faith that she would ever see him again. Was it not more than likely that the same would happen to me? But the worst thing by far was the fact that her father wanted her to apply to be put on the '*Volksliste*'. That would give her the status of a German with all that went with it. No more forced labour, no more wearing the scorned 'P' on her lapel. She would be able to live at home and get a good job and in a victorious Germany she would have a good future. Who could blame her father for trying to secure the future of his daughter when all the evidence pointed to a German victory?

In addition to all these worries Celinka was ill. She had lost a great deal of weight and, although her indomitable courage was unimpaired, I had the impression that her laughter and smiles were often forced. She wept frequently and, although she always insisted that her tears were tears of joy, I had grave doubts. Celinka feared for the future. She was a prisoner in so many more ways than I was. We often discussed the possibility of escaping together deep into Poland and joining the Underground Movement but she was afraid of the effect that would have on her parents and her brother and sister. The authorities would think nothing of wreaking their vengeance on them were she to disappear with a prisoner of war, for it would not have taken them long to put two and two together. Her family might be thrown into a concentration camp. The most dreaded concentration camp of all was on their doorstep – at Auschwitz.

One day, having swum across the canal, I was to be disappointed. Celinka didn't turn up. That was the first time she failed to keep an appointment. I felt immediately that there was something wrong. The following day the same thing happened. I was extremely worried. On the way back from work I saw Stasia and another Polish girl standing on the roadside so I moved to the flank for I felt certain they were waiting for me and had a message. I was right. As I went past Stasia slipped a piece of paper into my hand. It was to let me know that Celinka was ill, very ill, in her room.

The following day Stasia was waiting for me again with another message. Celinka had been taken to the hospital in Gleiwitz.

I felt a dreadful foreboding; something told me I would never see her again. I never did, for three days later Stasia was again waiting for me. I could see by her face what her message was. Celinka had died the previous day.

I believe I became a changed man from that day. Whereas before I had had the attitude of most soldiers to the war and to the enemy for whom there was little hatred, from then on I began to hate the system we were fighting against and all who supported it with an all-consuming hatred. For the first time since the beginning of the war I was personally involved. From then on my desire to be involved in it was greater than my desire to survive. Celinka was the first victim to bring home to me the horror of what was happening in Europe and especially in Poland. She was the victim of the barbaric system that had crushed her country, divided her family and had made the future too terrible for her to contemplate. It was that worry that had been the cause of her illness. I was resolved from then on that Celinka's people would be my people, their fight my fight. That is how I could best honour her memory, for above all Celinka was a Pole.

Sudetenland

Some time in early October fourteen names of so-called trouble-makers were read out on roll-call. My name headed the list, a fact of which I was very proud. It would not have pleased me at all had my name been second.

We were told to pack our belongings and be ready to move off early the following morning. I was glad. Laband held nothing for me any more except memories.

Before eight the following morning we were on the train, destination unknown. There was one comfort, there were some first-class chaps in the party. There were none of those who preached that as prisoners of war we should behave ourselves and win the respect and admiration of the Germans, show them by example what a superior people we were – English gentlemen in fact. Such good behaviour, they said, would earn us good treatment. We should not act like the Poles or the Russians who did not seem to mind what the Germans thought of them. Apart from the fact that I was not an English gentleman, I had other reasons for not caring what the Germans thought of me. The feeling I most wanted to instil in the Germans was fear.

Before we had been long on the train we managed to find out where we were bound for. It was a small village called Piltsh near the town of Troppau in the Sudetenland which until 1938 was part of Czechoslovakia but which Mr Chamberlain and M. Daladier had very kindly handed to Hitler *gratis*, without even the formality of consulting its real owners, the government of Czechoslovakia. They were merely presented with a fait accompli and told to lump it. This was done despite the fact that Russia had offered to present a united front with France and Britain to oppose Hitler and to tell him in unmistakable terms that robbery was not to be permitted.

Rather than join with the filthy Bolsheviks, France and Britain saw fit to call a conference attended by themselves, the robber and his accomplice Mussolini, the outcome of which was the transfer of the Sudetenland to Germany in a manner which lent the cynical and treacherous undertaking an air of legality. The people of France and Britain were cleverly duped, but that criminal act made European war inevitable. Stalin, far from being a fool, realized what the game was. He saw behind the professed peace-loving masks of the British and French governments and realized that Hitler had received a clear signal that any extension of territory he desired would not be opposed provided it was in an easterly direction and that when the time came to face the Germans he would have to do so alone. He took the necessary precautions which manifested themselves in August, 1939, and trumped Chamberlain's and Daladier's ace. I can just imagine the smile on his wily, Georgian face as he did so. I wonder whether *Pravda* carried a headline with the Russian equivalent of 'Knickers to you, Chamberlain and Daladier!' It probably didn't for I believe it regards itself as a 'quality' paper, but I have little doubt that that is how the editor must have felt. For the Molotov-Ribbentrop pact was indeed a brilliant stroke in which Stalin called the tune to which everybody else danced and to which Hitler ultimately danced to death in the ruins of Berlin.

We eventually arrived at the small station of Piltsh where our guards handed us over to what to us then appeared to be an old man wearing the medals of the First World War.

Having counted us he marched us off towards the village. In order to have a chat with him and to sound him out I fell in at the rear. The country around us was good, flat agricultural land but in the distance we could see the foothills of the Sudeten mountains and just below the smoke rising from the old town of Troppau. Turning to the guard I said, '*Eine wunderschöne Gegend, Herr Posten!*' (Wonderful surroundings, Mr Guard!)

'*Ja*', he said, '*aber Sie sprechen gut Deutsch!*' (Yes, but you speak good German).

I went on to explain how I had studied German at school, had taken an interest in Germany and its culture and I had longed to visit the country one day. Alas, not in the manner in which it had come about! The truth was I did not know a word of German until I landed in Laband.

The old guard said he knew how I felt and that he sympathized with us all. He had been a prisoner in the First War in Manchester.

What a stroke of luck! We were soon commiserating with each other and the old chap was accepting my proffered cigarette and thanking me in stumbling English. Not much trouble was to be expected from him. I could not help but sympathize with him, knowing the kind of people he was going to have to be responsible for.

In the village we were taken into a large guesthouse where we were to be accommodated in one of the public rooms which had already been prepared for our reception by the simple expedient of fitting iron bars to its one window and furnishing it with seven wide wooden beds, a long table and a number of stools. On each bed was a palliasse and pillow, both made of hessian which we took to a nearby barn and filled with straw. When we had been issued with two blankets per man our bedding was deemed to be complete.

There was no stove in the room so I guessed that it was not intended that we should be there for the winter.

The guard told us that the rest of the guesthouse was strictly out of bounds to us, that we were not to talk to any civilians we might chance to meet and that we would be locked in our room whenever we were not at work. He said all this in a kindly way, giving us to understand that these orders were not his but had come from above. He went on to express the hope that we would be happy at Piltsch and that he would do all he could to make us so.

Hardly had he finished when Nobby Clarke, a native of Sheffield and a hard case, called out, 'You can start by taking that b – d down!' indicating a large, framed picture of Hitler hanging on the wall.

'That is the Führer!' said the guard.

'I know who the b – d is!' said Nobby. 'Take it down and take it out of this room. I'm not having that fish-eyed b – d looking down at me!'

The guard looked at us appealingly but what he saw convinced him that he had no alternative but to comply with Nobby's demand. He called the proprietor and the Führer's picture was reverently taken down and removed.

We now knew for certain that we could do whatever we liked.

At about five o'clock we were marched to another guesthouse for our evening meal. It turned out to be a good hot meal of meat and vegetables followed by semolina pudding, served by two attractive young ladies, one not more than about eighteen, fair-haired and rosy-cheeked, whose toilet had obviously been specially made for the occasion, she, no doubt, having been eagerly looking forward to seeing the *Engländer*. Her maidenly simpering which showed her dimples to the best advantage showed that she had not been entirely disappointed.

After the meal back to Guesthouse Number One to be locked in for the night, as the guard thought. We thought otherwise and explained to him that it was quite unreasonable to expect fourteen men to remain in one small room for fourteen hours with no toilet facilities other than a bucket. It was contrary to all the rules of the International Convention for the Protection of Prisoners of War and we would not put up with it. If he wanted to consult his superiors he could go ahead.

The poor old chap was aghast and tried to reason with us. As group interpreter and representative I took him to one side and explained to him that he was dealing with very determined men, but he had nothing to worry about as I could give him my word that no one would try to escape or to do anything that would get him into trouble. If he were prepared to leave the room unlocked until nine o'clock I would guarantee that everyone would be present at that time and I stressed the need for cooperation and also the benefits that would accrue to him as a result of such cooperation, at the same time pressing a packet of cigarettes into his hand.

He was like clay in the potter's hand. Locking-up time was delayed until nine o'clock.

Jock Souter, Corporal, Royal Tank Corps and a native of Lossiemouth, and I took the air in the farmyard behind the guesthouse where we found two maids a-milking. When they discovered that, instead of rushing upon them and violating them, we addressed them in polite, passable German, they were delighted. Was it any wonder, starved as they were of the company of young men? When I politely asked one of them, whose name I soon discovered was Hedel, to give me her bucket and then sat down beside her cow and milked it they thought that the age of miracles had returned.

The arrival of the *Engländer* was the best thing that had happened to the guesthouse for a long time, judging by the crowd that filled the public bar that night. Instead of being treated as hated enemies we were treated as objects of intense curiousity by the rustic clientele who took great care not to ask us any embarrassing questions.

Jock and I sat with our newly acquired girlfriends who appeared to be completely unaware that they were fraternizing with the enemy and oblivious to any possibility of reprisals from the other villagers. I must have drunk pints of the heavy malt beer, but I could not have paid for any of it for I had no German money.

By the time the guard appeared at nine o'clock to remind us of our agreement Hedel had promised to make me a dumpling the following day!

In the morning we marched to Guesthouse Number Two where we were served an adequate breakfast by the same young ladies, already in their best clothes, their faces wreathed in smiles. We felt almost human again.

Then off to the railway-siding where we found huge heaps of sugarbeet and a row of empty railway wagons. We were welcomed by the station master and told that our job was to load the beets onto the wagons, that we would have a break between twelve and one o'clock and would finish at five. It was then eight o'clock, so it would be an eight-hour day, rather longer than we cared to work. The rest of the gang told me to negotiate a system of piece work. I tried but the station master pointed out firmly that the hours of work were as laid down. We decided not to push things that first day but to wait and see how matters developed.

We were right out in the country, rolling fields stretching for miles around, the village of Piltsch about a mile to the north and to the south Troppau and the Carpathian mountains; beyond, the rich provinces of Bohemia and Moravia, in 1938 a part of free Czechoslovakia but then a German Protectorate ruled by the infamous Heydrich whose assassination by Czech patriots resulted in the burning of the village of Lidice with all its inhabitants.

We started to load the beets with the large forks provided but did not strain ourselves overmuch. The old guard walked up and down stamping his feet. The poor old chap must have been bored stiff. It was much worse for him than it was for us.

Soon the farm carts started to arrive with more beet, driven either by Poles or Ukranians, some of them women. They were delighted to see us, particularly the Poles, and especially were they delighted with our forceful expressions of confidence that Germany would soon be defeated, a view we did not hold with any conviction but which we knew would be music to the ears of the Poles.

During our midday break I made another attempt to arrange piece work but the station master was quite adamant and turned rather nasty. For the rest of the afternoon we hardly did anything. Nor did we the following day, despite the shouts and threats of the boss and the plaintive pleadings of the old guard, to which I always replied by the offer of piece work – we would load four wagons if allowed to finish on completion.

On the third day we had piece work. We loaded our four wagons and were finished by about half-past two.

We now enjoyed our work and particularly enjoyed the good things the Poles brought us in exchange for items from the Red Cross parcels – half-loaves of good bread, sausages, eggs, apples, pears – they showered us with kindness.

After we had been there about a week the old guard was reinforced by a young soldier, a local lad of some influence who had managed to wangle himself the job while on leave from the Russian front. He started off by being perfectly obnoxious. The first thing he did was to cancel the piece work arrangements and insist that we work the full hours. He had obviously managed to convince the station master that he would stand no nonsense and would get much more work out of us.

He stood over us all the time, shouting and bawling and bullying the Poles and Ukranians whom he forebade to speak to us. He was also very fond of fingering the pistol he carried in a leather holster at his belt and indulged in insulting remarks about us having put our hands up at Dunkirk. My answer to that was to invite him to take his belt off and chance his luck with me alone, out of sight, behind one of the railway wagons and to taunt him with cowardice when he refused. Some of the lads tried to get round him with offers of cigarettes and chocolate but he pretended to be incorruptible and was obviously a young man who was too stupid to know what was best for him and would have to be taught the hard way.

That happened within a few days. I was standing on a farmcart talking to the Polish driver when I heard a commotion. Turning towards the sound I saw the young guard standing over a chap called Mackie, the oldest and the smallest member of our group, who was on the floor being kicked by the guard. I ran to the scene. The guard, seeing me and realizing my intention, turned and ran. Unfortunately for him he ran into the angle formed by two sides of the station building. As he turned to get out of it, I caught him with a mighty swipe to the kidneys. He fell like a stone, uttering a piercing squeal, just like a stuck pig. For a moment he lay still, then a couple of lads picked him up and stood him on his feet. He was groggy and his eyes were vacant. He probably hardly knew where he was. Someone stuck a lighted cigarette into his mouth at which he puffed instinctively. Meanwhile the squeal and the loud 'hurrahs' of the Poles and Ukranians had reached the ears of the station master and the old guard who came running from the former's office.

'*Was ist hier los?*' (What is the matter here?) shouted the station master.

'Nothing,' I answered, 'except that our young friend here and I have had a friendly wrestling match which he won.' Whereupon I lifted up the young soldier's arm and everyone took the cue and cheered again while he stared with a puzzled look on his face as if he were not quite sure of his part in this strange charade.

The station master ordered us back to work at once. I could see from the old guard's face that he was highly suspcious but he did not say anything.

When things had quietened down I went to the young guard and told him that, if he took the matter further, he would do well to remember that we had plenty of witnesses to his kicking Mackie and to the fact that he had also struck me first and that the whole episode had arisen from a dispute over a black market deal. Without giving him time to think, I added that, had the circumstances been reversed, I was quite certain that he, as a good German soldier ready to stand up for his comrades, would have done exactly the same as I had. I challenged him to deny it. After a slight hesitation he said: yes, he would have done the same for one of his comrades.

'There you are!' I said, 'I knew it. You and I are very much the same, except that you wear that uniform and I this one. And now let's smoke a cigarette together and be friends in future.'

He accepted a cigarette from me but insisted that I took one of his and we smoked together like reconciled brothers.

The next day he was the perfect guard, exchanged cigarettes with us and told us not to work too hard. We asked him to tell us about his experiences on the Russian front which he was quite delighted to do.

But our days at Piltsch were numbered. Numbered also the good meals and the smiling faces of the young girls who were becoming even more friendly. The following Sunday morning two strange soldiers burst in and gave us half-an-hour to pack before doubling us to the station to catch a train to a place called Bauerwitz – a place we could well have done without!

Bauerwitz

It was a really dreadful place – a mild version of Dante's inferno. The camp was in an old brewery and housed well over three hundred prisoners in one long, narrow room. Not only were there three-tiered wooden beds along each side of this room but there was also a row running down the middle. In between the beds were two rows of tables and benches and the only means of moving from one end of the room to the other was either under the tables or over them. We were literally packed like the proverbial sardines. The result was chaos. But this chaos was further compounded by the fact that we were divided into a number of different work-groups, each of which started work at a different time. One shift worked from six in the morning until six in the evening, one from nine in the morning until nine in the evening, one from midday until midnight, another from six in the evening until six in the morning, while still another worked from nine in the evening until nine in the morning. There was therefore a continuous coming and going. The guards would call for their shift to assemble and if they didn't in a reasonable time they just grabbed the required number of bodies and marched them off regardless. Some of them might just have returned from a twelve-hour stint. Protest was in vain! It was devil take the hindmost. Some hardly left the camp, others were hardly ever in it.

The men worked in a sugar-beet factory at a place called Leobschutz, some four miles away, and on the Monday morning soon after five o'clock Jock Souter and I trudged wearily along the frosty paving-stones on the way to our first shift at the sugar factory. It was drizzling, it was cold, it was miserable, it was the beginning of November, 1942. The winter was ahead; we were in a very poor camp where any kind of decent life was practically impossible and we were going to work twelve-hour shifts in a pretty awful place according to all reports. Morale was very, very low but our motto was *nil desperandum*. We were scheming.

When we arrived at the sugar factory we were lined up in two ranks. A number of German foremen came along and each picked a number of men. Before they were taken away two copies of their numbers were taken, one for the guard and one for the foreman. Jock and I were taken to a room and shown what we were to do, and a most horrible job it was.

The beets were emptied into a huge rotating drum where all the dirt was removed from them and expelled down a chute. Our job was to catch it in sacks, a huge pile of which was stacked at arm's length. The foreman showed us how to do it while the guard looked on. Why he attached himself to us I don't know, unless it was because we were new and perhaps looked rather bolshy. Having showed us how, the foreman told us to get on with it. We started. The dirt came down the chute at the rate of knots. The sacks were filling up sooner than we could replace them; a pile of dirt was building up on the floor and we could hardly breathe for dust. In a fit of temper I threw a sack on the floor and turned to the guard, telling him that the whole thing was impossible and that he should tell the foreman either to slow the process down or bring another man to help. I had shouted at guards before then but generally I had picked my man. On this occasion I acted a bit too hastily. I had picked on the wrong man! The guard swung his rifle off his shoulder and placed himself in position to deliver a butt stroke, at the same time yelling at the top of his voice, '*Verfluchte Engländer! Hau hin! sonst mach' ich dich kaput!*' (Cursed Englishman! Get on with it, or I'll smash you!)

One look was enough to convince me that he was not bluffing. He was certainly not a man to be trifled with. We got on with it and carried on getting on with it for the rest of the day, the guard hardly letting us out of his sight.

On the way back to camp that evening Jock and I swore that we had worked our last day at the sugar factory. And we had. Jock had been badly wounded in France; after the German surgeon had removed a large piece of shrapnel from his back he had left a hole into which one could insert a fist. So Jock would report sick the following day with the absolute certainty that he would be declared unfit for work and recommended for return to the main camp at Lamsdorf. That is exactly what happened.

I, however, was caught for the six o'clock shift, but as soon as we were lined up for selection by the foreman I made certain I was in the rear rank and hardly had we halted before I crept away and hid. When all the lads had been taken away I crept out of my hiding place, started to explore and eventually found the ideal hiding place. The beets having been cleaned were boiled in huge tanks, the ash from the fires which heated them fell through a grill into a huge cellar from which it was carried away in wheelbarrows by a gang of prisoners. The far corner of this cellar was dark and warm and that is where I lay all day, sleeping and waking and waiting for knocking-off time.

When I got back I learnt that Jock had indeed got his ticket back to Lamsdorf. It was now my turn to try. The sick parade every morning at the local military hospital was huge. Everybody wanted to get back to Lamsdorf. Dr Schwartz knew that and he had no doubt seen thousands of malingerers in his time. It was no use telling him that one had a pain in the back; if he could not see it or measure it, it did not exist and he uttered one word: *Arbeiten!* (Work!) So I had to use my imagination. When my number was called I did not stagger in to his consulting-room. Instead I walked in smartly and greeted him politely with a '*Guten morgen, Herr Stabs-Arzt!*' He looked up at me and almost mumbled, '*Guten morgen!*' But what he did say was, 'And what is the matter with you?'

'TB sir,' I said.

'.B?'

'Yes sir.'

'And how long have you had that?'

'All my life, sir. I was born with it.'

'Nonsense! If you had TB you would not be a soldier.'

'I am not a soldier, sir. I am a civilian. I was working in a canteen in France and should never have been put in a prisoner-of-war camp.'

'Take your shirt off!'

He examined me carefully and said, 'What are the symptoms of this TB of yours?'

'Shortage of breath and heavy sweating at night.'

'So! And you say you've always had it?'

'Yes sir. All my family has TB. My father died of it and so did my brother and sister.'

He picked up the telephone. 'I have an *Engländer* here, a prisoner of war but he maintains he is a civilian and that he is comsumptive. Isn't there a place for consumptive prisoners of war in Switzerland run by the Red Cross? That's the place for him, I should have thought. What did you say? Lamsdorf? Send him back to Lamsdorf? Right away? Very well then, I'll put him down as unfit for work and recommend that he be sent back to Lamsdorf.' He put the phone down and said to me, 'Did you understand that?'

'No sir,' I said.

'Put your clothes on then and clear out!'

I did not tell a soul apart from Jock, otherwise they would have all gone sick with TB and my trip to Lamsdorf would have been cancelled!

Lamsdorf

When I was in Lamsdorf in 1940 the camp was being extended; by now, November, 1942, the work had been completed and it contained thousands of prisoners from many nations. Although the majority were British, with considerable numbers of Australians, Canadians, New Zealanders and South Africans there were Americans, Indians, Arabs and representatives of most European countries, all speaking their own language, forming national groups and following their own way of life. That was not at all difficult, for, as far as the Germans were concerned, everyone could do just as he liked. They did not bother about what went on inside the perimeter fence, all they concerned themselves with was the prevention of escapes. In that they had complete success. As far as I know no one managed to escape from Lamsdorf, despite many attempts. Several tunnels were dug, but, as soon as they were completed, the Germans drove heavy lorries inside the perimeter fence and caused them to collapse. It was obvious that they had reliable sources of inside information.

The camp was surrounded by a double barbed-wire fence about twenty feet high. Between the two fences was a veritable thicket of coiled barbed-wire that even a mouse would have found difficult to penetrate. Every fifty yards was a high tower standing some hundred feet away from the wire. The tower was equipped with a machine-gun and a searchlight and was manned day and night. Some twenty feet from the perimeter was a warning wire about three feet high. Anyone crossing that wire was liable to be shot without warning. In addition there were armed sentries patrolling the perimeter day and night.

The Germans had found it impossible to maintain order within the camp and had abandoned the task. With a very few exceptions the men refused to recognize the authority of warrant officers and non-commissioned officers. I'm glad to be able to say, though, that this was not the case in my own regiment. The senior warrant officer in the camp was Regimental Sergeant-Major Sherriff of the Royal Welsh Fusiliers who had been a prisoner in Lamsdorf in the First World War. I believe he did his best to maintain some sort of discipline but since he had no means of punishing malefactors his task was practically impossible. The vacuum which resulted in the refusal of the Germans to accept responsibility for internal discipline and the inability of the prisoners to impose self-discipline on themselves was filled by gangs of strong-arm thugs, many of them armed with open razors. Their purpose was theft, theft of food from Red Cross parcels or anything else that caught their fancy. They succeeded through terror. Anyone resisting the gang would be beaten mercilessly, some having their faces slashed.

There was a flourishing market in the camp, the currency being cigarettes. On the stalls were the contents of the Red Cross parcels and of the personal parcels from home. Anyone with plenty of cigarettes could live really well; needless to say it was the gangsters who had the cigarettes. Anyone who thinks that prisoners of war are all on one level are greatly mistaken. Just as at home, there were rich and poor in the camps; the rich were the strong and unscrupulous while the poor were the weak and meek.

One could say that in Lamsdorf there were three social strata – a small minority employed in camp administration, who lived in what was known as the 'Rackets' compound where they had luxuriously appointed bunks made from the packing-cases in which the Red Cross parcels came and which were heated with the fuel that should have been shared evenly between all the various compounds. These administrators controlled the issue of rations, of Red Cross parcels and of mail; they were a sort of civil service whose ranks were closed and could only be entered by personal influence. They were the insiders, the haves.

The second stratum was the outsiders, the have-nots, prisoners who came in from working-parties for various reasons and recently caught prisoners. In their compounds there were not even beds, all had been broken up to provide heat in winter, and not only beds but also doors and window-frames. They slept on the concrete floor and stamped their feet to keep themselves warm. The only thing that kept them going was the Red Cross parcel, that is to say, that part of it that the armed gangs allowed them to keep, for it was on them the gangs prayed. The people in the Rackets compound were safe, for they had a Police Force, ostensibly to guard the Red Cross store. The third stratum was the armed thugs.

Lamsdorf was no place for Jock Souter and I, so we volunteered to go to a working-camp. Early in December we were on our way to Münsterberg, a small town on the River Oder, in the company of half-a-dozen other young men, among them my cousin, a Royal Marine aged nineteen who had been fished out of the Mediterranean by a German ship after his own, H.M.S. *Gloucester*, had been sunk during the evacuation of Crete. There was also a very cheerful character from Wrexham by the name of Glyn Salisbury who had been captured following the Commando raid on St Nazaire. Glyn had a daughter born on the day of the raid. He had sent his wife a strict order that she be christened Sainte Nazaire Salisbury! I visited Glyn after the war and discovered that his wife had failed to comply with his orders and had christened their daughter Blodwen!

Münsterberg

Münsterberg was a small town on the River Oder in the province of German Silesia a few miles from the old Polish Frontier.

The camp was a large house; its windows were barred and it was surrounded by a high barbed-wire fence. There were only about forty prisoners, all British apart from one New Zealander. They worked in a factory making earthenware pipes of all descriptions, and conditions of work were very good. In fact it was a very good camp. We were given two hot meals a day plus a ration of half a kilo of good, solid, dark German bread. Since we received a Red Cross parcel every week, some eight pounds of good food, we lived like fighting cocks and were all in excellent physical condition.

Relations with the German civilians in the factory were very good. Most of them, I would go as far as to say ninety per cent of them, were anti-Nazi. The two men I worked with were Communists and so were a large number of others who called in for a chat about the military and political situation whenever the opportunity arose. I am proud to say that they trusted me absolutely. They knew that, had I betrayed them, they would have landed in a concentration camp. They gave me a detailed history of the pre-war years in Germany, the growth of the Nazi party and the street battles that had taken place between it and the Communist party. They listened regularly to the BBC and to the Russian news service and kept me informed of what they heard. They were quite convinced that the Allies would win the war and said that when the Red Army arrived they would fight alongside it.

All in all Münsterberg was a very good camp although I nearly met my end there. I and a couple of other chaps had reported sick one day, more for the opportunity of a stroll to town where the Military Hospital was situated than for any other reason. It was in

February, 1943, a few days after the surrender of the German 6th Army in Stalingrad. The whole of the country was in official mourning, all flags at half-mast and people wearing armbands of black crepe. It was the first German defeat of the war and was, of course, a very major defeat, one that had shaken the people's faith in final victory. For the first time they realized that defeat was a distinct possibility. There was no need for black crepe to show how the people felt; their frightened and sombre mood was evident in their faces.

We were jubilant, of course, and made no attempt to hide the fact.

At the hospital the doctor took one look at our healthy faces and ordered us back to work. I believe he also rebuked the guard for bringing us there to waste his time. The guard was a young man in his early twenties who had been severely wounded on the Russian front. He double-marched us as soon as we were out of the hospital. About half way back to camp there was a level-crossing and when we arrived at it the gates were shut. While we were waiting for the train to come the gate-keeper came along and started a conversation with the guard. He suggested to him that we were malingerers and that a good hiding would do us no harm. He went on to say that we did not deserve any respect as we were obviously cowards who had put up our hands and surrendered rather than fight. Instead of telling him to clear off the guard encouraged him, so I ventured to tell him that under the Geneva Convention it was his duty to protect us from insults by the civilian population and not to encourage them.

I had again picked on the wrong man. The guard immediately unslung his rifle and came for me with the bayonet. He tried to turn me round but I kept facing him for I knew that he would have stuck his bayonet right into me had I presented my back to him and started to run. He was shouting frenziedly and it was quite plain that he was not putting on an act.

The bayonet was no more than an inch from my chest and I felt that my last moment had arrived. Just then the train came roaring past and the guard regained a little of his self-control. The gates opened and the guard yelled at us to get going. This we did with alacrity, but as I turned round I felt a searing pain in my thigh. I turned to face the guard but he gave me such a shove with the butt of his rifle that I went flying for yards. The other two lads then shouted at the guard before grabbing me by each arm and dragging me forwards. I could feel the blood running down my leg.

When we got back to camp the guard took us to the Underofficer in charge and told him what had happened without hiding anything. When I tried to intervene he turned to me and said, 'The next time, I'll shoot you dead!'

The Underofficer merely nodded and dismissed us.

I felt it was time I left Münsterberg and immediately started to plan an escape.

The Second Attempt

I had two good friends in the camp who were very keen on joining me in my attempt. They were George Bell of the Norfolk Regiment and Dick Mills of the Welsh Guards. Neither had made a previous attempt but George had had some hair-raising experiences in France where he had been on the run for months after the end of the fighting at Dunkirk. He had been hidden by a French family but had finally been betrayed to the Germans together with a number of other British soldiers in the area by a British soldier who turned renegade. The French people who had helped them had been sent to a concentration camp. George was a very bitter person.

It was difficult to decide which direction to take. Poland was the nearest country in which we might hope to find a friendly population, but there was no way out of Poland and the whole country was riddled with occupation troops. France and Switzerland were hundreds of miles away. Czechoslovakia was only some forty miles to the south. We could expect to find a friendly population there and far fewer Germans than in Poland. Beyond Czechoslovakia was Austria and Yugoslavia where Tito was carrying on a successful resistance and where we knew there was a British Military Mission. We decided we would try and join it.

So we started our preparations. As we were furnished with two-piece navy-blue working overalls with the letters 'KGF' (*Kriegs-gefangene*) on the back of the jacket civilian clothes was no problem. We simply sewed a patch taken from the leg of a spare pair of trousers over the letters. I also obtained a quantity of dye and dyed our battle-dress black. A civilian cap each from the same source completed our going-away trousseau. I also obtained a compass. As we intended to go on foot, walking by night and hiding by day, we needed a large quantity of food, so every week we put by biscuits and chocolates from the Red Cross parcels, also a large quantity of prunes, obtained mostly by swapping with the other lads against other commodities. Tinned food was not a possibility as all tins had to be opened on issue. This was to prevent the stocking-up of food for the purpose of escaping.

Breaking out of camp was not a serious problem. Escaping from the factory during the day would have been relatively easy except for the fact that our absence would have been discovered within four hours at the outside. We wanted a much longer start so we decided to try and break out from inside the camp early on a Saturday evening. With luck that might give us until Monday without being missed. The sergeant and the other lads were only too glad to do what they could to cover up for us. As no one had ever attempted to escape from the camp the Underofficer and guards were hardly alert to the possibility.

Red Cross supplies were kept in the attic of the house; there were two locks to the door, one key being held by the Underofficer and the other by the British Sergeant. On the second storey slept the Underofficer and guards while we slept on the ground floor. At about six o'clock every Saturday the store was opened by the Underofficer and Sergeant and the parcels were issued.

We planned to lure the Underofficer from the store just before the last parcel was issued, move our escape kit into the store and hide it and ourselves behind the packing cases. Then, as soon as it became dark, climb on to the roof through the skylight and climb down the wall via the drain-pipe.

Saturday the 24th of April was chosen for the break-out. Dick and George and I put on our escape clothes, rolled up our trousers to the knee and, with our army overcoats on, went up to the Red Cross store. Another couple of lads carried our escape food. With only some half-a-dozen parcels left to be issued, one of the lads shouted from the ground floor where the camp office was situated that the Underofficer was wanted urgently on the telephone. The call was taken up all the way up the stairs to the attic. The Underofficer told the Sergeant to carry on; he would be back to lock up, and off he went. We three immediately slipped into the room and hid behind the packing cases. Soon the Underofficer came back grumbling that whoever had been on the phone had hung up. As all parcels had been issued the door was closed and double-locked. It would be about seven o'clock in the evening. About an hour later it would be dark. We tried to open the window, but found we couldn't. The bar for lifting it had been removed and it looked as if the window frame had been firmly cemented as a security measure. Fortunately, however, there was a jemmy in the room used for opening the packing cases. With that we prised the window free and lifted it right out. Then by helping each other, all three of us managed to climb out on to the roof. The rain was falling in torrents and it was almost pitch dark. It was also very slippery and dangerous on that sloping roof. Fortunately, we had made a very accurate reconnaissance and knew exactly where the corner of the building was where the down-pipe was located. We lay flat on our bellies and let ourselves down very gradually until we felt the gutter under our feet; then we moved sideways until we came to the down-pipe. It was a tricky business but the three of us managed to get down safely. Climbing the perimeter wire was child's play and soon we were moving through the factory grounds and over the railway line making for the open country. The rain poured without cease. In a matter of minutes we were wet to the skin, but, what was worse, the endless ploughed fields through which we trudged were a quagmire into which we sank up to the ankles with every step we took. We could not have chosen a worse time for our escape had we tried to.

I had a sort of pillow-case on my back. I had tied a string on each end of it and slung it over my shoulders bandolier-fashion. It contained some twenty pounds of prunes but I am quite certain that within an hour each one of those prunes had soaked in some three times its weight in rain-water and that the pack then weighed about sixty pounds!

Having walked for about an hour we took our bearings with the compass and marched towards the south. It was too dark to pick out any feature at which to aim so we just went on blindly, hoping that we were at least putting some distance between us and the camp.

It was extremely hard going. We were in open country, in endless ploughed fields with neither hedge nor pasture to break the never-ending furrows. There was no stopping, for, in addition to being wet, the weather was also bitterly cold. And there was no shelter and not an inch of dry ground on which to sit or lie, not even a tree to lean against. We just gritted our teeth and trudged on. But there were no recriminations because we had foreseen that there would be danger and hardships and had promised each other that we would not quarrel on that score, all three of us having entered upon the venture with our eyes open.

After some four or five hours we were so tired that we could not go any further. But we had to remain on our feet, for had we gone down on the wet and muddy field we would never have got up again. Dick Mills was not as strong as George and I. He was very tall and rather thin and was feeling the strain much worse than we were. So we put our arms around his waist and told him to relax as much as he could while we held him up. Dick closed his eyes and managed to sleep for about a quarter of an hour. By then George and I would be so cold that we could stand it no longer. We would then drag Dick along for half a mile before repeating the process. We carried on thus till dawn when we arrived on the bank of a big river – the Neisse, the river which with the Oder now forms the western border of Poland.

We had known that we would have to cross this river but we did not know how big it was. We were afraid to try and cross by one of the bridges in case they might be guarded. Our intention was to swim across, or rather to wade if that were possible. It was still too dark to see the far bank so we decided to wait until it became lighter. And what a good job we did. When daylight came I literally shuddered when I saw how deep and wide the river was. After the torrential rain of the previous night the river was swollen up to its banks and flowed dark and swift and menacing. Had we attempted to cross an hour earlier we would certainly have been drowned. We had to find a more favourable crossing-point. We walked along the bank for about a mile until we came to a place where there were waves and ripples indicating that the river was shallower at that spot.

The rain had stopped and a cold, watery sun had broken through the clouds. We were extremely glad to see it. Beyond the river meadows and copses stretched towards a line of wooded hills which we guessed to be the foothills of the Altvater mountains beyond which was Bohemia, until 1938 part of Czechoslovakia. A few miles further up the river we could see the smoke of the town of Glatz (now Klodzko).There were two bridges there, we knew – a road-bridge and a railway-bridge, but it was out of the question to try and cross in daylight.

So we had to brave the water. It was decided that I should cross first on my own. I found a stout stick and waded into the river. The water was icy cold, and no wonder, as it flowed from the mountains where the snows were probably melting.

Leaning firmly on my staff, I waded slowly and carefully into the current. I moved sideways, facing upstream and moving my feet inch by inch, not daring to raise them, merely sliding them along the bed of the river; I had to ensure that both my feet were firmly on the ground, for had I raised a foot the current would have had the better of me, would have turned me round and carried me away. With the heavy bag of prunes on my back my chances of getting back to the land would have been slim indeed. So, leaning forward with all my strength on my staff and without raising it or my feet even a quarter of an inch from the river bed, I sidled across inch by inch.

The current was extremely strong, breaking in a wave across my chest and tugging at my legs behind the knees. By the time I got to midstream I knew that Dick Mills had not an earthly chance of completing the crossing. Being well over six feet tall and rather thin, he would never have been able to withstand the strength of the current. But I had gone too far to turn back; I had to go on to the far bank and rest.

When I climbed out of the river I turned and saw that George and Dick had already started to cross. I shouted at them to go back but they could not hear me and kept on coming. I jumped up and gesticulated like a madman for I knew beyond all shadow of a doubt that Dick was facing certain death. There was nothing for it but to enter the water again and to start the return crossing while continuing to wave the other two back. Seeing me coming towards them they got the message and turned around.

The initial crossing must have taken a lot out of me; I had hardly the strength for the return trip. I could hear the current roaring in my ears; I could see the river standing still while I was moving upstream at a speed of knots. I had to make a superhuman effort to maintain my self-control. I gritted my teeth, closed my eyes and told myself over and over again: 'I am not going to drown! I am not going to drown!' I defied all the might of the river and forced myself across inch by inch without daring to open my eyes.

Dick and George must have seen my distress for they plunged into the river to help me out. I collapsed on the bank. They undressed me and told me afterwards that I was literally blue with cold. They slapped me, rubbed me and beat me with twigs until I came round. I then ran and leapt about to keep warm while my clothes were drying on the bushes.

It was the 25th of April and the sun was fairly strong and, since there was also a stiff breeze, my clothes, although far from dry, were fit to put on before very long. Then, having eaten, we huddled together under the bushes and managed to get a little sleep. We woke up every twenty minutes or so shivering with the cold and had to exercise violently to get a little warmth back into our limbs.

We decided to try to cross over one of the bridges at Glatz but that would not be possible until after dark. As soon as it was dusk we walked along the river bank until we arrived at the railway bridge. There we sat down out of sight and watched the trains going over. Most of them were goods trains and had one of them slowed down sufficiently we would have jumped into a wagon and taken a chance on its destination, provided it was going in a southerly direction.

We waited for hours; we did not have a watch between us and ideally we didn't want to venture through Glatz until after midnight, when, we hoped, the streets would be deserted.

Eventually we climbed the embankment on to the bridge. We crossed without seeing a soul, then left the railway in case we landed in the station and found ourselves unable to get out. We were now in the town and terrified of being stopped by a policeman. Although we tried to walk as quietly as possible our footsteps in our hob-nailed army boots resounded like claps of thunder in the deserted streets. It was a largish town but we went through it without encountering a soul. The sky was clear, so we had no difficulty in maintaining direction. By this time our compass was waterlogged and quite useless.

At last we left the town behind us and before dawn we were climbing steadily through wooded country. We were heading south for the Moravian Gap, past the Glätzer Eisberg, some seven thousand feet high and still snow-capped, as we saw later that day. It was through this gap that Frederick the Great's Army marched against the Austrians, from whom he wrested Silesia. It was also this way that Bismarck's armies marched to the defeat of Austria at Sadowa, thus giving Prussia hegemony in Germany.

We were now marching through the Moravian Gap. What, we wondered, would be our fate.

The Three Bulgarians

We kept going until midday, marching through the forest parallel to the road. We were in very good spirits; our clothes were dry, we were warm, we had a major obstacle behind us and we were right on course. Also, we had enough food to last us for many days.

Having slept for a couple of hours we woke up stiff with cold and resumed our march. We kept going all night with short stops for food and a smoke. We were climbing steadily all the time.

The next morning we noticed that the appearance of the land had changed completely. There were no more ploughed fields to be seen, nothing but bog and scrub and forest, and in the distance the snow-capped Glätzer Eisberg.

Some time towards mid-morning we came across an isolated farmhouse and thought it might be a good idea if we called and got the farmer's wife to boil us some water for tea. We did not want to light fires in case we attracted unfavourable attention. We watched the farmhouse for long time before we ventured to approach it. All we saw was a young woman occasionally going in and out.

Cautiously we went up to the door and knocked. It was opened by a young woman of about eighteen and an extremely handsome young woman at that. I saluted her politely and asked her in German whether we could have some boiling water with which to make tea. The girl merely looked at us with round eyes; a voice, obviously the voice of an old woman, could be heard from inside the house asking who was there. We took that as an invitation and walked in.

It was a very poor, sparsely-furnished room into which we walked. At one end was the hearth on which a wood fire was burning; beside it sat a very old woman. On one side of the room was a long wooden table with wooden benches on each side of it and opposite an old sofa, on which the girl now sat, her legs tucked up under her.

The old woman began to cackle something, but in a language I did not understand. I now know that it was Wendish, the language of the Wends, a Slavonic people related to the Poles and Czechs who have managed to retain a semblance of their identity and language in that remote part of the country. I asked her whether she spoke German. She nodded but said that her grand-daughter spoke it much better. Turning to the girl I explained to her that we were Bulgarians who had been working in Germany but were now going home, walking as much as possible to save our money which we wanted as a down-payment on a small farm. The old woman kept butting in to find out what I was saying while the girl interpreted for her. I then asked the girl whether she would boil us a kettle of water with which to make tea. She agreed at once and lowered the kettle on to the flame before returning to the sofa and tucking her legs under her. I took a good look at her. I put her at about seventeen or eighteen – and very, very pretty. She had jet black hair with a bluish sheen to it, round, dark eyes, under arched brows, high cheekbones, a small well-formed nose and beautifully moulded red lips. A real beauty, blooming and blushing unseen in that remote wooden shack! She kept looking from one to the other of us and gave no hint of resentment at our uninvited visit. There was nothing demure about her; she did not drop her eyes when looked at but gazed steadily back.

We made the tea and gave the old woman and the girl a cup each, which they sipped, although it was obvious that it was a drink with which they were not very familiar. I asked the girl whether her father and grandfather were about and she replied that the former was in Russia in the Army and the latter dead. It seemed, therefore, that there were no men about the place at all. We discussed this point and suggested that it might be a good place to hide up for a few days and get a good rest. I asked the girl to ask her grandmother whether she would like some work done on the farm for two or three days; we didn't want any payment and we would eat our own food and sleep in the barn.

From the altercation that took place it was immediately obvious that what the old granny wanted most was to see our backs, and the reason for it was also quite obvious – she was worried about her grand-daughter.

After a few minutes, we decided that Granny was right and that the farm was far too dangerous a place in which to hang about. So, thanking them both profusely and giving the girl a bar of soap, we took our leave. The girl accompanied us to the door and as I said my final '*Auf wiedersehen*' I thought she gave me a look which almost amounted to an accusation of cowardice.

As the country was so desolate we decided it was safe enough to walk during the day, so we made very good progress. The weather was fine, the sun quite warm and the ground had dried well enough for us to lie down and snatch a little sleep.

By the following morning we were through the Gap and starting the descent. It was magnificent country, mighty hills and mountain peaks all round, huge forests, and in the distance the rolling plains of Moravia. Somewhere over there was the town of Moravska-Ostrava, a place where we might get help.

We were now going downwards through alternating areas of forests and clearings with the odd isolated farm dotted here and there. It was obvious that we were in a Catholic district from the number of crosses and images of the Virgin Mary that were a prominent feature of every cross-road, each accompanied by a text or a prayer and all in German. Although neither of us was a Catholic, nor were we particularly devout, we nevertheless, took some comfort from the sight of these sacred emblems.

About midday we went into the forest to eat and to snatch a couple of hours of sleep. It was warm and sunny and we all fell asleep. It was to cost us dear.

I was woken up by George. A man was aiming a rifle at us. We woke Dick. I then got up slowly, yawned and stretched and called to the man, '*Guten Tag, Mein Herr!*'

He did not reply. Instead he seemed to press the rifle more firmly to his shoulder.

He stood about twelve paces away. I started towards him.

'*Halt!*'

I obeyed and took stock of him. A fairly tall, well-built man wearing green breeches and jackboots, a green jacket and a green hat turned up on one side and decorated with wild-boar bristle. A forester or a game-warden, he had a healthy-looking well-tanned face, skin that looked like well-polished leather, a pair of eyes hooded like a falcon and a beak like an eagle. A man of the great open-air if ever I had seen one and a very determined-looking man at that. I cursed our folly for being caught napping by such a man.

'A beautiful day,' I said.

'What are you doing here?' was his reply.

'Resting,' I said.

'Forbidden!' he said, 'Trespassing in the forest is forbidden!'

'I'm sorry,' I said. 'We didn't know, but I promise we'll never do it again.'

'Where have you come from?'

'From Germany. We've been working in Dresden. We are Bulgarians and now we are going home and we are walking to save the train fare. Our parents need the money; they are very poor.'

If I expected to see a sign of sympathy on his face I was disappointed. I took a step towards him.

'Halt! Out of the wood and on to the road! I am taking you to the mayor!'

There were still some twelve paces separating us. Had there been just half-a-dozen I might have tried rushing him, for the thought of three of us being taken by one man was unbearable. I turned to the other two and told them what he intended to do with us and we discussed whether to defy him or to comply and wait for a better chance.

Hawkeye realized what we were up to for he took a couple of paces backwards and said in a very stern and not-to-be-ignored voice:

'*Auf die Strasse, marsch!*' (Quick march on to the road.)

We obeyed but tried to give the impression that we were only doing so out of politeness. He walked behind us, still maintaining an interval of twelve paces, and still holding his rifle in position for an instant shot. I tried to draw him into conversation, but it was no use. Whenever we stopped, he stopped. There was no getting rid of him and no getting round him. We had been well and truly caught and there was nothing to do but allow him to march us to the mayor.

Soon we arrived at the edge of the village. It was late afternoon and the children were out of school. When they saw us they came running and fell in beside us. They had probably seen the game warden coming home many a time with a hare or a couple of pigeons but this was the first time they had seen him drive three strange-looking men in front of him. What a hero he must have appeared to them.

We found the mayor waiting for us on the doorstep; our captor must have sent word ahead to warn him of our arrival.

The mayor was a shortish middle-aged man in a tweed suit with a swastika badge, indicating that he was a Party member, in the lapel of his jacket. He had a smiling, cheerful face and did not look at all forbidding. Our captor made his report, to the effect that he had arrested us for unlawful trespassing in the State Forest.

'You are Bulgarians?' asked the mayor.

'Yes sir,' I said. 'We are Bulgarians who have been working voluntarily in Dresden and now we are going home and walking to save the fare. The summer is coming and it will be quite pleasant to walk and sleep out. We are very sorry that we went to the forest but we didn't know that it was forbidden. Everyone can walk in the woods in Bulgaria.'

The mayor smiled politely.

'May I see your papers, please?'

'Papers? What papers?'

'Your passports, of course.'

'Passports? We don't have passports! We don't need passports in Bulgaria.'

'You must have passports,' said the mayor, smiling kindly at our naiveté. 'Otherwise you'll be arrested by the Police. You will not get far without passports. Perhaps I can help you. Wait a minute.' He smiled again and went into the house.

Soon he reappeared, saying: 'Someone who will be able to help you will soon be here.'

Yes, I thought and I have a good idea who that will be.

Before very long we heard the sound of a car approaching.

'It looks as if they are going to give us a lift,' said Dick.

A car drew up and two policemen got out of it. Having greeted the mayor with a Heil Hitler they turned to us and one of them said in a no-nonsense tone of voice, 'Who are you?'

'British prisoners of war,' I replied. The mayor's smile widened until it reached from ear to ear. Within seconds we had been searched, handcuffed and bundled into the back of the car. Then with another Heil Hitler the policemen got into the front and we drove off. We tried to wave to the game warden but he did not respond; he merely stood there impassively looking the very embodiment of virtue being its own reward.

The two policemen were quite friendly and not at all averse to accepting our cigarettes. They asked us where we had escaped from and why. I told them from Münsterberg, and that the only reason was boredom and our love of adventure. They thought that very amusing and on the whole very praiseworthy. They even went so far as to say that they would probably do the same. I tried to give them the impression we were three happy-go-lucky young men and not at all dangerous.

Having arrived in a small town we were lodged in the cell, all three together.

Although the window was barred and the door was locked our handcuffs were not removed. We were fastened together with George in the middle. Dick and I had an arm free but poor George didn't. We soon set up a howl and when a policeman arrived we requested most politely that we be set free. After a consulation it was agreed and although we were given a hot meal we had a very uncomfortable night. There was no bed in the cell, just a wooden bench and the walls were dripping with damp and the ironwork red with rust. We had slept out for five or six nights without catching a cold but after just one night in that cell we were coughing and shivering like consumptives.

The following morning we were collected in a truck by two soldiers and taken to the barracks in Glatz. The journey which had taken us four days on foot was accomplished in three hours by truck.

After three days in the guardroom where we were well treated and were objects of considerably curiousity to the soldiers, we were taken to the headquarters in Neisse.

My second attempt at escaping had turned out to be a failure.

From Camp to Camp

At Neisse we were marched in front of the *Gerichtsoffizier* (Disciplinary Officer). We were accused of escaping in civilian clothes, being in possession of German money illegally obtained, criminal damage to the attic window in the camp and trespassing in the State Forest.

This of course was merely a matter of form in order to justify the punishment, for escaping was in itself no offence. The possession of German money was a serious matter but all three of us swore that we had found it under a bench on the roadside somewhere beyond Glatz. It was obvious that the *Gerichtsoffizier* did not believe us; he nevertheless accepted our story. The alternative would have been to call in the civil police to interrogate us; that meant the Gestapo, but the German Military was always loath to hand over prisoners of war to the tender mercies of those people. Our interrogater knew quite well that we had received the money from the civilians in the factory where we had worked. He also knew that the Gestapo had a sure way of eliciting that information from us and what the consequences would have been for those unfortunate people.

We were sentenced to twenty-eight days in a punishment camp for the criminal damage to the window and for the wearing of civilian clothes.

The camp was a stone quarry in the Sudeten mountains. There were some forty prisoners there altogether, serving sentences for various offences, ranging from escaping to striking civilians and sabotage.

Life was hard. We were called at half-past-five every morning and marched to the quarry where we were required to load a certain number of skips – small trucks running on rails – with large hunks of stone, push them about a mile and unload them into a large crusher. There were two men to each skip and as each was unloaded we were given a disc. No one was allowed to finish until the last disc had been collected. It was a case of helping each other and rarely did we finish before five or six in the evening. We then marched back to camp and received our rations for the following day. We were locked in at all times apart from when we were at work.

When our time was up we were returned to Münsterberg looking very brown and fit after our restcure in the mountains.

There was a new Underofficer, the other one having been posted for allowing us to escape. George and Dick were allowed to join the other prisoners but I, as the instigator of the escape, was put in the bunker pending return to Lamsdorf. Who did I find there but two old friends in the shape of Johnnie Beatty and Charlie MacDonald, both of the Cameron Highlanders and real hard cases, but in the nicest way. They had been sent to the camp as replacements for us, but, finding the régime so strict as the result of our escape, they refused to work. Although threatened with all kinds of violence they had refused to budge, so the Underofficer was sending them back to Lamsdorf for court martial. That did not seem to worry them in the slightest.

In a couple of days we were on our way under armed escort.

Since typhus had broken out in a nearby camp for Russian prisoners and since it was believed that the disease was spread by lice every newcomer to Lamsdorf was deloused in an annexe before entering the main camp.

We too had to suffer this very undignified treatment. Some fifty of us were taken into a room and told to undress completely. Our clothes were taken from us and put into a huge steam boiler where they remained for hours. In the meantime we were herded into another room and as we entered each was given a daub of soft-soap on the palm of his hand and told to rub it over the whole of his body. Then, suddenly, without any warning, a boiling hot shower descended on us from above, causing every one to howl and leap like madmen to try and avoid it, but there was no avoiding it and in a matter of seconds we were scalded until we were as red as lobsters. But as suddenly as it had come, the shower stopped, to be followed in a few seconds by a shower of icy-cold water which brought even more cursing and leaping. The cold water stopped equally suddenly and we were left with the soft-soap lather still clinging to us most unpleasantly.

The door opened and we were allowed back into the room where we had undressed, only to wait what seemed like hours before finally receiving our clothes. And what a dreadful sight we were, all red and blotchy after the scalding we had suffered.

Finally our clothes arrived, hot and damp with steam and shrunken out of all shape. I swore to myself that I would never suffer such an undignity again and I never did.

As soon as we were out of the de-lousing unit Johnnie, Charlie and I fell in with a squad returning to the main camp after working outside. Once through the gates we slipped one by one from the ranks and made our way to the Working Compound, the place from which men were recruited for the working-camps. It was run by a German Underofficer nominally, but the real administration was done by Company Sergeant Major Charters, Grenadier Guards, whom I knew. We went to him and told him that we had been returned to Lamsdorf for punishment and asked him whether he could get us out onto a working-camp before the long arm of the *Gerichtsoffizier* got hold of us. Without a moment's hesitation he said, 'Boys! You are lucky. There is an Underofficer in from a forestry working camp. He brought three men in sick and unfit for work and he wants three men to replace them and to leave with him this afternoon. I'll take you to see him!'

We were taken to another office and introduced to a big, fat, sloppy, daft-looking Underofficer whom we saluted as if he had been a Field-Marshal. We stood to attention like three statues while Charters sang our praises and asked whether we would do. Fatface nodded and let himself in for a lot of trouble!

Within an hour we were sitting in the train opposite Fatface who looked fatter, lazier and more surly and sloppy than ever. He did, however, accept a cigarette, but when I tried to engage him in general conversation I was told to hold my snout. It was a beautiful June day and we had a delightful trainride through the Upper Silesian countryside where the farmers were harvesting their winter wheat. It was an idyllic scene and ages removed from war, want and fear.

Eventually we arrived at our destination and de-trained. Awaiting us was a dapper young man wearing what appeared to be blue battle-dress trousers and an open-neck check shirt. His hatless head was beautifully groomed. He greeted the Underofficer and took his briefcase. He then led the way out of the station to where a pony and trap stood and got into the driving seat. The Underofficer took his seat next to him; we were told to get into the back where there were no seats and with a cluck of the driver's tongue we were off at a gentle trot.

'A Sunday School trip,' said Charlie. 'I wonder where we are off to.'

'The Inverary Inn,' said Johnnie, 'to see the wee lassie therein!'

Soon we saw the driver bring a packet of Red Cross cigarettes out and offer one to Fatface. They both lit up and puffed away with obvious pleasure.

'I suppose we'll have to smoke our own,' said Johnnie, bringing his cigarettes out. Then, tapping the driver on the shoulder, he said, 'Are you a prisoner, mate?'

The driver looked around in obvious annoyance and replied shortly, 'Yes. Why?'

'Nothing,' said Johnnie, 'except that from behind I thought you were a German, you seem to have such a square head!'

He turned his head away with an offended air. Whereupon we started to discuss him in detail, and his probable relationship to the Underofficer. But he chose to ignore us.

Once we were out of the small village we were on a farm track. On each side stretched miles of rural Silesia and in the distance a line of dark conifers indicating where the forest for which we were bound began. The golden wheat was ripe and the harvest in full swing, the labour being provided mostly by horses and women, the latter bare-footed and with colourful kerchiefs around their heads. We whistled and waved to them and they waved back, raising their sunburnt, smiling faces from their work with obvious pleasure. Fatface shouted at us to hold our snouts and it was plain that the driver strongly disapproved of our undignified behaviour. We decided to modify it a little, not because we cared tuppence for our betters but because we decided to postpone a showdown until we had had a good look at the camp.

We contented ourselves instead with looking at the wonderful, unspoilt countryside. Although there were no hedges, the patchwork of various crops that were grown in the open field prevented any hint of monotony. Each crop had its own peculiar colour, from the golden yellow of the wheat to the lush dark green of the alfalfa and lucerne. The corn stood almost shoulder high and as the mowing machine went through it, drawn by a pair of mane-tossing, sweating horses, the birds rose from it in a cloud. And all the time there was the incessant droning and buzzing of insects. Looking at it brought a lump to my throat and an overwhelming feeling of *hiraeth* (yearning) – *hiraeth* for the farm where I was born and brought up.

At last we arrived at the camp which was situated on the edge of a little village. We were taken in but no one took much interest in us. We felt that there was a very strange atmosphere in that camp. The building was a public house which had been adapted for the purpose by the addition of iron bars to the windows and a high barbed-wire fence around the precincts.

Sometime in the early evening we noticed a couple of prisoners washing and shaving with considerable care, then putting on civilian shirts and ties, and, having combed their hair meticulously, enter the room in which the guards were housed. We asked one of the other prisoners where the two were going and were reluctantly given the information that they were going out to work. Very curious. We tried to get more precise information but that was not forthcoming. When we asked about the issue of Red Cross parcels we were told that individual parcels were not issued. They went to the kitchen and certain items were sold to provide extra rations, the whole being organized by the Camp Committee, which we were told consisted of six elected members. Curiouser and curiouser!

The following day we went to work in the forest. It was really marvellous. Some of the lads were employed in felling the trees with saws and axes while the others sawed them into lengths, stripped the bark off and stacked them. There was no pressure. The forester in charge marked the trees to be felled, prescribed the lengths they were to be cut into and where they were to be stacked. The guard just sat around sun-bathing and smoking – Red Cross cigarettes. I suppose that it could have been boring every day but we were not to suffer that – we only worked there that one day!

That evening we saw three prisoners dolling themselves up and going to the guards' living-quarters. Committee members we wondered! We were most curious and also determined to have a share of whatever there was going.

We went out into the small compound to have a look around. It was a beautiful June evening. Fields of corn stretched as far as the eye could see and here and there were gangs of people, mostly women, getting in the harvest.

'What about a stroll?' said Charlie. 'There's nothing nicer than roaming in the gloaming on a summer's evening.'

Johnnie and I agreeing whole-heartedly and, there being no guard visible, we climbed over the barbed-wire fence and walked leisurely towards the harvesters. They were most surprised to see us but we explained that we were now allowed out in the evenings because the war was nearly over, Germany being on the point of capitulation. In reply to their amazed disbelief we answered that the British and American armies had landed in France and that the Russians were already in Poland. Our listeners didn't know whether to believe us or not, neither were they sure whether to cheer or not. The peasantry in Upper Silesia were Roman Catholics, the older people spoke a Polish dialect and the church services were conducted in Church Slavonic and not in German. Furthermore, they did not relish the fact that their young men were being maimed and slaughtered on the Russian front.

Having sown alarm and despondency among them, we strolled back to camp; we climbed the wire and jumped down on the other side. I was the last and as I landed on the ground I heard a roar like that of a mad bull. Fatface came rushing out of the camp building. He charged straight for me and aimed a terrific swipe at my head. I managed to duck and before he could aim another one Charlie and Johnnie had rushed upon him and seized him, shouting at the top of their voices, '*Verboten! Verboten! Das ist verboten!*' Words that every prisoner knew.

I then rushed at him and put my fist under his nose, saying, 'Don't you ever do that again or we'll knock your head off! We know what is going on in this camp and if you are not careful we'll report it to the authorities!'

He was petrified, white as a sheet and shaking like a leaf. He did not say a word or attempt to struggle. We released him and he went inside, looking like a dog that had been kicked.

Later that evening a British Sergeant asked us whether we would like to return to Lamsdorf. We decided we would and were told to report sick the following morning. This we did and were declared unfit for work. In two days we were back in Lamsdorf.

Sandowitz

We dodged the undignities of the de-lousing unit and made our way to the working-compound and Sergeant-Major Charters. His first question was, 'Haven't you gone yet?'

'Yes,' we said, 'and we are back again. The camp didn't suit our purpose. We would like one on the Swiss frontier or work on a ship carrying coal to Sweden!'

The Sergeant-Major laughed and looked at me rather oddly. Then he said, 'Your elder brother was here yesterday and he has made a request that you be allowed to join him at his camp. There is a note in the office about it. Wait a minute.'

He was soon back with a piece of paper.

'Here it is,' he said. 'Guardsman Kenneth Elwyn, Welsh Guards, POW No 9983, at Sandowitz working-camp. What is your POW number?'

'9982,' I replied, showing him my disc.

'That is it!' he said. 'Do you want to go? The Underofficer has agreed.'

It was my old friend Ken Elwyn who, having obviously come across a good thing, wanted me to have a share. Having every faith in him I replied without hesitation, 'Oh yes. I would like to join my brother. We were separated last October. When can I go?'

'Tomorrow if I can arrange it.'

And indeed the following day I took leave of my two friends and travelled to Sandowitz under armed escort. It really was marvellous the way I was able to travel about Germany!

I was welcomed by Ken like the proverbial prodigal son. It is true that he did not have a fatted calf to give me but he had practically everything else in the way of meat, eggs, bread and schnapps. He was literally in clover.

'You're doing well here, Ken,' I said.

'Well!' he said. 'You haven't seen anything yet! You name it, I've got it, or at least I can get it. Would you like a woman?'

'A woman?'

'Yes. I could fix you up with any one of half-a-dozen!'

'Good Heavens! You'll make your fortune after the war! Where are these women then?'

'Come with me and I'll show you!' He took me to the window. We were on the second storey of a public house, and he let out a high, shrill whistle.

'Watch that window over there!' he said, pointing to a house opposite about thirty yards away, the gable-end of which was facing us. No sooner had he spoken than a woman's head appeared at the window. All I could see was a tanned face surrounded by a mop of thick, black hair.

'That's Franziska,' said Ken, then pushing me right into the window he shouted, '*Bruder! Bruder! Heute Abend! Zehn Uhr!*' (Brother! This evening! Ten o'clock!)

Franziska waved and disappeared.

'Ken,' I said, 'I always knew that you were a smart operator but this beats everything. What is she like?'

'She's cross-eyed,' he said, 'but you are not superstitious, are you?'

'Not at all,' I replied, 'but I think I'll wait until I see the other five before I decide. After all, I'm sure you want your young brother to have the best.'

'Honestly,' said Ken, 'I could not have had a better camp had I designed it myself. I do just as I like at work and I've got the guards here eating out of my hand.'

There were about thirty-five or so prisoners in the camp, all British apart from two Australians and excellent chaps they were. We were all housed on the upper floor of a public house, the guards in an adjoining room on the same floor. The storey below was occupied by the owners of the pub, a woman and her children, the husband being on the Russian front. Outside was a small yard containing the water pump surrounded by a high barbed-wire fence. The windows were barred. Some twenty-five of the prisoners worked in the forest, the others, including Ken, in a timber-yard belonging to the Count de la Croix, a descendant of a Huguenot family that had settled in Germany following the massacre of St Bartholomew. Ken arranged that I should work there. He was the Count's right-hand man, being one of those fortunate men who could turn his hand to everything. That, added to his tremendous personality, powers of persuasion and irresistible charm had enabled him to get the position of trouble-shooter. Any piece of machinery that went wrong he fixed in double-quick time. His inventive mind found the means of overcoming all obstacles and difficulties, while his sunny nature made him everybody's friend.

The Count had built a new house in the grounds of the timber-yard. Any problems arising there, such as a leaking tap, a blown fuse or a squeaking door were grist to his mill. He would be called to fix it and on the way to and from the house he invariably did two things. On the way there he gave Kaspar, the Count's billy-goat, a kick in the back-side that caused it to leap like a bucking bronco; this was in repayment for a butt that Ken had suffered at their first encounter. On the way back from the house he visited the poultry-house and helped himself liberally to eggs.

I remember one day when the Count and Ken and I were walking across to the house, the billy who was grazing nearby looked up and on seeing Ken leaped into the air and galloped away throwing his back legs as if he were about to do a somersault.

'*Kaspar! Kaspar! Komm doch! Komm doch!*' called the Count, but Kaspar was deaf to his call. 'I don't know what has come over Kaspar recently,' sighed the Count, 'he used to be so friendly. I fear some of those young boys have been tormenting him.' He spoke excellent English.

'Yes, that's what it is,' said Ken, 'and if I catch them I'll put my foot under their backsides with such force that they'll land in the Malapane' (the local river).

'Yes indeed, Ken,' said the Count, 'you do that. They deserve it. And another thing. The Countess tells me that she is sure that somebody is stealing eggs. I wish you would keep a sharp look-out for the thieves.'

'Leave it to me,' said Ken, 'I'll catch them.'

To say that we worked at the timber-yard would be an exaggeration. It was more of a rest-camp than a working-camp. There were only a few civilians there, all either unfit, too old or too young for military service and not one, not even the young lads who were members of the Hitler Youth, had any enthusiasm for it.

The régime in the camp itself was also extremely liberal and we were given a great deal of freedom. Frequently in the evenings a guard would take us to the Malapane for a swim. It was there, one evening, that I thought my end had come. I was standing on the parapet of the bridge with two or three young Germans. We were all fully clothed. Some thirty feet below us was the water – a raging, white torrent which had just been released from the weir upstream to turn the huge water-wheel of the mill which stood just behind us; the spray from it was thrown higher than our heads. One of the lads who worked at the timber-yard, a brown-faced devil-may-care youngster of sixteen nicknamed 'Bomber' challenged me to jump into the seething waters. I asked him whether he thought I was mad. His reply was a white-toothed grin and a leap into the river. I turned to the other lad and said, 'He'll drown!'

'*Keine Angst!*' he said (No fear!) and jumped in after him. My heart dropped for I knew I had no alternative but to follow them, and I was absolutely certain that I would drown. I jumped. It seemed ages before I hit the water. I felt it singing in my ears as I sank to the bottom. Then I realized that I was on the surface again, being carried downstream at great speed. Gradually the current abated and I was able to swim to the shore, some thirty or forty yards down from the bridge. Waiting for me on the bank were the two young lads, dripping wet, smiling and shouting 'Bravo!'

I took care not to stand on the parapet of the bridge again.

The Malapane was a delightful river. Apart from the steep gully just below the mill where the bridge stood, the river meandered slowly through lush, flat meadows between poplar- and willow-lined banks, its water clear and limpid. On each side was a well-trodden path along which the people of the village, young and old, took their evening walk. But what endeared it to me so much was the absolute peace that reigned there, that eternal peace that exists only in the countryside and among country people. No one shook his fist at us in Sandowitz or made any kind of rude or threatening gesture. On the contrary, they waved to us and each one of us knew that they wished us nothing but good.

Ken's expertise as handyman was well-known in the village and his services were in great demand. I always accompanied as interpreter and Dick Jones, another Welsh Guardsman, from Holyhead, and an Australian by the name of Keith Carr went along as assistants under instruction. A guard provided the escort. All four of us shaved and washed and combed our hair very carefully before leaving, dressed in our best battle-dress beautifully pressed. It was always well pressed because, being Guardsmen, we folded it meticulously under our mattress every night and took care to sleep to attention!

In most cases the request for Ken's services was only an excuse to invite us to supper and have a jolly social evening in which the guard was also allowed to share, albeit reluctantly, and provided he behaved himself! And what suppers we had – home-made bread and butter, home-made sausages and salami, home-made caraway-seed cake and home-made schnapps. Why did the people do it? The most probable reason is that, although they were Reichsdeutsche (natural-born German citizens), they regarded themselves, as Upper Silesians, as being a race apart who wished to have nothing to do with Hitler and his war.

We had some odd adventures, but the one I remember best is when a farmer came to the camp and asked whether there was a vet among the prisoners. In answer to the question Ken bawled out, 'Yes! I was training to be a vet when I was called up for the Army to fight a war for which I was not responsible!'

After a hurried but careful toilet the do-anything, go-anywhere gang accompanied by an armed but lame guard was on its way. The farmer walking ahead.

Arrived at the farm we were taken to a loose-box where three or four men stood leaning against the wall contemplating a horse lying on a bed of straw.

'This horse was working all right yesterday,' said the farmer. 'I put him in last night and gave him a good feed but this morning he was lying down and I have been unable to get him up all day and he has not eaten or drunk anything.' The horse was lying on his side with his neck stretched out.

'Ask him if he has given him anything,' said Ken after walking round him cautiously and shaking his head knowingly.

'Yes,' said the farmer, 'I gave him a dose of this,' handing him a large bottle containing a dark liquid. Ken removed the cork and sniffed it and turning to us said in Welsh, '*Pi-pi mul!*' (Donkey-pee)

'You haven't given him enough,' he said. 'Hold his head!'

The man knelt down on the horse and held his head and with the aid of a jack-boot with the toe cut out Ken poured the contents of the bottle down the horse's throat.

The animal remained perfectly still for a few seconds, then with a mighty effort he collected his legs under him and threw the men off. Then, breaking into a white lather of sweat, he struggled to his feet. A tremendous shiver shook his whole body and he leaped some three feet into the air and fell flat on the ground and with a horrible gasp stretched his neck out and lay perfectly still. I could swear that I saw his eye turn glassy.

There was a deathly silence for a few seconds before the farmer leant over the horse and examined him. Straightening up slowly he said in a strangled voice, 'You've killed my horse.'

I looked at Ken and the others and saw them disappear through the door. In no time I was after them. When I got to the yard Ken and the other two were strung out on the path and going for all they were worth. Looking round I saw the guard hobbling behind me and behind him was the farmer with a pitchfork in his hand!

The guard shouted and Ken called back, 'What is he saying?'

'He wants you to wait,' I called.

'Wait?' said Ken. 'Tell him to run unless he wants a few more holes in his backside!'

I stayed about six weeks at Sandowitz. It was an idyll. I could have stayed there until the end of the war, safe, well fed and happy but my mind was on escaping, escaping to Poland to join the Underground. My heart was in Poland with Celinka's people. She was a true Pole who would have given her life willingly for her country and that was what thousands of young Poles were doing just then, fighting against overwhelming odds, sacrificing their lives in the most heroic manner for what they believed in above everything – the freedom of their country.

I wouldn't dream of escaping from Sandowitz although nothing would have been simpler, because that would have spoilt the camp for everybody. So I told Ken that I wanted to return to Lamsdorf and, of course, he fixed it!

Ratibor

Having once more dodged the de-lousing parlour, I presented myself to Sergeant-Major Charters with a request that he find me a camp near the Polish frontier and near a main railway line.

He complied with pleasure and early in August I was on my way to Ratibor sugar-factory in the company of my cousin, the Royal Marine.

The military situation was changing rapidly. For Germany the days of victories were past. The Allies had cleared them out of North Africa and had taken Sicily. In the East the Russians had opened up their mighty offensive on the central sector between Orel and Bielgorod where they were poised for an advance towards the Polish border. I knew that the Resistance movements in Poland would be getting ready for major operations and I wished to take part in them.

Like Bauerwitz, Ratibor was a wide-open, free-for-all camp, where everyone fended for himself and the devil took the hindmost. The factory worked day and night and the lads were divided into shifts covering the whole twenty-four hours. The usual chaos reigned with everyone dodging work as much as they could. Many of the prisoners were new to the game, having been brought up from Italy when that country was facing collapse, so they were the ones that caught it most. The old hands went to the factory only when they needed sugar to make home-made schnapps or to sell it to civilians over the wall at night. We used to carry the sugar into camp in long elongated bags tied inside the legs of our trousers.

There was much drinking of home-made schnapps – pure alcohol and truly terrible in its effects. Some of the lads used to drink it until they became as stiff as corpses, some suffered temporary blindness, some became fighting mad and some, I was told, had become permanently blind.

The Author in 1944, wearing the clothes he was given in Sweden.

British Prisoners of War, Germany 1941. This was before Red Cross parcels started arriving regularly.

(*left*) Little Wanda: photograph taken just after the war.

(*below left*) Krystyna Perkowska after the war.

(*below*) Kazimiera Kaptacz after the war.

The Author at OCTU in 1944 – middle row, centre, wearing lanyard.

Group Captain Jackson, Defence Attaché, British Embassy, Warsaw; Pani Krystyna Perkowska; Pani Wanda Malinowska; Pani Kazimiera Kaptacz; RAF Sergeant. This picture was taken in August, 1986.

I remember one night my cousin and I and a chap called George Cook, a Glaswegian, were sitting at a table drinking this dreadful hooch. George took an open razor out and started to strop it on the palm of his hand. He talked of his life in Glasgow and how he had been a member of a razor-gang. He described battles that he had taken part in against rival gangs and of the slashings that had occurred. He himself had two or three nasty scars on his face which, he claimed, had been caused by razors. He had drunk a lot and was becoming quarrelsome and aggressive. He seemed to be itching to have a go at us but it was also quite obvious that he was sober enough to realize that he would be risking his life. We watched him very carefully and made it quite plain to him that we were doing so.

Eventually he staggered to his feet and said he was going to bed which was in the next room but separated from us only by an open doorway. He had not been gone a few seconds before we heard a scream. We rushed there and saw George standing by a bed, his razor in his hand and a man sitting up in the bed, his hand stretched out and dripping blood. I asked him what had happened but before he had time to answer George said, 'It was an accident! I asked him for a cigarette and he flung his arm out and struck the razor. It wasn't my fault. It was an accident!'

I grabbed him immediately and sent him flying across the room. My cousin picked up his razor and jumped on it several times before throwing it into the stove. I then asked the lad again what happened, telling him not to be afraid. He said, 'It was just as George said. It was an accident.'

I did not believe him. It could not have been an accident, but I understood why he chose to lie. He was terrified that George might slash him across the face if he were to tell the truth.

Most of the lads in the room in which my cousin and I slept were sailors, survivors from H.M.S. *Bedouin*, sunk off Pantellaria. They had been prisoners in Italy until the collapse, when they were brought to Germany. In the next room, separated only by an open doorway, in which stood the communal stove, the majority were South Africans, mostly Afrikaners. They had been caught when Rommel took Tobruk in June, 1942, and were suspected by the British prisoners taken in that campaign of having surrendered the garrison deliberately to the Germans. There was, therefore, very bad blood between them. The result was constant fighting. I was to have my share too.

One day a train loaded with tomatoes stopped on the track just outside the camp. I, with a few others, went snooping around it. We eventually returned with a box of tomatoes, quite a rare treat. I had a big iron frying-pan which I filled with the loot and then placed on top of the stove. To do so I had to move a tin mug full of water about one inch. No sooner had I done so than I was grabbed round the throat by a big Afrikaner. I had both hands on my frying-pan but, fortunately, my cousin was standing next to me.

"Hold this!' I said and thrust the pan into his hands. Then I struck the Boer right in the eye with the left and as he let go of my throat I hit him again with my right on the point of the jaw and sent him back-pedalling across the room.

That was the signal for pandemonium. The Afrikaners rushed to the aid of their compatriot while the sailors leapt in to help us. I grabbed the big frying-pan from my cousin and defied the Boers to come within arm's reach. Tomatoes were flying everywhere. The enemy being heavily outnumbered, they beat a retreat. They were given a solemn warning that in the event of their starting anything they would be massacred. It was probably not an exaggeration.

The Third Attempt

In the meantime I had been making preparations to escape, had collected a tidy sum of German money and had prepared suitable clothes.

I would have preferred to have gone on my own but my cousin insisted on coming with me, as also did a Welsh sailor from Barry by the name of Bryn Jenkins.

Our destination was Poland, our aim to join the Armja Krajowa (The Home Army).

One Saturday morning we went out with the six o'clock shift, our escape clothes on underneath our overcoats. As soon as we reached the factory we slipped out of sight, took off our overcoats and jumped over the wall on to the main road which ran along the River Oder and led to the town. It was dark. No one had seen us. We had blue overalls over our battle-dress and a civilian cap each, just like any ordinary working-man.

We walked through the empty streets to the railway station, clearly discernible by the dim, blue lamp outside. Then we got our first shock. Two SA men (Storm Troopers) were standing in the hall with collecting-boxes for the *Winterkriegshilfe* (a charity in aid of the troops). Our first reaction was to turn on our heels, but instead, with a '*Heil Hitler*', we each put a coin in the proferred box. I then had to go to the ticket-window and buy three tickets for Heydebruck, a junction some twenty-five miles away. It was with a sense of considerable relief that we passed on to the platform.

The train came in and we got on and stood in the corridor. Since neither my cousin Idwal nor Jenkins spoke German I had to try and intercept any conversation addressed to them, but despite all my alertness I was caught out when the lady-guard approached from my blind side and demanded to see Jenkins' ticket. He looked dumb, which aroused the guard's ire, so I hurriedly intervened, presenting to her our three tickets. She looked at them and threw them back at me saying something about us requiring a '*Susatz-karte*'. I apologized and offered her a twenty mark note, whereupon she issued us with three additional tickets. It appears that a '*Susatzkarte*' is required for a certain type of train, which ours obviously was – a '*D' Zug*, meaning a through train. She pushed past muttering something about '*Dumbe Polaken*' (dumb Poles.) It was a near thing because the attention of other passengers had been drawn to us.

We arrived eventually at Heydebruck where we got out to get tickets for the next stage. Our ultimate destination was Katowice, a large town just over the border in pre-war Poland but at that time, of course, annexed to Germany and Germanized. I left Idwal and Jenkins on the platform with strict orders not to attract attention or speak to anyone. I then went through the barrier, waited about ten minutes, bought another three tickets to Gleiwitz and went back on to the platform. When I got there I was alarmed to see a German soldier shouting and shaking his fist at my two companions. I went up to him and said, 'Excuse me, Sir, but these two are feeble-minded. They are not responsible for their actions. I am looking after them. I am very sorry if they have annoyed you.'

Fortunately I managed to mollify him and he moved off. He had gone up to them and made some inquiry, whereupon Jenkins had made signs that he was deaf and dumb and Idwal had burst out laughing, at which the soldier had taken considerable umbrage.

We got our train to Gleiwitz and arrived there without mishap. Having got off I took my companions to the toilet and told them to stay there until I came for them. Then I went out through the barrier, handed in my ticket to the collector, beside whom stood a policeman, and went outside. Having waited about a quarter of an hour I returned, bought three tickets to Katowice and went through the barrier, foolishly presenting three tickets. As I was leaving the policeman said, 'What are you doing with three tickets?'

I replied, 'Two of them are for my friends.'

'Where are they?'

'They are on the platform.'

'Didn't I see you go out a few minutes ago?'

'Yes,' I said. 'I went out to buy the tickets.'

'And your two friends, didn't they have tickets then?'

'Yes' I said. 'I handed them in as I went out.'

'There's something fishy going on here,' said the policeman. 'Where have you come from?'

This is it, I thought, the next words will be – show me your papers! Having nothing to lose I decided that attack was the best form of defence and said in an exasperated tone, 'While I'm talking here with you my train will be gone. I only get one weekend a month off. Its all right for you in your good uniform and nothing to do but waste people's time. I want to get home to see my mother. *Auf Wiedersehen!*'

I strode off in what I hoped was a good passing likeness to injured innocence, expecting every second to hear a stentorian '*Halt!*' But nothing happened.

When I got to the toilet, Idwal and Jenkins were in a near panic; they thought I had been caught.

We got on the train and arrived in Katowice in the early evening. Outside the station we saw a sign: *Eintopfrestaurant* (a restaurant serving vegetable soup without coupons). We went in to see if we could make any contacts there and were served with a basin of quite good vegetable soup for sixty pfennigs, about ninepence in pre-war money. The waitress who served us was obviously Polish. I managed to convey to her that we were French at which she showed some interest. But, there being no chance for any extensive conversation, we left and went out into the street.

The first thing we saw was a tram with destination 'Sosnowitz' on it and the sign '*Nur für Polen*'. Sosnowitz was the Germanized form for the Polish town of Sosnowiec and the sign meant 'Only for Poles' We ran to it and jumped on just as it was about to leave. A Polish conductress came to us and we bought three tickets to Sosnowiec. I asked her whether she would be kind enough to let us know when we got there. She agreed with a smile, probably thinking we were French, of which quite a number were working in the area. That was the way the French were able to get their prisoners of war released, by supplying a civilian worker for each released prisoner.

When we arrived in the centre of Sosnowiec the conductress gave us the nod and we got off. It was almost dark and the people in the streets seemed to be in a hurry to go home. There were no loiterers to be seen on street corners but we saw several patrols of Gendarmerie walking in pairs and armed to the teeth.

We walked along the streets trying to give the impression that we had somewhere to go. In fact we had, because we intended to walk through the town and out into the open country, if possible in an easterly direction. Before we had gone very far we noticed a young man following us at a distance of some ten paces. We quickened our step. He did likewise. We slowed down, hoping he would pass. He chose to stay behind. To make sure we turned into a sidestreet and then into another. He was still behind us. We stopped. He stopped and addressed us in Polish. We didn't answer, just stood and stared at him. He said something in French. There was something about him that looked very suspicious, even treacherous. We moved on; he followed and spoke to us in German. I asked him what he wanted in the same language; he muttered something incomprehensible so I rushed at him. He turned and fled. And so did we in the opposite direction.

We felt for certain that he was a Police spy and that in no time the Police would be warned to look out for us. We had to get off the streets and quickly.

Soon we saw two young men coming towards us. As they came I could hear them talking to each other in Polish. I looked right into their faces and felt intuitively that they could be trusted. I bade them good evening in French. They stood stock-still. I then told them in French that we were French prisoners of war who had escaped from a camp in Germany and that we were looking for shelter for the night.

One of them answered in perfect French and asked me something which I did not understand. When I tried to reply I could see on his face that he had realized we were not French. Fear was plainly written there. He must have thought that we were *agents provocateurs*. There was nothing for it but to tell them the truth.

I explained that we were British prisoners and to prove it showed them letters addressed to us through the Red Cross. I asked them whether they spoke German. They did, so we carried on the conversation in that language. I explained that we had pretended to be French because we knew what a close relationship there was between Poland and France.

'No more,' they said, 'not after what happened in 1939, when eighty French divisions stood on the Maginot Line and let us face the whole German Army on our own!'

Having examined the letters very carefully and having listened to us speaking English to each other, they believed us and shook our hands warmly. Then they said, 'Follow us at a distance of some twenty paces. We shall get on a tram. You do the same. We will get the tickets for you and when we get off you do likewise and keep on following us!' Having made quite certain that we had understood, they set off. They stopped at a tram-stop, so did we. They got on and we followed. We saw them get our tickets and give the nod to the conductress. We were in a tram for Poles only. When they got off so did we.

We were on the outskirts of the town. They led us along a narrow lane for about half a mile. Then they stopped and allowed us to catch up with them and said, 'We are going to take you to a camp for French civilian workers. They will put you up for the night. Tomorrow morning at about eight o'clock we will call for you and take you to the railway station and put you on the train for Myszkow. We will explain what to do after tomorrow morning. Stay here and we'll fetch a French friend of ours who will arrange to put you up for the night.'

Before long they returned with a Frenchman whom they introduced as Georges.

The latter agreed to take us in, but reluctantly, because the majority of his companions were virulently anti-British. That was probably due to our desertion at Dunkirk and to the sinking of the French fleet at Mers-el-Kebir. Be that as it may, we had to stay outside the camp for hours, until everyone there had gone to bed and Georges was able to conduct us unseen to an empty room.

There were a number of beds there but they were so indescribably filthy that we did not dare sleep on them, although we were nearly dropping with fatigue. Instead, we sat on a bench with our heads resting on our folded arms on a table and although we were frozen to the bone we couldn't possibly cover ourselves with the filthy blankets on the beds.

We did not have a comfortable night and were very glad to see the dawn. Soon after it was light our Polish friends arrived with Georges bringing with them a can of hot coffee and a packet of sandwiches. While we were eating and drinking they explained what was going to happen.

They were going to buy us tickets on the train to Lelow, a village some forty miles to the east and on the frontier leading to the Generalgouvernement – i.e., that part of Poland which had not been annexed to Germany, although occupied and policed. The frontier was very well guarded to prevent any contacts between Poles living on either side. There, we were to go to a chemist shop run by a Pole named Grabowski and tell him that we had been sent to him by the man who distributed the papers in Sosnowiec. After that we would be in his hands.

Having thanked Georges, we followed the Poles from the camp and arrived at the station by tram. Leaving us outside, one of the Poles went and bought our tickets. When they heard the train arrive at the station they shook our hands, wished us good luck and told us to get on the platform. We got on the train just as it was about to leave.

There were very few passengers and all appeared to be Poles. They looked very poor and depressed and so did the surrounding countryside. It was early winter and the land was bare. Poland had already suffered four years of occupation and the country had been stripped bare of its livestock. Hundreds of thousands of people had been killed in reprisals, hundreds of thousands had been carried off to Germany for forced labour and the entire Jewish population of some three million was either in concentration camps or enclosed in ghettoes. The country was being crucified, but despite all the oppression not a single major Quisling came forward to offer cooperation with the invaders. The Poles resisted actively and passively just about one hundred per cent. Scores of resistance units were training in the forests and carrying out raids on German positions. The German army was forced into defended garrisons and strongpoints, leaving the country at large to the Polish partisans.

It was a slow train, stopping at every station with country people getting in and out. No one addressed us beyond the normal greeting offered to the carriage in general as people entered or left but it was obvious that we were the object of much concealed curiousity – three young men travelling together must have been quite an unusual sight. All young men of our age were either conscripted into the German army or to war-work in Germany or were in the Polish Forces fighting in Russia, Italy or in Britain, or in the forests with the partisans.

At last we saw the name Myszkow on a station and got out. The village was a one-street affair and we soon spotted Grabowski's shop. Instead of going there we walked out of the village and, while my companions hid themselves in a field, I returned to the shop.

As I entered the door-bell rang. A middle-aged woman appeared from the living-quarters. I said good morning in her in Polish and she returned the greeting and asked what she could do for me. As I knew only a few words of Polish I asked her whether she spoke German. She answered that she did and I could see her whole attitude change and become alert and apprehensive. I then asked whether her husband was in. She said he was out and asked whether she could help me. I said, 'No, madam, I must speak to Pan Grabowski.'

'What do you want to speak to him about?'

'I'm sorry, madam, I cannot tell you. I must see him. I'll wait until he comes back.'

She was now visibly quaking. Her lips were trembling. She said, 'Wait there please,' and disappeared into the living quarters. In a few seconds she was back, a man by her side who said, 'I am Pan Grabowski. What can I do for you?' I said, 'I have been sent by the man who distributes the papers in Sosnowiec.' He stared for a few seconds, then said, 'What papers? I don't know anything about any papers in Sosnowiec! I don't understand what you mean. Tell me what you want.' I repeated, 'I have been sent by the man who distributes the papers in Sosnowiec,' feeling very uncertain of myself.

The man said, 'Who are you? What do you want? I know nothing about any papers in Sosnowiec or anywhere else!'

They were both obviously terrified, believing me to be a German who was trying to trap them. I said, 'I am an escaped British prisoner of war,' and showed him my letters and photographs of myself taken in a prisoner-of-war camp.

They both examined them carefully. I asked them if they spoke English; they didn't but they asked me how it was that I spoke such good German. I said that I had learnt it at school and had perfected it in the three years I had spent in Germany.

Eventually they believed me and asked what I meant by my reference to the man who distributed the papers in Sosnowiec. I told him about the two young Poles. Then he said angrily, 'What exactly do you want?'

I said, 'I and my two friends want help to cross into the Generalgouvernement so that we can join the Armja Krajowa and fight against the Germans.'

'I'm sorry,' he said, 'I can't help you. It is far too dangerous. I have no one I can send with you any more.'

'Can you give us any advice at all?' I asked with a sinking heart.

'Yes,' he replied, 'the children. The children can help you. They cross backwards and forwards all the time to smuggle. That is the only advice I can give you.' I thanked them both and walked out. The other two were still hiding in the field.

We returned to the road and walked along it in the direction of the frontier. Soon a middle-aged man came towards us. I greeted him in Polish and he returned my greeting. He was obviously a simple peasant and, not having much to lose, I decided to try and enlist his aid.

'Do you speak German?' I asked him in that language.

'A little,' he replied, stiffening with fear.

'Do you speak French?'

'No,' he said.

'Do you speak English?'

'No, only Polish and a little German.'

'We are British,' I said, showing him the letters and the pictures. He could see the Red Cross sign on the letters and the German Censor's stamp which obviously impressed him quite a lot. I explained that we had escaped from a prisoner of war camp in Germany and wished to join the Armja Krajowa.

His face lit up immediately. He said, 'I'll help you! You must cross into the Generalgovernement, that's where you'll find the Armja Krajowa. I would come with you if I could, but I've got three little children and what would happen to them if I went? But come to my house until it gets dark.'

He took us to a little cottage and introduced us to his wife who immediately set about preparing a meal for us. It turned out to be macaroni soup, which although not very nourishing was extremely welcome.

While we were eating I questioned the man about the frontier. He told me not to worry and said that he would see to it that we crossed safely as soon as it got dark. When I asked him how, he replied, 'The children. My children will take you across.'

'Your children?'

'Yes,' he said, 'my three little girls. They'll soon be back and they know every path across the swamp where there aren't any Germans. They go backwards and forwards all the time to visit our relatives and bring food back from the farm.'

Soon the girls came in. The eldest was thirteen, the next eleven and the youngest, Wanda, just eight. They stared with round-eyed surprise at us. When they were told who we were they each came to us, curtsied beautifully and kissed our hands. We were touched to the quick and discussed whether or not we should allow them to risk themselves for us. We conveyed our doubts to their father, but he insisted absolutely, assuring us that there was no risk and that it was an honour for his family to help us and to do whatever was in their power for their country. He had fought in the 1939 campaign, he said, and would fight again when the opportunity came. In the meantime the least he could do was to help three strong, young men to join the resistance, as every man was needed.

The Poles made considerable use of the word "honour" and I believe quite sincerely that they do put honour before expediency, and that, I have since found, is something extremely rare among nations.

Over the Border

As soon as it was dark the three little girls put on their coats and scarves and left the house. We said goodbye to their parents, their mother kissing us on both cheeks while the tears streamed down her face. We followed the little girls, just keeping them in sight. We were going along a straight road leading directly to the frontier-post which we could see lit up about four miles away. The girls father had told us that the post was strongly manned day and night and the frontier on each side patrolled by Gendarmerie with Alsatian dogs. Only people with special permits were allowed to cross.

Before we had gone more than about a mile we were overtaken by a young man on a bicycle. He was upon us before we realized it, so we had no chance to hide ourselves. He greeted us in Polish but we did not reply. He got off his bicycle and walked beside us, speaking in Polish. We ignored him completely and carried on going. He kept up his attempt at conversation for a full five minutes until we were almost desperate and definitely considering falling upon him and rendering him *hors de combat*. However, he saved us the trouble by jumping on his bicycle, saying '*dobranoc*' (goodnight) and pedalling off into the night. I called a very grateful '*dobranoc*' after him.

Soon after that the girls left the road and took a path across the fields to the left. We were then walking parallel to the frontier and we heard the barking of the dogs. They were undoubtedly *Schaefer-hunde* (Alsatians), the dogs which tend German sheep and children and when the latter grow up they follow them to war.

The little girls kept up a good pace and soon we were winding our way through woods and swamps. Every now and again they would stop and wait for us to catch up in order to guide us through a particularly dangerous swamp, on more than one occasion actually leading us by the hand. My admiration for them knew no bounds.

After another half an hour or so the girls stopped. The eldest said, 'Little Wanda is not coming any further. It is too dangerous for her. We are very close to the frontier now. She will stay here under this tree until we come back.'

Little Wanda stood there smiling and quite fearless in her little coat and with a scarf over her head and tied under her chin. We each picked her up and kissed her and so did her two sisters. I tried to persuade the eldest girl to let us go on on our own but she would not hear of it, saying that we would be sure to lose our way. Reluctantly we moved off. The last I saw of Wanda she was waving goodbye to us. My heart almost stood still.

Half an hour after leaving her we were led into a farmyard. The girls went up to the door boldly and knocked, saying to us, 'You are safe now! You are in the Generalgouvernement!'

A man came to the door and when he saw the girls he clasped them both to him, pulling them into the house. But they pointed to us and told him who we were. We were invited in and offered shelter for the night, but, feeling that we were too close to the frontier, we decided that the best thing was to push on.

The girls kissed us goodbye and hurried back to their little sister. When I think of medals for bravery I wonder what award would be worthy of such heroism. But heroism seems to come naturally to Poles, men, women and children.

Having thanked the farmer, we moved off. It was a clear, frosty night, so keeping direction was no problem. Keeping the North Star on our left shoulder we strode on firmly towards the east. But coming across another isolated farm within a few hours and, feeling tired, we decided to have a rest. Finding a loose-box, we went in and laid ourselves down on the straw. Unfortunately, however, we were not the only lodgers. Besides us there was a goat, a calf and a rabbit and they gave us no peace.

The calf kept sucking our sleeves and the legs of our trousers, the goat kept butting us and the climax came when the rabbit hopped on my shoulder and pee-ed down my neck. Feeling the warm liquid running down my back I jumped to my feet and said, 'Out! Let's get out! I can't stand it any longer!'

And out we went. It was nearly dawn and before long we could see endless, flat, open fields stretching ahead of us to infinity. We went past several small villages of wooden houses where the people stared at us with a mixture of curiousity and fear and mumbled a Polish greeting. But we were still too near the frontier to try to make contact with anyone.

Towards midday, coming across an isolated cottage, we knocked on the door which was opened by two bare-footed children. I asked them whether their father was in, which sent them scurrying back to fetch a young lad of about eighteen, obviously their brother. I told him we were British and we were invited in. It was an extremely poor establishment. In front of the stove stood a thin middle-aged woman baking small, flat loaves which she made from dough contained in a basin. They were baked in a matter of minutes and handed to the children who ate them greedily. She offered some to us but we refused, saying we had just eaten, which was not true, but one glance at those children convinced us that their need was much greater than ours. For anyone wanting to know what are the fruits of war, the answer was there in that cottage – poverty, misery and starvation.

The young lad had a bottle from which he drank and which he offered to us saying it was vodka. We each took a sip. I could feel my stomach rising into my throat and the tears shoot out of my eyes. If anything, it was worse than the fire-water we made out of sugar in Ratibor. He offered to sell us a bottle and we accepted but we did not take it with us when we left.

The poor woman took no interest in us at all; she was obviously too worn out by privation to concern himself with anything that was not absolutely necessary. We took our leave feeling quite depressed.

We walked steadily all day. Towards evening we came to a village and I noticed a young, beautiful and well-groomed girl standing by a gateway leading to a house.

'*Dzien dobry, panienko,*' I said, touching my cap.

'*Dzien dobry panu!*,' she replied.

'*Parlez-vous Français, mademoiselle?*'

'*Oui, Monsieur.*'

'*Do you speak English?*'

'*Comment, Monsieur?*'

'*Vous ne parlez pas Anglais, mademoiselle?*'

'*Non, monsieur.*'

'*Nous sommes prisonniers de guerŕe Brittaniques.*'

'*Un moment, monsieur,*' she said and disappeared into the house.

In a few seconds she was back with her mother and another girl who was the spit image of herself.

'*Venez, messieurs*,' said the mother, '*Entrez!*'

We went into the house. Inside we saw about a dozen teenage girls sitting in a circle. At a word from the woman they all got up and disappeared. Then she started to question us in fluent French, a language I was not very fluent in at that time. I asked her whether she spoke German; she said only a very little, but her husband spoke it fluently and would soon be home.

Armja Krajowa

We were given a good meal and the two girls came to keep us company. They were seventeen-year-old identical twins, very attractive, well-groomed, extremely well-mannered and quite decidedly Polish. It is said that one can always tell a Polish woman because she has such a regal air about her. That is quite true in my experience and I ascribe it to the status that the Polish woman has gained for herself by her courage and steadfastness throughout the ages. Being surrounded by powerful and acquisitive neighbours and having almost indefensible frontiers, Poland has had to struggle very hard to maintain her independence. The women played their full part in that struggle. During the partition of Poland between 1795 and 1918 when the country ceased to exist as an independent entity and when Polish schools were not allowed, it was the women who taught the children and inculcated in them patriotism and national awareness and when the need arose they fought side by side with their men. In some of the occupied countries the women consorted with the enemy, but not so in Poland. There, thousands and thousands of women fought actively in the underground movement.

Finally their father, Pan Kowalski, and his son, aged fifteen, came home. He was about fifty and looked to be a man not easily fooled. He questioned us very closely in perfect German and took a keen interest in my account of the young men in Sosnowiec and the chemist in Myszkow. His last question was, 'Who sent you to this house?'

'No one,' I said. 'I just happened to see your daughter at the garden gate and felt that she was an intelligent girl.'

'So,' he said, 'you did not know that you came to exactly the right place and that I am the representative of the Armja Krajowa for this area?'

I looked at him in complete surprise but I could see that he was a man well used to authority.

'You will stay here now,' he said, 'until I have checked your particulars with London. After that, if all is well, you will join the Armja Krajowa.'

'How will you communicate with London?' I asked.

'By radio,' he said. 'We have a direct link with our government in London and they will make enquiries with the British Government. Of course, you might be German spies, but if you are we are sure to find out, and do you know what will happen to you?'

'I have a good idea,' I said.

He then told us to follow him. He took us out of the house and into the farmyard where several round haystacks stood. Removing some hay from the side of one, he went inside, telling us to follow. When we got in we found that the stack was hollow and that there were mattresses and blankets there.

'This is where we hide people,' he said. 'When the Gendarmerie patrols are in the neighbourhood the girls often sleep here. You will stay here now without coming out until I come for you. There are toilet facilities here and you will be fed. I must tell you that you will be well-guarded and that it would be extremely dangerous for you to go out. Make yourselves comfortable. I'll see you in the morning. Goodnight!'

But he saw us before the morning, for sometime in the middle of the night we were awakened by a bright light shining in our faces and the voices of men. I heard one of them say in French, '*Ce sont de types anglais*.'

Then someone said in English, 'Tell me your names!'

We did. Then we were asked our military numbers, our units and other questions. Finally we were told to sing 'God save the King' which we did, and we did not feel foolish as we fully realized the gravity of the situation.

After that the voice said, 'I am an officer of the Armja Krajowa. By tomorrow I will have transmitted your particulars to London. If everything is all right we shall welcome you into our army. If not you will be given time to say your prayers before leaving this world. Don't think of trying to escape because you are guarded day and night. I hope everything is going to be all right. Pan Kowalski will take good care of you. Good night!'

'Good night,' we said, but it sounded more like 'Amen'.

The following morning we were taken into the house and given breakfast. Then we were returned to the haystack where we stayed for four days.

On the fifth morning we were again taken into the house where we saw three men in military uniform – the Polish pre-war uniform of khaki jacket, breeches and jack-boots and the four-cornered kepi. One had the silver braid of a sergeant. All three were armed. Pan Kowalski introduced us and made a dignified speech and we all drank a glass of vodka. We said farewell to the Kowalski family and left with the soldiers.

The sergeant was a man of few words but the other two were quite prepared to answer questions. They told us that their job was escorting recruits to a collecting centre from where they were sent on to various units in the forests.

Late at night we arrived at a large mill. We were taken into the house and given a good meal. There were some dozen or more uniformed soldiers there who gave us a very warm welcome. We had to tell our story to them many times over. I was amazed at their confidence in themselves and found it difficult to realize that I was in a country occupied by the German army. The Poles acted as if the campaign of 1939 was merely a battle lost.

After eating and drinking we all went into a large barn to sleep, a strong guard being maintained around the area.

The Battle

It was a Saturday towards the end of November when the word came that we were to move to one of the units in the forest beyond Kielce and that we would leave the mill around midnight. Apart from the regulars there were some thirty recruits, young men who had crossed over from the unannexed territories, among them three brothers, all strapping young men. They had yet another brother serving with the Polish Navy somewhere in the Atlantic.

There was to be no more walking – we were going to be carried on wagons, each drawn by two light draught-horses, long-coated very tough horses of which the Poles thought the world. The Poles have always been great horsemen and their cavalry has been famous throughout European history, from 1410 when their Winged Hussars imposed that crushing and decisive defeat on the Teutonic Knights at Grunewald, right through the Napoleonic wars where they fought on every battlefield, to the Second World War when in 1939 they mobilized twenty-three cavalry brigades and actually charged the German mechanized units. To this day the ceremonial head-dress of lancer regiments in all countries is based on the Polish four-cornered kepi.

That evening, before leaving, we all went into the mill for a meal. The vodka flowed freely. By midnight we were all quite merry, including myself, but, fortunately as it turned out, I was very quickly and rudely sobered. As I jumped into the back of the wagon the horses moved forward and I fell backwards right into a pool of water. The ice broke under my weight and I was drenched to the skin. So low was the temperature that my clothes froze to my back. Had it not been for the vodka I had drunk I might have been frozen to death. I was certainly sobered!

There was straw in the bottom of the wagons and as soon as we moved off most of the men stretched themselves on it and were soon fast asleep. My frozen back kept me wide awake, however, so I sat next to the driver and chatted to him.

After about an hour we halted. An officer walked from wagon to wagon and warned us that we were approaching a German road-block. We were going to go through the road-block but without a fight if possible. A section of about a dozen men got off the wagons and took up positions on either side of the road. Then the order was given to move forward slowly, the officer in front.

Everyone was now awake and holding his weapon at the ready. Soon we say lights ahead and as we approached we could see a number of German soldiers.

Someone shouted, '*Halt! Sonst wird geschossen!*' (Halt or we'll shoot.) Across the road was a long pole. On each side of it we could see levelled rifles. Our officer walked slowly to within a few yards of the Germans, a pistol in his hand; behind him were a dozen men, their rifles pointing at the Germans. I could hear the officer speaking to the Germans but did not catch his words. The I saw the pole being raised and we moved forward slowly, passing within feet of the Germans on either side of the road. As we passed them we covered them with our rifles and machine-pistols. There was one hair-raising moment when an Alsatian dog rushed at the horses, causing them to rear up. But not a shot was fired and the whole convoy passed through the road-block. I found the whole thing astonishing and asked one of the Poles what the explanation was.

He told me that our officer had explained to the Germans that they were surrounded and heavily out-numbered and should they resist they would all be killed. That made sense to me, but why did we not kill or at least disarm the Germans? The answer was that it would have been self-defeating as the Germans would then have sent a large punitive expedition to the area, thus endangering the security of the mill which was a very important base.

In less than a couple of hours we were suddenly challenged from the shadows at the side of the road. A password was given and two Polish soldiers appeared. They spoke to the officer in charge and the convoy moved off again. After going a mile or so we turned off the road and drove through a gateway and along a drive into a big courtyard outside a large country house. The wagons drew up in line and halted. Everyone got out and formed up in single rank in front. A colonel in full Polish uniform then appeared, accompanied by his adjutant. He inspected us, shaking every man's hand and saying a few words. He then gave a short address of welcome to the recruits after which we all trooped into the big house.

I was amazed at what I saw – a huge room full of people and most of them looking like left-overs from a previous age. Many of them were old people, the men dressed in tails and white waistcoats and the women in long dresses and wearing jewellery. They all seemed to be smoking cigarettes in long holders. In occupied Poland it was a truly fantastic sight. I was told that they had been celebrating some important event and that since it had always been their custom to dress up for it they could not see why they should change just because of the German Army! Tables had been laid out with an excellent meal for us and soon we were all tucking in with gusto.

I sat next to a young Polish corporal, a real fire-eating partisan if ever there was one. He had fought as a lancer in the Autumn Campaign, had been taken prisoner and carted off to Germany from where he had escaped and made his way back to Poland, where he had joined one of the first partisan units. For some time he had been employed as an executioner. German officials accused of inhuman treatment of the Polish population were tried *in absentia* by an Armja Krajowa court and if found guilty were sentenced to death. The verdict would then be carried out by an official executioner, such as my corporal friend, who would watch his victim until he got a suitable opportunity when he would dispatch him with a pistol-shot or a hand-grenade, regardless of any risk to himself. This young corporal had successfully carried out several such operations. Among his victims was a Chief of Police of a district.

He had no false modesty and no love for the British or the French, whom he accused of fighting to the last Pole. He reckoned that both Britain and France had betrayed Poland in 1939 and in any case Britain was only interested in business and expanding her empire at anyone else's expense. And, as to our fighting qualities, he derided them. According to him we had done nothing except run away from the Germans, citing Norway, France, Greece, Crete and North Africa. The more he spoke the hotter I got under the collar, the more so because he delivered his tirade in a way that brought peals of mocking laughter from the other young Poles.

The crunch came when he asked me how many Germans I had killed.

I replied, 'There were so many I couldn't count them all.'

'Where was this?' he asked.

'In France,' I said.

'In France? You were only there for three weeks before you all ran away or stuck your hands up!'

This brought a peal of laughter. I was now very angry, so I said, 'I've only got your word for all the heroics you boast about.'

That did it. He jumped up and aimed a blow at my head. I avoided it and threw a punch at him which he failed to avoid. Whereupon he grabbed his sten-gun and jabbed it against my chest. There was a pistol on the table which I promptly grabbed and pointed at his head. I thought my last moment had come. There was a completely reckless light in my opponent's eye. A deathly silence descended as we glared at each other. It must have only lasted for seconds but to me it felt like an age. I knew that the corporal could not possibly retract; his reputation alone prevented that. And could I, after all the insults I had endured? But I was saved when an officer stepped up to us and took the sten-gun away from the corporal. I put the pistol down and never have I been more glad to put anything down. The officer sent for the colonel.

The latter came and inquired what the trouble was. On being told that a fight had broken out between one of his corporals and a British soldier he exploded, putting all the blame on the corporal. He read him a most severe lecture, pointing out that we were supposed to be allies and that the Germans were the enemy. The poor corporal was literally trembling. Discipline in the Armja Krajowa was extremely strict. In appropriate cases the death sentence was awarded, but perhaps the most dreaded sentence of all was a dishonourable discharge. Anyone suffering such a penalty faced the life of Cain, becoming a permanent pariah among his own people.

Having delivered his admonition, the colonel ordered us to shake hands. The corporal was not satisfied with that, however; throwing his arms around my neck, he kissed me repeatedly on both cheeks. Then, calling for two glasses of vodka and giving me one, he insisted that we drink '*bratswo*' – brotherhood, by linking arms and emptying each other's glass at one gulp. This brought a storm of applause and for the next few minutes I was a hero. All the Poles praised my courage in standing up to the redoubtable corporal, the ex-executioner and bravest of the brave, and he himself was the most lavish in his praise. The look on his face was proof of his sincerity.

Soon after that the party broke up. We trooped out to the courtyard where orderlies had the horses and wagons ready. The corporal, whom I shall call Janek, insisted that I rode with him. We mounted and moved off in line ahead, saluting the colonel as we marched past him.

I told Janek that I had been brought up on a farm and asked him whether I could drive the horses. He agreed at once and handed me the reins. Sitting down next to me in the front of the wagon he told me about the Armja Krajowa, its organization and aims. The words mean Home Army and as such it was merely one of the Polish Armies that was fighting on the Allied side. There was another Army in Russia, there was one in Italy under General Anders and another in Britain waiting to take part in the invasion of France. The Commander-in-Chief of all the Polish Armies was General Sosnkowski who was in Britain. Commanding the Armja Krajowa was General Bor-Komorowski. Its aims were manifold. Firstly, to maintain a uniform military organization within Poland despite the German occupation. Secondly, to train cadres and units and to recruit against the day when an all-out offensive could be launched. Thirdly, to harass the enemy and to carry out operations of a specialist nature. Fourthly, to protect the civilian population as far as that was possible and to maintain their morale in the face of the dreadful oppression they were undergoing. As far as my friend was concerned Germany was merely the enemy of the moment. He foresaw the defeat of Germany and the re-establishment of the Polish State, but he had considerable reservations as far as Russia was concerned. He knew that Russia laid claim to certain territories in Eastern Poland, but for him the pre-1939 frontiers in the east were inviolate and he was quite prepared to fight the Russians should they attempt to change them. His words send a chill down my spine. I could see myself spending years in the Polish forests after the end of the German war. There was no arguing with him and no chance of reasoning. He was one of those Poles, personified by Marshal Pilsudski, who, given half a chance, would have claimed the frontiers of 1772 which would have included the whole of Lithuania and most of the Ukraine.

The horses went forward over the flat country track at a steady trot for mile after mile. At last I could see the first grey streaks of dawn appearing in the sky ahead and gradually it started to get light. We were on an immense plain, the land sloping very gradually towards the east. To the south I could see the dim, dark line of a forest. As it grew lighter I could see a layer of mist ahead in the distance towards the lower ground. Gazing into the mist I imagined I could see shapes reminiscent of a herd of cattle, but doubted whether the Germans had left may cattle after their ceaseless requisitions.

I nudged Janek, who was asleep. He sat up and asked what was wrong.

'German cavalry ahead!' I said but only as a joke.

'Where?' he asked. 'The more the merrier!'

He snatched the whip from the side of the wagon and cracked it over the horses' heads. As we careered down the slope the mist lifted and not two hundred yards away was a horse-drawn convoy of scores of vehicles, but not a man to be seen. Then, before we had time to appreciate what we were meeting came the sound of machine-gun and rifle fire. I stood up and pulled as hard as I could on the reins. The horses slithered to a standstill. Meanwhile Janek jumped out of the wagon, calling on the others to follow him. Everyone jumped out and started firing furiously at the Germans. Janek and another young Pole, being armed only with sten-guns, were out of range, so, pulling hand-grenades out of their belt-pouches, they ran forward. Before they had gone a dozen paces they had both been mown down. I saw their bodies twisting on the ground under a hail of bullets. Then I heard the horses scream in their death-agony as the bullets tore into them. Looking round I could see the other wagons pull up and the men jump out and take up firing positions. One glance at the enemy convinced me that our position was quite hopeless. We probably had no more than twenty rifles; the men armed with machine-pistols were able to contribute nothing except their bodies as targets, for the range was too great for them. I could see Idwal and Bryn Jenkins lying in the field with enemy bullets falling all round them. The Germans were using a high proportion of *Leuchtkugel* (tracers) which made the surface of the field look like a sheet of flame.

I crawled back as quickly as I could towards my two companions and told them to follow me to the rear if they wanted to stay alive. One being a sailor and the other a Marine, they had never faced small-arms fire before and were most reluctant to lift their heads. I knew that to stay where they were meant certain death so I forced them to move. But they were quite unused to crawling, not being infantrymen, and their progress was slow. So, jumping to my feet and running forward zig-zag with my head down for about ten paces before throwing myself flat on the ground, I called on them to do the same. In that way we covered some fifty yards towards the rear without being hit, although bullets were thudding into the ground all round us.

Looking round the battlefield, I could see that all the horses apart from one pair were in their death throes. The pair still alive were walking round in a tight circle, their heads to one side. I rushed up to them. I saw that the reins had caught in the hub of one of the wheels and I tried to undo them but could not. So, putting my foot on the hub, I tugged at the reins with all my strength and managed to break them. Jumping into the wagon I drove towards Idwal and Bryn and picked them up. Then I saw an officer waving me towards him. He jumped into the wagon and told me to drive round the field. We picked up another two men. By this time the Germans were concentrating most of their free on us. The officer ordered me to gallop away as fast as the horses could go. We flew back along the track pursued by a hail of enemy bullets but soon we were out of range. We did not slacken our pace until we reached a village about a mile away. There the three Poles jumped out, telling us to make our way back to the big house where we had stayed during the night.

We set off again at a cracking gallop for I felt sure the Germans would unhitch a troop of horses and gallop after us. But after a couple of miles I could see that our horses were all in. I pulled them up and jumped out. The poor creatures were a mass of lather, they were trembling and their heads hung nearly on the ground. I could ask no more of them, so I unharnessed and separated them so that they could move freely and fend for themselves. We then abandoned the track and struck off across country, hoping that we could find some sort of shelter by nightfall.

After going hard for about an hour we crawled under some bushes for a rest and a council of war. We were in a fix. Jenkins was completely exhausted and in a state of considerable shock. He had no stomach for that kind of fighting. Idwal had no definite opinion, merely stating that he was prepared to follow wherever I led, but he had no great enthusiasm for the Polish cause. They had both realized by now that there was no escape through Poland and that the only thing that lay ahead for them was fighting and probably dying.

In any case Jenkins was a non-starter and I was faced with the dreadful alternative of either abandoning him there and then or of trying to get him back somewhere where he could be returned to a prisoner-of-war camp. He had escaped with me because he thought it was a great adventure, but he had not thought out the possible consequences and as a result he was not prepared for them. I, on the other hand, had had no illusions. This was the sort of thing I had expected, so it came as no surprise.

It was decided between us that we should try and cross back into the unannexed territories where Jenkins could be picked up by the Police and handed back to the military authorities. He would then land in a prisoner-of-war camp from which, he said, he would never again escape. There was no dishonour in that. On the whole, escaping was a foolish adolescent adventure in which, for the most part, innocent people suffered – the people who helped the foolish, selfish, immature escapee. On being caught he was returned to a prisoner-of-war camp, where after serving a few days' solitary confinement he was able to boast of his exploits. The people who had helped him landed in a concentration camp from which they never returned.

We set off again in a westerly direction. Towards evening we came across lonely cottage, a mere hut. We knocked at the door and a woman's voice bade us enter. We went in and saw, near a miserable fire burning on the hearth, a bed in which lay a woman. Going up to her I saw that she had a young child with her. She appeared to be a young woman but looked extremely thin and weak. I explained to her that we were escaped prisoners of war and that we were looking for shelter for the night. She said we were welcome to stay in the cottage provided we did not mind lying on the floor; she had no other beds and added that she could give us no food as both she and her child were starving.

As we had approached the cottage I had seen a haystack and I decided there and then that we had no right to accept the poor woman's hospitality, particularly since it would endanger her and her child's life should we be caught there by the Germans. So, thanking her for her kind offer, we wished her well and went outside.

We stuffed ourselves as deeply as we could into the haystack and huddled together, We managed to keep warm enough to sleep until dawn.

The next day we kept going almost unceasingly despite our hunger and the severe cold. We did not see a soul. That night we found another haystack in which we slept.

The following day was a Sunday. We set off as soon as it was light. By now Jenkins was in a really bad way and had continually to be urged to keep going. On occasions we even had to drag him along.

Around midday we were approaching a village and although we were really desperately hungry I judged it unwise to go near any human habitation. We therefore made a detour and just when we thought we were clear we heard a voice shout, '*Rece do gory!*' (Hands Up!)

Turning towards the sound we saw a young man standing in a pony-trap and pointing a machine-pistol at us. We raised our hands. The pony-trap approached at a gallop driven by another young man. It drew up in front of us with a flourish and the first young man jumped out and menaced us with his machine-pistol saying, '*Zydzi przeklenci! Ja was zazrtele!*' (Cursed Jews! I'll shoot you!)

'We are not Jews,' I said, lowering my hands.

'*Rece do gory!*' screamed the young Pole, jabbing the barrel of his machine-pistol into my stomach. I obeyed instantly for I could see that I was dealing with an extremely dangerous customer.

'We are not Jews,' I said. 'We are British airmen. I am a pilot and we are on our way to Cracow under arrangements with the Armja Krajowa where an aeroplane from England will pick us up.'

'Lies!' said the young Pole. 'You are members of that Jewish gang of bandits who killed that woman the other day. And now I am going to kill you!'

'You'll be sorry,' I said, 'when you find out too late that we are British airmen. I have letters and photographs in my pocket which will prove to you that I am telling the truth.'

'Show them!' he said.

I took out the letters and the photographs and handed them to him. His companion jumped from the cart and they both looked at them, trying to read the letters. The next moment the letters were on the floor.

'*Zydowski jezyki!*' said the young desperado. (Yiddish)

I then thought it was all over and I consciously prepared myself to meet my death. I could feel my whole body go taut, my teeth clench, and I had that dreadful feeling of utter loneliness on realizing that my life was over. I was staring into the face of my would-be executioner and I could see a change coming over him too. He was no longer the blustering, bullying, bluffing extrovert. He was a very young man who had talked himself into killing three young strangers and now he had to go through with the dreadful act rather than let his friend think him a weakling. I am certain there was more terror in his face than in mine. But it gave me no comfort.

Then, suddenly, in a flash, he jabbed the barrel of his weapon against my leather waist-belt and said, 'Take it off!'

I loosened my belt, wondering what peculiar humiliation he had in mind. He then pulled my trousers down and examined my penis, calling his friend for a second opinion. In a flash I realized what he was doing. The next moment the machine-pistol was on the ground and my would-be assassin was embracing me as if I were his long-lost brother. Tears were actually running down his face and he was blubbering, '*Przepraszam brata, Ja myszlalem ze ty zyd. Ale ty nie zyd. A ja chciatem cie strzelic!*' (Forgive me brother, I thought you were a Jew. But you are not a Jew, and I wanted to shoot you!')

We finished up by my consoling him! We were now subjected to an embarrassment of kindness and concern.

'Dont bother about the *Armja Krajowa*,' said the young Poles. 'They are mad, they are. They are fighting the Germans and getting killed like flies while we are robbing the *Szlachta* (Aristocrats) and living like lords. Join up with us and you can live like lords too. You'll get plenty of food, plenty of vodka and plenty of women! Death is all you'll get in the *Armja Krajowa*. Poland is finished and will never be free again. Fighting the Germans is a waste of time. Eat, drink and be merry, that is the best. Look.' And they dragged us towards the cart. It was full of weapons and ammunition. 'What would you like? A Schmeisser, a Sten or a Luger. Take your pick!'

We thanked them most profusely but insisted that we were under orders to make our way to Cracow where an aircraft was to pick us up to take us back to Britain, so that we could fly again and bomb Germany.

Bombing Germany seemed to appeal to them and they said, '*Dobrze, dobrze, pojdziecie do Anglii aby rzucic bomby na Berlin. Wszystko zniszczyzc!*' (Good, good, go to England in order to drop bombs on Berlin. Destroy everything!)

They were all for destroying everything! But they were not prepared to let us go without enjoying their hospitality. We were made to jump into the cart which then careered off at breakneck speed towards the village. They pulled up in front of a cottage and told us to follow them in. The man and woman inside looked in amazement and alarm at us and even more so when the two desperadoes demanded food and drink for four immediately. They protested that they had no food, whereupon one of the bandits rushed out into the yard. Within seconds there was a piercing squawk and he was back with a dying hen in his hand which he threw at the man, telling him to pluck it forthwith. He then told the woman to get potatoes. He did not have to tell her twice. She disappeared and soon returned with a large basket of potatoes. Having seen to the meal, the young bandit jumped into the cart and galloped off. When he returned about ten minutes later he had a couple of bottles of vodka. Opening one he stood it on the table and, dispensing with a glass, took a sip much in the way that a diner samples his wine. Pronouncing it '*dobra wodka*', he passed the bottle round. We polished that bottle off before the meal was ready and smoked innumerable cigarettes of which our unwanted hosts seemed to have an endless supply.

The meal eventually appeared – a boiled hen in a big basin, surrounded by boiled potatoes, no plates. We merely took a spoon each and dug in, washing the mess down with gulps of vodka. Our hosts were in great form and were glad to see how impressed we were by the fear they had instilled in the poor occupants of the cottage. I was impressed all right but not in the way they thought. I was impressed by their savage depravity and would have gladly sent a bullet through them. But, of course, they too were victims. Victims of the total breakdown of society as a result of the German occupation. But I am glad to say that of all the thousands of Poles I met these were the only two villains.

Finally we were allowed to go, but not before we had been kissed on both cheeks many times and reminded of our promise to bomb Berlin to smithereens.

It was with a feeling of great relief that we set off. We didn't feel safe until we were well away from the village. We left the road as soon as we were out of sight and hurried off across country.

How the young Poles were able to tell that I was not a Jew from the examination they carried out I just do not know, because I certainly had been circumcized. The only suggestion I can make is that, since there was a very large Jewish population in Poland, some three million, the Poles were familiar with the Jewish way of doing this operation and that it is different from the way the Christian doctors do it. Be that as it may, the old Welsh doctor who performed on me was not to know that his orthodoxy and dexterity was to save my life one day!

My aim now was to try and get back over the frontier and to Sosnowiec, find the French camp and try and contact the young Poles who had first introduced us to the Armja Krajowa. Our direction was west and we stuck to it, going forward with absolute determination regardless of hunger and fatigue. The weather was bitterly cold but dry and there was no snow, so progress was not difficult. The most important thing was to avoid the villages where we would have been singled out immediately as suspicious characters. The young bandits' suspicion of us being members of a Jewish raiding gang was quite natural for there were many such gangs and that too was quite natural. The position of the Jews was indeed desperate. They had either been carted off to concentration camps or enclosed in ghettoes in the big towns where they were starving. By the time that the events I describe were taking place Hitler's so-called Final Solution had been put into effect in the Warsaw Ghetto. Thousands and thousands of Jews had been murdered, countless thousands carried off to concentration camps and the ghetto had been razed to the ground, Many young Jews had escaped into the forests from where, if they were to survive, they had to make raids into nearby villages to get food. This brought them into conflict with the Poles, so internecine war broke out between them. And, of course, it is true to say that the Poles, like every other European nation, were anti-semitic. Anti-semitism has been endemic in Europe for centuries. Poland was no worse than any other country. In fact it was much better, which is the reason why there were three million Jews in Poland – one tenth of the population. They came into Poland when that country was a part of the Russian Empire because of the official anti-semitism of the Tsarist Government and of the Orthodox Church. Poland was a far more liberal country and proved to be a haven for hundreds of thousands of Jews. Nevertheless, there was anti-Semitism and not unnaturally, since certain businesses and professions became the preserves of Jews. In addition, throughout Eastern Europe devout but ignorant peasants blamed the Jews for having crucified Christ. There was also anti-semitism in France; the Dreyfus case proves that beyond all doubt, as there also was in England, but in a much more subtle way. It was certainly rife among British prisoners of war. I knew of several instances where British prisoners told the guards that such and such a person was a Jew, and on each occasion that person was removed from the camp.

I remember in 1940 in Lamsdorf a German Officer standing on a table addressing thousands of us and saying: 'All Jews are to step out in front of the parade!' One solitary man went out and he, I believe, is the bravest man I have ever seen. I was stunned at first by his stupidity. Then, on reflection, my heart was filled with admiration for him. But what appalled me was the fact that we allowed him to step forward alone. We should have all stepped forward and said, 'This is our comrade! We demand to share his fate!' But we didn't. We stood and allowed him to go forward alone to face his enemies, enemies who refused even to grant him his human dignity, to recognize him as a man. But the worst thing of all was the fact that his mates from his own unit allowed him to go forward alone. That was not anti-semitism of course, that was the innate feeling of self-preservation that is in all of us, another name for cowardice.

One day, having skirted a village and by my reckoning not being very far from the frontier, we noticed that we were being followed by three young men. We were heading west so we immediately changed course towards the north. The young men caught up with us and greeted us in Polish. I replied and added that we were French escaped prisoners of war heading for Czestochowa, which I knew was to the north, where we were expecting help from the Armja Krajowa. They pointed out that we were very close to the frontier and that we had, in fact, been heading straight towards it. I pretended to be shocked and said that we must have missed our direction. The young men looked extremely suspicious and I have no doubt at all that they were armed. They walked with us for some miles and were most insistent that we return with them to the village. I was equally insistent that we keep going, explaining that we had to get to Czestochowa in the least possible time. It was an extremely trying experience and needed every ounce of resource and determination to persuade them to allow us to continue. Finally, however, they left us, albeit very reluctantly, and we continued in a northerly direction.

As soon as it was dark we changed course and headed due west. We had no idea what sort of obstacles we might meet at the frontier but we had no choice. There was only one way for us – forward, whatever lay ahead. We walked all night without hindrance. Luck must have been with us for by dawn we were over the frontier, having literally dragged Jenkins along for most of the night. He was by now at the very end of his tether; both my cousin and I were also ready to drop.

When we came to a main road we abandoned the fields and walked along it, not caring anymore what lay ahead. We had not gone far when we were overtaken by a Feldgendarmeric vehicle. On being asked for our passes I told them without hesitation that we were escaped prisoners of war, showing them our identity discs which we wore on our chests, next to the skin, suspended from a piece of string tied around the neck.

They took us to a Police Station in a nearby town. Later that evening we were moved into the civilian prison in Sosnowiec, a sinister move.

Shakespeare and the S.S. Colonel

We were placed in the same cell. That night we heard several volleys of shots and suspected that executions were taking place in the prison courtyard. This was confirmed the following morning when we were greeted by a voice which seemed to come from the ceiling: 'You are Englishmen?'

We looked up and saw a face in a tiny gap in the wall just under the ceiling.

'Yes,' we replied. 'Are you?'

'No, I am a Polish Jew.'

He asked us how we came to be there and when we told him that we were British escaped prisoners of war he said that we were very lucky as the Germans did not hate the English. They hated Jews and Poles but not the English. Nothing terrible would happen to us, he said, most likely we would be handed over to the army. As for him, he said, he knew that only death awaited him. He said it in the most matter of fact way, something that he had completely accepted. We asked him about the shots in the night and he said that it was the SS shooting communists.

That afternoon we were taken to see the prison governor. He was an *Obersturmbannführer* in the SS, equivalent to colonel in the army. A tall, handsome man with close-cropped hair and an elegant black uniform, highly polished jack-boots and SS insignia. I called my two companions to attention and saluted him Guards-fashion. I could see immediately that he was impressed. He ordered the guard to leave and then said, 'Ah Tommies! To be or not to be, dat isst ze question. *Nicht wahr?*'

'I beg your pardon, Sir?' I said.

'Ze question, Tommy, isst to be or not to be. *Sein oder nicht sein, mein lieber Tommy*. Ha, ha, ha!'

'Oh, I see, Sir. Shakespeare. You know Hamlet?'

'Of course, Tommy, I know Schekspir, *Der Prinz von Danemark*. Do you know *Der Prinz von Danemark*?'

'Of course, Sir. I know Shakespeare well, but I also know Goethe, the German Shakespeare. I am very pleased to learn that Shakespeare is admired in Germany. We in England certainly admire Goethe.'

'You know Goethe, Tommy?'

'Yes, Sir, and Schiller as well and other German poets.'

'Ah Tommy, you have *Kultur*. I also love *Kultur*, but ze war, Tommy, there is no time for *Kultur*. We must fight against ze Bolsheviks and ze Jews. Ve must fight for ze *Kultur* of Europe. Ve are not fighting against ze English. Ze English are our friends. Ze Germans are not *Barbaren*. Goethe and Schiller are not *Barbaren*.'

'Of course not, Sir. They were great poets.'

'You speak German, Tommy?'

'*Jawohl, mein Herr!*'

'So,' he said and spoke in German. 'You must realize that your lives are in my hand. You have escaped from your camp, have put on civilian clothing and come to Poland where the Polish sub-humans are shooting our soldiers in the back while we are defending Europe from the Asiatic Bolshevik hordes. We are fighting to save European civilization. England ought to be fighting on our side but your government has been corrupted by Jewish gold. I know that the ordinary people of England hate the Jews and the Bolsheviks as much as we do, but if they fight against us what are we to do? You have chosen to come to Poland to consort with our enemies and by wearing civilian clothes you have forfeited the right to be treated as prisoners of war. As you have chosen to pose as Poles, haven't we the right to treat you as Poles and deal with you accordingly? Wouldn't that be fair?'

'*Nein, Mein Herr*,' I said. 'You know perfectly well that we are not Poles but British soldiers and it would be dishonourable of you to pretend otherwise. It would be a stain on the good name of Germany. Everyone knows that Germany is a civilized country and the most cultured in Europe. My father was a soldier in the Great War and he had nothing but admiration for the fair way in which the German soldiers fought.'

I knew that our fate was in the balance and that the *Obersturmbannführer* alone could tilt it in our favour. Only a few miles away was the most infamous concentration camp of all – Auschwitz. Were we to be sent there no one would be any the wiser and we would disappear in smoke and ashes. I did not consider the prison governor to be either a fanatical Nazi or a particularly vicious person. I took him to be a typical lower-middle-class German with a secondary school education who had entered the SS via the Police Force as so many of the higher ranks had. He was certainly an intelligent man, had quite a lot of conceit and also that sense of self-preservation which typifies the lower-middle-class.

I gambled that my assessment of his character was right and argued my case accordingly. Above all I must not cringe; that would have been fatal.

'Sir,' I said, 'I am convinced that whatever decision you will come to, it will be an honourble decision, of which you, your family and your nation will not be ashamed.'

He looked at me for a long time, a half-smile on his lips but a deadly serious look in his eyes. Finally he said, '*Ach Tommy, du bist ein feiner junger Kerl. Ich werde mal sehen* – to be or not to be.' (Ah Tommy, you are a fine young fellow. We shall see –).

Back to the cell.

The next day I was taken again to the Governor's office. His wife and teenage daughter were there, obviously having come to see the German-speaking *Engländer*. I saluted the Colonel smartly and bowed towards the ladies. I was very pleased to see them for I took it to be a very good sign.

'Tommy,' said the Colonel, 'ze question isst – to be or not to be.' He looked towards his wife and daughter to see if they were suitably impressed by his knowledge of English.

They were beaming. I said to his wife, 'The Colonel speaks very good English, *gnädige Frau*' (gracious lady). She smiled.

The Colonel said, 'Now, now Tommy, no flattery.' He was speaking in German, 'I want to know what to do with you.' I was surprised that he should mention my fate in front of his wife and daughter but I guessed that perhaps he wanted to impress them with his power of life and death over people, even *Engländer*. I decided to give him an opportunity to show them how magnanimous he could be.

'As I mentioned yesterday,' I said, 'I am quite sure that whatever you will do will be just and honourable. I have not the slightest fear on that score.'

'You think I should hand you over to the Army?'

'Yes, Sir. That's what I think you will do.'

'Ha! Ha! Ha! Who would have thought that a British soldier would be so fond of the German Army? Ha! ha! ha! We shall see Tommy. We shall see!'

Turning to his wife, he said, 'Tommy knows Goethe, what do you think of that?'

She smiled and said, 'Is it really true that you know Goethe?'

'Yes,' I said, 'and I like his poems very much.'

'Can you recite one of his poems?'

'With pleasure, gracious lady,' and I repeated a verse from *Erlkonig*.

'Wer reitet diese Nacht durch Sturm und Wind
Es ist der Vater mit seinem Kind – '

The three listened and looked at me as if I were performing a miracle. The Colonel had a particularly proprietorial look on his face, like an impressario who had just discovered a new star of stage and screen.

Fortunately, they did not ask for any more, for the only other German poem that I knew was the *Lorelei*, but that was written by a Jew, Heine, who by then had become a non-person.

'When is the war going to finish?' asked the Colonel.

'Next year,' I replied.

'And who is going to win?'

'The Allies.'

'Why do you say that?'

'It's quite obvious,' I replied. 'As soon as America came into the war the fate of Germany was sealed. However good the German soldier is, he cannot win against overwhelming odds. It is American industry that will win this war. Its ability to produce weapons is almost limitless. You have failed in Russia. Stalingrad was the turning point. Since then the Russians have mounted a non-stop offensive. The whole of the German Army is unable to hold them. The British and Americans already have a foothold in Italy but the main offensive will undoubtedly come with an invasion in France. Meanwhile German cities are being razed to the ground by the British and American bombers. I believe Germany's position to be quite hopeless.'

'And what do you think Germany should do?'

'Try to come to terms with the British and Americans.'

'And do you think that is possible?'

'Everything is possible, Sir.'

'We Germans do not believe that the war is lost.'

'I would not either, Sir, if I were a German.'

'Ha! Ha! Ha! *Ist Tommy nicht ein feiner Kerl?*' (Isn't Tommy a fine lad?)

'*Was machen wir mit ihm?*' (What shall we do with him?)

'*Gehen – lassen*,' (Let him go) said his wife.

'Good Tommy,' said the Colonel. '*Wegtreten!*' (dismiss)

He rang the bell for the guard. I stood stiffly to attention, saluted him and said, '*Ich danke Ihnen, Herr Obersturmbannführer, fur Ihre Güte*.' (I thank you for your kindness.)

Bowing to his wife and daughter, I marched out with my warden-escort.

Oppeln Prison

About midnight we were taken into the prison courtyard where a double row of prisoners was lined up, each man handcuffed to his opposite number. We were placed at the end of the row. Idwal and Jenkins were handcuffed together. I was handcuffed to a man who turned out to be an Ukrainian. On the platform above the courtyard was a machine gun manned by an SS man. For a moment I thought we were going to be shot, but on reflection I thought that unlikely after they had gone to the trouble of handcuffing us. This view was strengthened when I saw some half-dozen SS men in what appeared to be marching order. If we were to be shot it would be done elsewhere. We were obviously leaving, but what was our destination? Judging from the appearance of the prisoners – young men almost without exception – we were on our way either to forced labour or to a concentration camp.

After waiting what seemed to be an endless period the gates of the yard were opened and we marched out under our armed escort.

We marched through the dark, deserted streets of Sosnowiec to the railway station where we were loaded into a prison train. The coaches had small cells on each side of a long corridor. The train had its own complement of wardens who threw us into the cells, up to half-a-dozen into each.

Soon the train moved off. I asked my cell-mates where we were bound for. They said they did not know but were pretty certain that we would land up in a concentration camp. Had I therefore failed to influence the SS colonel in our favour? It would appear so. All that flattery, and all my eloquence had been in vain. I wondered whether he had deceived his wife and daughter too. I had felt certain that they had been on my side.

As soon as the train moved off the young Poles started to sing. I immediately recognized the song – '*Serce w plecaku*' (My heart in my rucksack.) It was one of the most popular songs of the Armja Krajowa and had a most heart-rending, sad and haunting melody. The words were also extremely touching, about a young soldier of the Armja Krajowa who always carried a white rose in his rucksack to remind him of his sweetheart whom he had to leave to answer the call of his country which he loved with an even greater love. The song tells of victories, incredible sacrifices, of blood and tears that flowed like a river, of suffering and catastrophic losses, of the supreme sacrifice, of the unconquerable spirit of the young men and their passionate love of their country.

The warders yelled at them to stop singing but they were wasting their breath. Even going to a concentration camp was bearable in such gallant company. The young Poles, even handcuffed, and on their way to almost certain death, were unconquerable.

The train stopped several times during the night, but whether to drop prisoners or to pick up more I do not know. The time seemed endless. There were no windows so we knew not whether it was day or night. We received no food or drink. But eventually we three were yanked out, thrust along the corridor and out of the train. We were standing on the platform of Oppeln Station, a town I knew to be not more than about thirty miles from Lamsdorf. My recitation of *Erlkönig* had not been in vain after all!

We were handed over to the care of two uniformed and armed men who took us out of the station and loaded us into a prison van. When we got out of it a few minutes later we found ourselves in Oppeln Civil Prison. That was a bit of a blow but it was a great consolation to know that we had not landed in a concentration camp. This was a prison for ordinary offenders, thieves etc. We were put together in a cell containing three low wooden beds on which there were two blankets. The only other article of furniture was a bucket for the usual purpose. There was no heating.

The following morning we were awakaned at the crack of dawn and ordered to empty the bucket into a large container in the corridor outside. We were given a broom and told to clean out our cell and were also informed of the procedure to be followed whenever a prison officer entered our cell, which was to stand stiffly to attention, give our names and numbers, the offence for which we had been committed, the length of sentence imposed, the length of time we had served and the time remaining. This presented us with a problem as we had no prison number and had not been sentenced. We compromised by giving our prisoner-of-war numbers and leaving it at that.

Having cleaned out our cell we were given breakfast – a dish of *ersatz* coffee without milk or sugar and a slice of bread. At the same time we were given an armful of string tied in knots which we were to untie and arrange in neat bundles of ten lengths. The provision of supper was dependent on us completing this task by six o'clock in the evening. We set to without stopping and only managed to fulfil our task by a few minutes before six. Our fingers were almost raw. We got our supper – a dish of warm, thin soup and a slice of bread. We were some five days in the prison – five days that seemed like an age, the more so as we had no idea how long we were to stay there.

Then one Saturday morning a prison officer appeared unexpectedly and said, '*Komm mit!*' (Come with me). He took us to the Governor's Office where the Governor read us a short, sharp lecture on the dangers of escaping and told us how lucky we were to have got off so lightly. We were then handed over to a soldier who marched us out of the prison, through the streets of Oppeln to the railway station. I asked him where he was taking us. 'To Lamsdorf,' he replied. What a relief!

Another Trip to the Sudetenland

We could not escape the indignity of the de-lousing parlour and as it was December we nearly froze to death while waiting stark naked for the return of our clothes from the steam boiler.

Then straight to the *Strafe* Compound (Punishment Compound) where the Head Warder, known to all the old lags of Lamsdorf as Ukraine Joe, clapped us into solitary confinement in a freezing cold cell.

I think we spent about fourteen days there before we were released, but, wonder of wonders, we were not called in front of the *Gerichtsoffizier*. That was very lucky for me for he would most certainly have given me an extra dose of solitary, but worst of all he would have ordered my papers to be stamped LV – *Lager Verboten* (Forbidden to go on working parties). That would have meant the end of escaping, for Lamsdorf camp was absolutely escape-proof.

Having done our stint, we were released into the Working Compound which meant that we were again available for outside working camps. There I met a few old friends, including Bill Peascod, a sailor from the *Bedouin* and a native of Carlisle, Sonnie Hay and Shorty Crowther of the Cameron Highlanders and a few others, all excellent chaps and ready for anything.

We called to see Sergeant-Major Charters, Grenadier Guards, who, under a German Underofficer, was responsible for sending men to working camps. We were in luck. He told us that a new working camp of only fourteen men was being formed in the Sudetenland. It was to be in a quarry somewhere in the mountains. The new working party would take with it a six-week supply of Red Cross parcels. What better could we ask for? We asked the Sergeant-Major to hold everything while we collected fourteen men together, and of course they would be hand-picked! He agreed, but stipulated that one of them had to be a Sergeant. No problem, we knew the very man – Sergeant Dave Smith of the Argyll and Sutherland Highlanders, a man we knew to be game for any adventure. Within a couple of hours we had our fourteen men.

We left Lamsdorf about the middle of January with a consignment of about eighty Red Cross parcels. We had no intention whatsoever of doing any work. On the contrary, we intended to live like lords on the contents of the parcels which we reckoned would last us a couple of weeks and then make a mass escape and scatter southwards through Czechoslovakia and make for Yugoslavia if possible.

We were accompanied by two guards who were to stay with us. They were both fine chaps, one only about twenty and obviously unfit for front-line service. I could not help feeling sorry for them, for I knew that they would have nothing but trouble with us.

Having reached a small village in the depths of the Sudeten mountains, we de-trained and marched some two miles uphill to the quarry where a brand new wooden barrack had been built for us.

'God help them!' said Bill Peascod on seeing the brand-new building, 'they might as well have saved themselves the trouble. We shall only be here long enough for the house-warming party.' His words turned out to be only too true.

The trouble started the following morning. We had been told the night before to be ready to leave for work by a quarter to eight. When the guard arrived a good half of us were still in bed. He started to shout and to threaten but we told him that we refused to go to such a dangerous place as a quarry until it was perfectly light and that would not be until about nine o'clock. He disappeared and came back in about a quarter of an hour with the younger guard. Dave Smith went up to him immediately with his hand held out and asked him to shake hands as a gesture that everything was all right. The foolish youth did so and Dave, who was a gorilla of a man, grasped his hand and pumped it up and down at least a dozen times, meanwhile stroking his face with his other hand. Dave then bawled for silence and, calling me to him as interpreter, ordered me to tell the guards what the routine was to be concerning work: firstly, we would not leave camp before half-past eight until the spring, secondly, only nine men to go out to work, five to remain in camp – one to cook, one to clean up, two on sick-list and he himself, who, being a Sergeant, was not liable for work.

The senior guard refused to accept any terms from us, maintaining that he was the one to lay down terms , not us. He did, however, agree that Sergeant Smith should not work. He was also agreeable to one man staying behind as cook, but that was the limit. Before he had finished speaking Dave said to me, 'Tell him to shut up!'

I looked at him. 'Go on,' he said, 'tell him to shut-up!'

I said to the guard, 'The British Underofficer says that he is senior to you and that you are to keep quiet.'

The guard exploded with rage. Dave stepped up to him and yelled at him to shut up. Expecting far worse to come, we all closed in on the two guards. They were petrified. Dave told me to tell them that the terms he had given them were the terms of work agreed in Lamsdorf and that we would not work on any other terms and, if they were not acceptable to them, they could take us back to Lamsdorf that very day and that was final.

The guard said that he personally did not care a damn whether we worked or not but that the quarry authorities expected fourteen men in the quarry by eight o'clock every morning. We told them to leave the quarry authorities to us, we would deal with them. Realizing that there was nothing they could do without calling up reinforcements, the guards caved in. We immediately made a tremendous fuss of them, reminding them that we soldiers should stick together and present a common front to any threat from civilians. We persuaded them to accept cigarettes and a bar of chocolate each. They capitulated.

I went to the quarry about twice. It was a huge hole in the mountain into which one descended on a kind of escalator.The work consisted of loading large pieces of rock into skips and pushing them along railway lines to a crusher. I didn't take to it at all.

I was ready for another escape and Bill Peascod was to come with me. But I wanted to go to Poland not to Yugoslavia and the Sudeten mountains was no starting point. There was nothing for it, therefore, but to return to Lamsdorf, for the mass breakout had been wisely postponed to the spring, the mountains being no place to hang about in during the winter. But I could not wait for spring. I wanted to be in Poland as soon as possible for I guessed that as soon as the Red Army reached the Polish frontier there would be a general rising and I wanted to be in on it.

It was therefore arranged that Dave Smith should warn the guards that Bill Peascod and I were trouble-makers and should be got rid of. This was done and within three days we were on our way back to Lamsdorf and taken straight to the *Gerichtsoffizier* who had quite a file on me. We were given fourteen days' solitary and told that we were to be sent to a special camp from which escape was impossible.

After serving eleven days we were taken from the *Strafe* Compound and, with about a dozen others, most of whom I knew, were marched down the long hill to Annahof Station where we entrained for the camp from which there was no escaping. Among the other lads was Jonah Jones from Doncaster, an ex-miner, a good boxer, a hard case but a first-class chap. Then there were the two paratroopers, Roy Weston and Dusty Miller, both of whom had escape experience, and Digger Springfield, an irrepressible Australian who was ready for any adventure.

Our escort consisted of two guards who had obviously been warned that we needed careful watching. It was only after the most persistent efforts that I managed to draw them into conversation and to get them to tell me where we were bound for. It turned out to be Peiskretscham – a location that was just made to measure for me. It was about half-way between Laband where I had spent over two years and Gleiwitz, a large town on the pre-war Polish border and about fifteen miles away. Turning to Jonah who was an old friend from Laband days and with whom I had boxed scores of rounds, I said, 'Jonah, we're bound for Peiskretscham. Do you know where it is and anything about the camp?'

'Yes,' he said. 'You could call it Peiskretscham by-the-sea. The camp is in the middle of a desert of sand, miles from anywhere and the prisoners who are all from the RAF work in a huge sandpit. It is worse than Sing-Sing. Houdini himself could not escape from it!'

'How far from Gleiwitz is it?'

'About fifteen miles.'

'Did you hear that, Bill? That means that we will not be above forty miles from Sosnowiec.'

'So what?' asked Jonah.

'I'll tell you so what,' I said. 'I have a contact in Sosnowiec. Today is Saturday; I shall be there on Wednesday night!'

The Fourth Attempt

There were about forty RAF prisoners in Peiskretscham when we arrived. All were housed in one wooden barrack. All windows had iron bars. Outside was a compound surrounded by a high barbed-wire fence, in the corner of which stood the toilets and ablutions. The perimeter fence was lit up all night and patrolled by an armed sentry.

The men worked in a sandpit about a mile away and were guarded by four soldiers armed with rifles. The site stood in a vast sandy plain completely devoid of any cover and escape from it would have been extremely difficult. The camp had been in existence for two years during which time there had not been a single escape.

I began my preparations at once by going to see the senior Warrant Officer. After a general conversation I broached the subject of escaping and asked him whether anyone had made an attempt. No, he said, but two lads had been preparing to escape when they were suddenly removed from the camp by the authorities. I asked him whether he thought they had been betrayed and he said that he did, and moreover that he had a good idea who had been responsible. This was very bad news but it was a difficulty which could be overcome.

I asked the Warrant Officer point-blank what his attitude was to escaping, having regard to the fact that life would be very unpleasant for the inmates of the camp following a successful escape. He replied that he was all in favour of people escaping regardless of the consequences and would do anything to help. I then told him that four of us intended to escape at the earliest possible opportunity and that the remainder of our gang would deal very severely with anyone who stood in our way.

The following day was a Sunday and a rest day. We examined

the camp carefully and came to the conclusion that the best place from which to break out was from behind the ablutions, the outside wall of which was only a couple of yards from the perimeter fence. We would loosen the planking from the inside. This would be done by non-escapers while others watched the guard. Then at a signal the escapers would arrive in the ablutions one by one, the planks would be removed and an escaper would crawl through the hole, climb the barbed-wire fence, jump clear and run beyond the range of the lights. We reckoned each escaper should not take more than three minutes to clear the perimeter fence. We walked around the fence and estimated the distance to be some one hundred and fifty yards. We then set men to watch the sentry. They reported that he walked constantly at a steady pace and on an average took some ten minutes to complete a round. For half of that time the ablutions would be out of his sight, thus leaving at least five minutes for the escape. The escape would have to be done within about an hour after our return from the sandpit because after that we would be locked in the barrack-room until morning.

The following day we went to work. I placed myself at the end of the column in order to have a word with the guard who walked behind.

'Very cold this morning,' I said to him.

'Yes,' he said.

'What's the latest news of the war?'

'That is none of your business. Look to your front and get a move on!'

'No need to be angry,' I said. 'The war is very much my business. I can't go home until it is over.'

He snatched his rifle off his shoulder and threatened me with it, whereupon I started to shout, '*Hilfe! Hilfe!*' (Help! Help!)

One of the guards from the front ran back to see what was wrong. I told him that the soldier was threatening to shoot me, that he had gone mad and I pretended to be greatly distressed. He was an *Obergefreite*, a corporal, and in overall charge. He calmed his subordinate down and took me with him to the front of the column, telling me not to be afraid, that he would see that the other soldier would not hurt me!

I had several conversations with the *Obergefreite* during the day. He was not averse to smoking Red Cross cigarettes nor to discussing the war and the general situation. He seemed to be quite promising material.

The next day, Tuesday, Jonah and Dusty Miller reported sick

and were given two days off work by the Medical Corporal. Their job then was to prepare our escape clothes by dyeing our battle-dresses black and altering the neck of the jackets to make them look more like civilian jackets. I always carried a good supply of black dye, adding to it at every opportunity.

When we returned from work that evening our two friends had been very busy. Four sets of battle-dresses had been dyed and altered; all that remained to do was to dry them. They should be ready by the following evening.

The following day, Wednesday, we returned from work at about six o'clock to find that the atmosphere in the camp was extremely tense. The majority of the men knew that something was about to happen.

Jonah and Dusty had prepared us a slap-up meal. Our escape clothes were ready, dry and ironed neatly. We would have to be clear of the camp within one hour, because at seven o'clock the Underofficer would come into the barrack-room; we would have to stand by our beds as he counted, each man standing in his stockinged feet with his boots in his hand. After having been counted we would file into an adjoining room and deposit our boots there. That room would then be locked until morning. On leaving, the Underofficer would lock and bar the barrack-room door, which would not be opened again until six o'clock the following morning.

Having eaten our meal we put on our escape clothes, rolled up the trousers to the knee and then put on our overcoats. Jonah then went out to the ablutions, taking with him the large iron poker belonging to the barrack-room stove. He was to remove a sufficient number of planks from the ablution wall to enable us to crawl through to the perimeter fence. Two other men were sent to keep an eye on the sentry.

I then went to the Warrant Officer and told him that four of us were going to escape within the course of the next quarter of an hour and suggested that he call everybody into the barrack-room. He agreed at once but asked how we were going to get through the barbed-wire. I told him we intended to climb it, whereupon he put his hand inside his palliasse and pulled out a pair of brand-new wire-cutters.

'Any use to you?' he asked.

'Wherever did you get these?'

'From a guard,' he said. 'I intended to use them myself, but you might as well have them. It will impossible to hide them in any case after your escape. The guards will go through this place with a fine tooth-comb. I suggest you take them with you and hide them under the first bush you see. I might be able to get them back one day.'

Having got all the RAF prisoners together, I got on a table and addressed them. I told them that four of us were going to break out of camp within the next few minutes, that we had a definite place to make for outside, where help would be waiting and that we had a fair chance of being successful. I apologized in advance for the restrictions I knew would be imposed on them but reminded them that it was everyone's duty to escape and if one could not escape oneself one should certainly help others. I asked them to behave perfectly naturally but to keep away from the ablutions.

They looked very surprised but no one said anything.

After saying goodbye to the Warrant Officer, Dusty Springfield, Roy Weston, Bill Peascod and I went out to the ablutions in pairs with a towel over our shoulders. Jonah and his mates were ready for us, the planks were entirely loose and only needed lifting off for a hole to appear in the wooden wall. I handed him the wirecutters. He lifted them to his lips and kissed them reverently. They made the job of getting through the fence a piece of cake.

The next step was to watch the sentry go past the ablutions, along the fence to the next corner, turn left and continue until he was out of sight behind the barrack-block. We would then have at least five minutes, sufficient time for all four of us to go through one behind the other. Before getting the wire-cutters we had only envisaged one man going through at a time which might have meant the whole operation taking anything up to half-an-hour.

From just inside the ablutions' door we watched the sentry approach, dressed in his extra-long overcoat and his felt over-boots and a thick scarf round his neck, and he needed them for the temperature was well below ten degrees centigrade. He shuffled along, stamping his feet, his rifle slung over his shoulder and his hands buried up to the elbows in his overcoat pockets. Had anyone suddenly rushed the fence, climbed it and jumped over right under his nose he would have had an even chance of getting away with it before the half-frozen, half-dozy sentry could have done anything about it. He shuffled round the corner behind the ablutions and along the fence, round the next corner and away from us until he gradually disappeared behind the barrack-block.

Jonah had already removed the plank. Crawling through the hole, he cut the wire in about ten places and bent it up, leaving a hole through which we could comfortably crawl on our hands and knees.

'Off you go, lads, and good luck!'

We crawled through one after the other and crawled beyond the reach of the lights. A quick shake of hands and we separated, Digger and Roy going in one direction and Bill and I in another.

An Attempted Break-in

We moved off rapidly in the direction of the village of Peiskretscham about a couple of miles away. We intended to try and catch the first train for Gleiwitz.

Having reached the road we walked along the verge, ready at the slightest danger to retreat out of sight into the field. We had not gone far when we saw a bicycle approach from the direction of the village. We withdrew a few yards and measured our length on the ground. It was one of the guards from the camp and we smiled as we thought of the uncomfortable night that awaited him.

When had passed we returned to the road and reached the village without seeing anyone. Having walked through a few streets we heard the unmistakeable noise of a railway station and went towards it. Soon we saw the blue light. Just as we were going through the entrance to the station yard we saw two policemen standing at the door leading to the platform. We turned back immediately in case they asked us to show our identity cards. We might have been missed already and the police informed.

We cursed fluently for we had depended on getting a train to Gleiwitz that night. There was nothing left but to walk and what better than the railway line? So we skirted the village towards the east and crossed the fields until we came to the railway track. At least we could not lose our way.

We didn't walk, we ran. In about an hour or less we saw the lights of a prisoner-of-war camp. It could not have been anything else because only prison-camps were allowed to break the black-out restrictions. For one dreadful moment we feared that we had returned to the camp from which we had escaped, but from the size of the camp it was quite obvious that we had not. We left the railway track to have a closer look. The place looked somewhat familiar to me. I stared and stared, then turning to Bill I said, 'This is Laband Camp. I was here for two years and I am sure there are still many of my friends there. I also have quite a few excellent Polish friends in this area. Do you know what we will do?'

'What?'

'We'll break in and get my friends to hide us. It should be dead simple because it is a very easy-going camp, a real home from home. Tomorrow I can send someone to my Polish friends and we'll see what develops from that. Are you game?'

'Well,' said Bill, who was the best chap I ever escaped with, 'if you say it's a good idea I'm with you, but I must say that breaking out of one camp should be enough for anyone without thinking of breaking into another one.'

'It will be child's play, Bill. You watch!"

We went as close as we could to the camp without making ourselves visible. There were five big barrack blocks and a large compound lit up like daylight. Several men were walking between the blocks probably visiting each other for there were no restrictions in Laband until lock-up at about eight o'clock.

After watching for a few minutes I saw a chap I knew. He was a Welshman known as 'Big Dai' – an excellent chap but not the quickest on the uptake. I shouted, 'Big Dai!'

He stood stock still.

'Big Dai. Do you remember Taff Elwyn, Welsh Guards?'

'Yes' he said, 'but he left here over a year ago!'

'Well, he's back. It's me! I'm coming in! Watch the guard for me!'

Just then a Sergeant whom I also knew very well arrived. I could see him asking Big Dai what was happening and the latter telling him. Then the Sergeant sang the following words, 'Go to the other side of the camp. Whistle when you get there. I'll give you the sign to come over the wire!'

We did as he advised and, having arrived there, I whistled. We were standing outside the wire immediately behind the camp ablutions on the other side of it. We could see the whole of the compound and most of the perimeter fence apart from the side hidden by the barrack blocks and immediately to the right of the ablutions. We could not see a sentry anywhere although I was certain there was one prowling about somewhere.

Soon the Sergeant who was standing in front of one of the barrack blocks gave us a sign to climb over the wire.

'Let's go,' said Bill.

'No, wait a moment.'

'But he's giving us the sign.'

'I know. But I don't like it. I can't see the sentry. Let's wait until we see him.'

The Sergeant was still waving us on.

'It must be safe,' said Bill, 'otherwise he wouldn't wave us on.'

I was uneasy. Why hadn't the sentry appeared on his round?

'You crawl that way, Bill,' I said indicating one direction, 'and I'll crawl this way. We might be able to see the sentry.'

Bill went one way and I went the other. As soon as I cleared the corner of the ablution I saw the sentry. He was creeping up on us, his rifle at the ready, and not more than ten yards away and on the outside of the perimeter fence! 'Bill, look out!' I rose to my feet and was off like a hare with Bill hard on my heels. A bullet and then another whistled past us. Then we were beyond the reach of the lights and racing over the dark field. We ran for about five hundred yards and looked back. We could see the sentry standing by the fence and hundreds of prisoners out in the compound.

'That Sergeant tried to get us shot,' said Bill. 'I thought you said he was a friend of yours.'

'No,' I said. 'He was never a particular friend but I don't think he would have me shot just the same.'

'The guard was between us and him. He should have seen him,' said Bill.

'That's true,' I said. 'An explanation is required and if I ever see him again I shall expect one and it had better be a good one!'

We returned to the railway track and continued towards Gleiwitz.

The Gestapo

Gleiwitz was nearer than we had expected. We went straight to the station and at half past nine got a train to Katowice and from there a tram to Sosnowiec, arriving there at half past ten. I managed to find the tram-stop from which I had earlier travelled to the French camp and jumped on the first tram that came along. I really had no idea when to get off but I thought that we had travelled for about a quarter of an hour on the previous occasion. I was quite sure of one thing, we had got off at a stop beyond the town.

There was nothing for it but to trust my judgement and to take a chance. When I thought the quarter of an hour was up and, noticing that we were beyond the town limits, we got off and walked on. After about five minutes we saw a lane leading off to the right and turned into it. Before we had gone a few steps I felt convinced we were going the right way. Sure enough, a couple of hundred yards further on we saw the barracks in which the Frenchmen lived.

But how to get hold of Georges? We stood near the wall where we could not be seen. Before long a man arrived from the direction of the town. Just as he was about to go in I stepped out of the shadows and greeted him in Polish. He returned my greeting in French. I told him that I needed to see Georges urgently.

'Georges?' he said, '*Je ne le connais pas.*' (I don't know him.)

Obviously not his proper name, so I described him – a tall bespectacled young man wearing a beard.

'*Ah,*' he said, '*c'est Alphonse peut-être. On parle anglais?*' (It is Alphonse. He speaks English?)

'*Je ne sais pas, monsieur.*' (I don't know.)

'*Oui, m'sieur, vous le savez, mais cela ne fait rien.*' (Yes, you know, but that does not matter.)

He told me to wait and disappeared into the barracks. He must have been a friend of Alphonse, or Georges as we had known him. Luck was definitely on our side.

Soon Alphonse came and gave us a warm welcome, although he was amazed to see me and someone else with me this time. He imagined me to be somewhere in central Poland. But he was far too wise to ask many questions. He took us into the room that I had occupied on the previous occasion and promised to contact my Polish friends the following day.

The room was as dirty as ever and we spent the night very uncomfortably on the benches. Alphonse brought some bread and coffee in the morning before leaving for work and warned us to stay where we were until he returned in the evening. We spent a long, cold and hungry day.

About six o'clock in the evening the two young Poles arrived. They were both astounded and saddened when they heard my story about what had happened and about the heavy losses the unit of the Armja Krajowa had suffered.

They then took us to the home of the fiancée of one of them who lived with her widowed mother in a top-floor flat and whose neighbours were mostly Germans. They had two rooms only, a living room and a bedroom containing one double bed which we were given while the two women slept on the floor in the next room. They could not be persuaded to allow us to sleep on the floor. Such is Polish hospitality.

In the course of the evening we were visited by another Pole, an elderly man of some importance in the underground organization and with whom we discussed the general situation at considerable length.

It was the beginning of February, 1944. The Russian army was approaching the eastern borders of Poland which would soon become the battleground. It was feared that the Germans would destroy the country as they retreated. But the greatest fear arose from the breaking off of diplomatic relations between the Polish Government in Exile in London and the Russian Government as a result of the Germans finding the mass grave of some thousands of Polish officers, each of whom had been shot, in the forest of Katyn and of the publication of the report of a tribunal of inquiry, allegedly independent, accusing the Russians of having been responsible. This was a very serious development since Poland was not an entirely united country. While probably the majority of the people supported the London Government a not inconsiderable minority supported a Polish organization which had come into being in Russia. This dichotomy was reflected in the fighting forces as well as in the political parties. The Polish forces in the west took their orders from London as did the Armja Krajowa in Poland, while the Polish forces fighting alongside the Russians in the Eastern Front as well as the Armja Ludowa in Poland (The People's Army) took their orders from the organization in Russia. Those people in Poland who knew what was happening, as our friends did, were desperately worried. The war against the Germans was being won, victory was almost within sight. That was something the Western Allies and their peoples could look forward to with confidence and happiness as the realization of all their dreams. But what had the Poles to look forward to? Rift, division, civil war and disintegration? Was it for that they had sacrificed literally millions of lives?

It was a very sad evening. What could we say to comfort them? Nothing. It would be arrogant of us to try. I only hoped that they knew that I felt for them with all my heart. But I felt something else too and that was that we were nothing but a damned nuisance to them and that we were unnecessarily endangering their lives. They had trouble enough without us. Had the Germans caught us in that flat they would all have lost their lives and the maximum we might have suffered would be twenty-eight days' solitary. I felt utterly ashamed of myself.

We discussed the Armja Krajowa and learnt that it was not men that were needed but weapons of which not enough were available for the men already serving. This news, which ought not to have been news had I used my common-sense, only reinforced my feeling of shame and guilt. Nevertheless they gave us an opportunity to join a unit of the Armja Krajowa if we really wanted to.

We discussed the alternatives. Escape to France meant crossing the whole of Germany and the only way would be by train. Without identity papers such an undertaking was impossible. The same applied to trying to get to Switzerland. South through Czechoslovakia was out of the question in winter.

We said we would like to join the Armja Krajowa if they thought we could be of some use. They replied that people who were really keen were always wanted, but we would be of no use to them locally in Sosnowiec as the work there was of a very specialized nature. We would, therefore, have to cross over to the Generalgouvernement and join one of the fighting units. They could not get us across through Myszkow because the chemist there who was responsible for getting people across was not prepared to help escaped prisoners of war as he did not consider the risk worth the effort. I agreed with him inwardly a hundred per cent. They would get us railway tickets to Tarnowice, a small town near the frontier and not far from Czestochowa. We would have to make our own way across and then go to Jasna Gora, the big monastery on the hill, where we would be certain of finding someone who would put us in touch with the Armja Krajowa. Jasna Gora is where the picture of the Black Madonna, the patron saint of Poland, is kept.

This is what was agreed. The following morning the two young Poles took us to the railway station where they bought the tickets. Having given them to us they warned us not to go on to the platform too early because it was a happy hunting ground for the Gestapo. They then shook our hands, wished us luck and left.

We had about twenty minutes to wait for the train. Having waited about a quarter of an hour we went into the station where we could see the clock. We knew what platform the train was to leave from. With about a minute to go we walked quickly over the bridge. When we arrived on the other side we saw a train pulling out and ran for it, but we were too late. We had missed it.

'Quick Bill!' I said, 'let's go to the toilets.'

We walked quickly back along the platform towards the bridge, over it and down the other side, making for the sign '*Herren*' (Gentlemen). As we were about to enter the toilets I heard a loud: '*Hallo! Halt da!*' (Stop!)

Looking round we saw two men in long overcoats and trilby hats. There was no need to ask who they were – the *Gestapo!* (*Geheimestaatspolizei*) – Secret State Police. But we carried on to the toilets. Within seconds they were behind us.

'*Ausweise vorzeigen!*' (Show your identity cards!)

'*Bitte?*' I said.

'*Ausweise vorzeigen! Schnell!*' (Quickly)

I pretended to search through my pockets, then I said apologetically, 'I'm sorry, I've left it in my other clothes.'

'Has your friend done the same?' he asked.

'*Vite, ton passeport!*' I said to Bill. He pretended to search through his pockets, but also in vain. He shrugged his shoulders.

'Who are you?'

'We are Frenchmen. Volunteer workers in the Oberhuetten works.'

'Where did you intend to go to on the train?'

'To Tarnowice to visit some friends who are working there.'

'*Komm mit!*' (Come with us!)

They took us to the station officer.

'What's your name?'

'Jean Berthier.'

He gave me his pen and told me to write it on a piece of paper.

'Write your friend's name as well.' I wrote Paul Dumas.

'And where did you say you were working?'

'In the Oberhuetten works.'

I had seen them as we came through Sosnowiec in the tram.

He lifted the telephone and phoned the works. I could hear him speaking with someone on the other end while his mate watched us like a hawk. I knew it was all over with us but one had to try.

Number one put the phone down and without any warning hit me in the face and sent me flying across the room. Number two then took a pistol out of his pocket. 'Who are you, you Satan?' he asked. 'Quick, before I put a bullet into you!'

'We are British prisoners of war escaped from a camp in Germany,' I said.

'Which camp?'

'Peiskretscham.'

The both looked at each other and smiled.

'When?'

'Two days ago.'

'So!' he said, 'we have been looking for you.'

'You didn't take long to catch us,' I said.

'No. Nobody avoids the Gestapo for long.'

'The Gestapo!' I said and looked at Bill as if we had been greatly honoured.

'Do you know what the Gestapo is?'

'Yes. The same as Scotland Yard. Detectives. Do you know Scotland Yard?'

'Of course. We admire Scotland Yard very much.'

'I'm sure they admire you too. I am going to be a policeman after the war. I would like to be a detective.'

'Good,' he said, 'and now you are going to have a taste of Gestapo hospitality. I hope you'll have nothing to complain about.'

They took us out of the station and then on a tram to their headquarters. I wasn't greatly impressed by them for they failed to search us, so I was able to stuff all my German money down the back of the tram-seat. I smiled at the one who had hit me and said, 'Tell me. Are you a boxer?'

'Yes,' he said.

'I thought as much. I never saw a man move so quickly as you did when you hit me. I never had a chance to defend myself at all and I'm a boxer.'

Teschen

We were searched at the Police Station and deposited in a cell. What next, we wondered. The following morning we were shoved into a car and moved off we knew not where but were most agreeably surprised when we drove into a prisoner-of-war camp not more than a few miles away.

'Two prisoners from Peiskretscham,' said the policeman to the Underofficer. 'They did not like it there so they escaped. I hope you can entertain them better here.'

'Oh, we have just the place for them,' said the Underofficer. 'We'll send them to our holiday-camp in Teschen*!'

Having taken our escape clothes from us were issued with a suit of battle-dress and were then allowed to join the rest of the prisoners, pending our removal to Teschen. The men worked in a nearby coalmine and were pretty demoralized. Some of them had been there for years working an eight-hour shift every day of the week.

I was extremely pleased when we were moved to Teschen. The last thing I wanted was to land down a coalmine. Teschen is a large industrial town on the Polish – Czech border, the population being quite mixed. In those days it was claimed by both countries and was the cause of much friction. It was a huge camp containing several thousand Russians and few hundred French and Serbians and some forty British – all waiting court-martial for various offences. I suppose that was what awaited us too.

The commandant was an officer of the rank of captain, quite a senior officer to be in charge of a prisoner-of-war camp. We were lined up in front of him and received our sentence, Bill – fourteen days solitary, me – twenty-eight days.

* Now spelt Cieszyn

The bunker contained some twenty cells. There was no heating and the temperature was anything down to minus twenty centigrade. The cell contained a wooden board and two blankets to serve as a bed, and a bucket. Nothing else. It was much too cold to sleep for more than a few minutes at a time. I got into the habit of jumping up and down until I was warm and exhausted and then wrap the two blankets around myself and lie down on the wooden board. It is doubtful whether I slept more than twenty minutes at a stretch during the whole of the twenty-eight days. In the morning we received a bowl of *ersatz* coffee and a thick slice of bread. Mid-morning we marched around the bunker compound under the supervision of a warder for about half-an-hour. In the evening we received a bowl of soup and a piece of bread. And that was it.

The only other inmates were five Russians who had been sentenced to death for murder and were awaiting execution. One of them occupied the cell next to mine; in the intervening wall was a hole some half-an-inch in diameter, obviously made by some enterprising former inmate, through which we were able to converse quite freely. All five were sailors of the Red Navy. Very strong and very cheerful young men who did not seem to worry one jot about their impending doom.

My neighbour told me how it had all come about. They were in a working camp where the Germans had selected the biggest and strongest of them as supervisor and given him extra rations and privileges. As a result he became oppressive and literally tyrannized the others, making them work like slaves and maintaining an iron discipline. So these five murdered him, hanging his body from a beam in the barrack-room to make it look like suicide. But unfortunately for them the Germans found out it was murder and by bribing a few weaklings with extra rations they got the perpetrators.

My Russian neighbour was a very interesting character and a great fan of Fenimore Cooper and Jack London. We spent hours discussing *The Last of the Mohicans* and *The Call of the Wild* through the hole in the wall. He had been a baker before the war. Whether he was an ardent communist I could not tell but he was certainly a patriotic Russian who knew the history of his country well. He took great pleasure in recalling what had happened to Napoleon when he tried to conquer Russia. He assured me that the same fate would befall Hitler.

After Bill had completed his sentence things improved for me, for every morning during exercise he and several others used to come up to the fence. One of them would throw a packet containing one cigarette over the wire, apparently surreptitiously, but in fact making sure that the warder would see it and pounce on it. While he was doing that Bill would pass me a full packet of cigarettes with several matches inside. It never failed to work. Needless to say I shared the cigarettes with the Russians.

Eventually my sentence was served and I was released. I was very thin and weak but Bill had been saving food for me and after a few days I was well on the way to recovery.

The British prisoners had a larger room to themselves with the usual double-tiered wooden beds and a large stove plentifully supplied with coal. On the whole we lived quite comfortably, particularly so since we all received a weekly Red Cross parcel.

Bill and I became friendly with a mixed bunch of Australians, Canadians and New Zealanders. We pooled our rations and Red Cross supplies and took our turn at cooking.

There were also a number of South Africans there, one of whom was trying to attach himself to us. He was an argumentative person who seemed to be always trying to cause trouble. One day he put his spoke in when an Australian and I were having an argument. I told him to shut up. He immediately took that to be fighting talk and invited me to make him shut up. Naturally I could not refuse such a challenge and asked him to come outside. He rushed me without further ado, grabbed me round the body and pressed me against the stove which was almost red hot, saying, 'I'll fry you!'

He would have done so too, for he was a big hefty chap while I was well below form after my solitary confinement and starvation rations, had not the other lads intervened and pulled him off me.

'Outside if you want to fight,' they said.

I did not want to particularly, for I did not fancy my chances overmuch, realizing how much stronger he was. But there was no avoiding it. Out we went and squared up. Suddenly my opponent rushed me, obviously intending to repeat his performance in the barrack-room. But I had room to move and avoided him easily. Then, jumping in, I struck him with my left on the point of the jaw which brought him up stock-still. Before he had a chance to recover I struck him again with my right on exactly the same spot and down he went. He staggered up but fell back again. He made another attempt to get up but just as I was measuring him for the final blow I was held from behind and a voice said, 'That's enough. Do you want to kill him?'

Back to Lamsdorf

About a week later eight of us were quite unexpectedly sent to a camp in Czechoslovakia. Things went wrong the moment we arrived there. The camp was made up entirely of South Africans. Whether that was the reason we had been sent there I am not sure, but it is quite possible, for the Germans were well aware of the bad relations existing between us.

As soon as we arrived in the camp we made a dish of tea and sat down to enjoy it. A Sergeant came to the door of the room in which we were and shouted, 'Who is in charge of your party?'

We looked at each other. Then someone said, 'He is,' pointing at me.

'Why haven't you reported to me?' asked the Sergeant. 'Come here at once!'

'Wait until I've had my tea,' I said.

'I'm giving you an order!' he said. 'Get up!' and he came over to the table. I got up and aimed my fist at his head. At that a general mêlée broke out with about a dozen South Africans joining in. Fortunately for all concerned the Underofficer appeared and called us to order. He then took the Sergeant away with him and he was followed by the remaining South Africans.

Having drunk our tea we went out to inspect the camp. Two civilians were engaged in strengthening the perimeter fence by adding an extra wire slanting inwards to the top of it.

'*Guten Tag*,' I said.

One of them replied, '*Guten Tag*,' but I knew immediately that he was not a German.

'*Dzien dobry, Pan czech?*' I asked.

'*Tak*,' he said '*my czechi*' (We are Czechs)

'Aren't you ashamed of yourselves strengthening the wire to

prevent us from escaping when we are your friends and allies?' I asked.

'We are very sorry for you, friend,' he said, 'but it is very hard for us too. We have to do what the Germans tell us. We have wives and children who would suffer if we didn't.'

'Of course,' I said. 'I fully understand. I was only joking. In any case no fence could possibly hold us if we wanted to get through it. Iron bars are the greatest obstacle to us. Do you think you could get us a hack-saw?'

'Yes' he said, 'we could bring you one tomorrow providing you promise not to tell where you got it from in the event of your being caught.'

'I promise,' I said.

The following day they brought me the hack-saw which I immediately sewed into the inside of the slit in the back of my greatcoat.

Most of the South Africans were Boers, although there were a few of British descent but they were very much afraid of the former. One of them told me in confidence that many of the Boers were members of the Osseva Brandwag, the South African Fascist Party, and were hoping for a German victory.

The second day in the camp the Sergeant came to me in a very conciliatory mood and said that there would be a meeting of the camp committee at seven o'clock that evening in the cook-house and would I attend. All eight of us decided to go, which was just as well for we immediately saw that a fine reception party had been arranged for us. About a dozen of the biggest chaps in the camp were gathered there.

'Come in and close the door,' said the Sergeant, 'we don't want everyone to know what we are going to talk about.'

It was obvious that they were rather disappointed that all eight of us had turned up. There was an awkward silence for a few minutes, then the Sergeant said, 'This is a very good camp and we don't want it spoilt. I have a very good relationship with the Underofficer who is prepared to do all he can for us provided we behave reasonably. Tell me, what are you intentions?'

'Why?' I asked.

'Because we dont want any damned trouble-makers here,' said one of the Boers.

'And what makes you think we are trouble-makers?'

'I'm not saying you are,' said the Sergeant, 'but I'm warning you. Don't make any plans for escaping. If I suspect that you are planning to do so I will immediately report the matter to the Underofficer. I am not going to have this camp spoilt by you. We want to keep what priveleges we have.'

The rest of the Boers were looking as if they were about to attack us. On the table near where we stood was a meat chopper. One of our gang, a chap by the name of Geordie Watts from the Durham Light Infantry, picked it up and running his thumb along the edge said, 'I bet I could chop somebody's head off with this with one blow,' swinging it at an imaginary head.

'It seems to me,' I said to the Sergeant, 'that you are a lot too friendly with the Germans. They are supposed to be our enemies.'

'I don't give a damn what you think,' he said, 'but I'm warning you all that if you cause any trouble I'll have you removed from the camp.'

'In that case,' I said, 'you had better go and see your friend, the Underofficer, and have us removed for we are not going to give any undertaking.'

That night we hardly slept in case we might be attacked. The following morning all eight of us were marched to the station and entrained for Jaegerndorf where we were lodged in the guard-room of the military barracks. The next day we were moved to Lamsdorf, It was 17 March, St Patrick's Day.

The RAF Escape Committee

About a couple of days after my arrival in Lamsdorf I bumped into Jock Souter, a corporal in the Royal Tank Corps and an old friend from Labard and Bauerwitz. He was on the Staff, working in the Record Office of the camp and living in style in the Rackets Compound.

Having told him about my four escapes he said, 'There is a man you ought to see in the RAF compound.'

'Oh. Why?'

'Because he is the chairman of the RAF Escape Committee and he has resources that you have never dreamt about.'

'What sort of resources?'

'To begin with, all sorts of identity cards complete with photos and German stamps, civilian clothing and money.'

'Very interesting. When are you going to take me to see him?'

'Not so fast,' he said. 'It will depend whether he is prepared to see you. I'll have to make inquiries first.'

'Is he so very important?'

'Yes, he is. It is he that took over from Wing Commander Bader before he was removed to Colditz.'

'He must be quite a big shot then.'

'He is. He is known as Big X, a Canadian Warrant Officer. But he is only interested in helping aircrew to escape. That is where you would come in useful with your experience. Aircrew have never been out of Lamsdorf. They have no idea what things are like outside. Big X might want you to take one of them with you, as a guide if you like. In exchange you would be issued with identity cards and money.'

'Sounds very interesting, Jock. See what you can do.'

The following day Jock came to see me and said, 'I've arranged for you to see Big X tonight.'

He turned out to be a Canadian Warrant Officer in his late twenties. He opened the conversation by saying, 'I've heard that you have made four escapes. Will you tell me something about them?'

I recounted my experience. He then asked, 'How good is your German?'

'Pretty fluent,' I said.

'Do you speak French?'

'Not much, but I get by. I could fool a German provided I can maintain the initative and channel the conversation my way.'

'Do you intend to escape again?'

'If I get the chance.'

'Where would you make for?'

'Poland.'

'Why?'

'It is the easiest place to get to and I can always depend on the Poles for help.'

'Wouldn't you prefer to get to Sweden? You could return to Britain from there.'

'Maybe, but how would I get to Sweden?'

'Through one of the Baltic ports, Danzig or Stettin. You could get a Swedish ship there. Do you think you could get to Stettin?'

'If I had the money to pay the train-fare I reckon I could get there. From a working-camp of course.'

'Do you reckon you could escape from any working-camp?'

'Yes.'

'I could help you on certain conditions.'

'And what are they?'

'That you take one of our pilots with you.'

'And what help can you give me?'

'Identity papers as a French volunteer worker, a permit to travel by rail to Stettin and enough money to cover the fare and anything else you might need.'

'May I see this pilot before I decide?'

'Yes. You come here at twelve o'clock tomorrow and you'll meet him.'

I was there at the appointed hour the following day and met Desmond Simpson, a Londoner, a tall, slim, pale-faced young man of twenty-three. He did not at all seem to be the escaping kind. Having been shot down in North Africa he had been in Lamsdorf about a year and a half. He had never been in a working-camp, did not speak a word of German and had no idea of conditions outside Lamsdorf. Not very promising.

We were left on our own for about an hour to sound each other out and to decide whether we were prepared to trust each other. He told me how he had been shot down and what had happened to him since, while I told him about my escapes. We also discussed getting out of Lamsdorf and into a suitable working-camp, not far from the main railway line and the various possibilities of escaping from the camp. I told him that as soon as we were out of Lamsdorf he would have to trust me absolutely and allow me to make all decisions. He demurred a little at this, suggesting that we should consult together before doing anything. I refused that categorically because from experience I knew that someone would have to take the decisions, right or wrong, and since I was the more experienced it would have to be me. He agreed reluctantly. I was not satisfied with that and told him that I was making it an absolute condition, otherwise the deal was through. He accepted.

When Big X came back he asked us whether we had agreed to make the attempt together. I asked Desmond to answer him. He said, 'Yes. I am prepared to go with him.'

'And I am prepared to take him,' I said, 'on the conditions we have agreed between us, the main one being that in all things to do with the escape my word is to be final.'

'Are you quite sure you are agreeable to that, Desmond?' asked Big X.

'Yes,' he said.

'Good,' said Big X. 'Both of you come here by seven o'clock tonight and may I remind you of what I've told you before. You are not to breathe a word about this. Not even to your closest friend!'

That night I had my photograph taken in an RAF collar and tie with the jacket having been altered to look exactly like a civilian jacket. The same happened to Desmond.

'The next thing,' said Big X, 'will be to get someone to change identities with Desmond. We'll have to find someone who resembles him very closely or he'll never get past the man checking the documents as you go out of Lamsdorf. But we'll find somebody.' Turning to me he said, 'Meanwhile you try and find a suitable working camp not far from a main railway station. I'll have your documents ready within a week.'

The business of swapping identities was all-important for Desmond because as aircrew he was not allowed to go to a working camp. The authorities were most anxious not to give aircrew any chance of escaping. As each prisoner went out of Lamsdorf main camp he was checked very closely against his record-card which contained all his particulars plus his photograph. It was necessary therefore for Big X to find someone resembling Desmond and then ask him to change identities with him. This was a fairly common practice as not only aircrew were banned from leaving Lamsdorf, the ban also applied to 'L.V.' prisoners, that is, men who were not allowed on working parties because they were known escapers. As a result many a man in Lamsdorf was answering roll-call in someone else's name and also receiving his mail from home.

Meanwhile I went to see my old friend Sergeant-Major Charters to inquire about a suitable working camp, preferably a small camp near a main railway line. His first words on seeing me were, 'What! You again! Haven't you been shot yet?'

'Yes, me again,' I said, 'but I hope this is the last time I'll trouble you. When I get back to Blighty I'll recommend you for an OBE!'

He asked me for how many men he had to find a place.

'Four,' I said.

'I'll do my best,' was his reply, 'and when will you be ready to go?'

'In about ten days,' I said.

After my experiences with the South Africans I was not going to take any chances. I wanted two men with me who could ensure that no one would hinder us in our breakout from the camp. There were two men in Lamsdorf at that time who were eminently suitable for that job; they were George Cook the Glasgow razor-man who had been with me in Ratibor and a little chap called Hughes from the Haymarket, Edinburgh, who also carried an open razor for his protection!

I went to see them and, without giving anything away, told them that I was in a position to do a very special escape which might very well be successful but I needed their help to get away from the camp. They both agreed to come with me without hesitation.

Desmond and I were to leave Lamsdorf wearing RAF trousers and shirt underneath our khaki battle-dresses and overcoats. Our false passes and German money would be inside our socks, between our feet and the shoes. We would each have an RAF tie tied round our waists next to the skin.

Within a few days a New Zealander with a passing resemblence to Desmond had been found to swap identities with him who then had to memorize the details of his new identity – name, date of birth, place of birth, regimental number, where captured, etc, etc.

According to our false passes I was François Dupont and

Desmond was Albert Lebrun. We were both French volunteer workers, electricians and were proceeding to Stettin to work in the naval dockyard. One paper was an Identity Card and the other a permit to travel from Gleiwitz to Stettin. Both were properly stamped. The only thing wrong with them was that they were not made with the actual type of paper of which such documents were made. But the Identity Card only purported to be a temporary document issued to us because our original documents had been destroyed in a fire. Each Identity Card was contained in a genuine Identity Card wallet as used by all Germans, the photograph showing prominently. It was hoped that all we would have to do at a routine check such as was commonly made at railway station barriers was to flash the wallet with its prominent photograph at the policeman and we would pass through on the nod. Should the police, however, take the Identity Card out of the wallet and examine it closely there would be some awkward questions to answer. The travel permit should not cause any trouble as it bore the stamp of the Polizei Praesidium, Gleiwitz o/s (Upper Silesia) and was boldly signed in Gothic script.

Both Desmond and I had to learn the particulars on our Identity Cards and satisfy Big X that we knew them word-perfect.

Our final instructions were: 'Get to Stettin anyway you can and go to the public house 'Zur Ostsee' in the Kleine Oder Strasse. It is a public house exclusively for non-Germans but mainly for foreign sailors, Swedes, Norwegians, Finns and Danes. Try and get into contact with Swedish sailors and persuade them to take you on their ship. If not lucky with the Swedes try the Norwegians first, then Danes. Don't have anything to do with the Finns as they are allied to the Germans. If unlucky with the sailors try and stow away on a Swedish ship. The best place to hide initially is the cable-locker. It will be empty when the ship is in harbour. Do not hide in an empty hold in case you are buried alive when they start loading the ship. If you are caught at any time you must try and destroy your passes. Should you fail you must say that you got them from French prisoners at Teschen. If you are tortured tell the truth. Should you manage to hide on a ship don't give yourselves up to the ship's officers until you are at least a day's voyage out of Stettin. You can tell the Swedes that, should they help you, they will be handsomely rewarded by the British Minister in Stockholm. Good Luck!'

Desmond and I then moved into the Working Compound where I went to see Sergeant-Major Charters.

Derschau

I have places for four men in a camp at Derschau, a small village about seven miles from Oppeln. Will it do?'

'Absolutely made to measure,' I said and gave him the four names. 'When are we going?'

'Any day now a guard from Derschau will be coming to fetch you.'

'I shall certainly recommend you for that OBE!'

'You do that and good luck!'

We left on the 5th of April. Bill Peascod came to say goodbye and gave me a going-away present. It was a leather lumber-jacket with a fur collar.

'Where did you get that, Bill?'

'It was a present from a Yank,' he said, 'but he doesn't know it.'

'What! You mean to say you pinched it?'

'Yes, I thought your need was greater than his. It will make an excellent part of your escape kit. All you need with that will be your RAF trousers, just as they are. Don't wear your RAF shirt and tie, they look too much like a military uniform. Make a collar for your khaki shirt and then dye it black. You won't need a tie. You'll be just right as you are.' Bill was right.

Having said goodbye to him and Jock Souter, and the escort having arrived for us, we were moved to the Vorlager where everyone leaving Lamsdorf was carefully checked. Everything depended on getting through without being detected, not only our chances of escape but also the survival of the Escape Committee because, had the documents and money been found on us, the authorities would soon find a way of making us tell where we had got them from.

But, fortunately, we went through the check-point without any mishap. It was with an audible sigh of relief that we passed through the main gates and marched down the long hill to Annahof Station. I tried to remember how many times I had walked down that hill hoping that each time was the last. Would I ever walk down it again?

There were some fifty prisoners in Derschau, among them about a dozen or so South Africans. The camp was a former public house adapted for the purpose – iron bars on the windows and a barbed-wire fence around the yard outside. We occupied the second floor while the guards occupied the ground floor. At about seven-thirty every night we had to hand in our trousers and boots which were then locked in an adjacent room. The men worked in a saw-mill about a mile away from the camp and from where it would have been quite easy to escape. I, however, favoured a break-out from the camp during the night to enable us to reach Oppeln Station some seven miles away to catch an early morning train for the north. Our route would lead through Breslau, Frankfurt-an-der-Oder and on to Stettin, some three hundred and fifty miles away, following the River Oder right through to its estuary on the Baltic.

Having had a good look at the camp I said to Desmond, 'Today is the 6th of April. At two o'clock in the morning on Monday the 17th of April we will make our escape!'

He looked rather taken aback and said, 'Would it not be better to wait until the weather gets warmer in May and to give me a chance to pick up a bit of German.'

'No,' I said, 'the weather is not a factor as we are going to be travelling by train and you won't pick up any significant amount of German between now and May. We must have a firm time and stick to it.'

'But what if the circumstances are not favourable at that time?'

'We'll have to make them. It is no use waiting for a favourable opportunity to turn up. There are thousands of prisoners who have been doing that ever since they were captured. They are still waiting and will carry on waiting until the war is over. No, we must start getting ready now and break out at two in the morning on Monday the 17th.'

Within a couple of days I had made a collar from the tail of my Army shirt and sewn it on quite neatly and had dyed the whole black. My RAF trousers and leather lumber jacket were hidden inside my mattress. The only thing left was to find some way of not handing in my shoes in the evening prior to escaping. That little problem was easily solved. Many of the prisoners had wooden clogs which they wore in the evening after handing in their boots. I acquired a pair and made uppers for them with stiff cardboard. I then made lace-holes in them and threaded through a pair of laces. Having then blackened them, they did not look unlike a pair of boots, particularly half-hidden by a pair of trousers thrown negligently over them.

Desmond was all right for escape clothes for he had come out of Lamsdorf wearing an RAF uniform which had been converted into a very good imitation of a civilian suit. This he had worn beneath his battle-dress and had hidden it inside his mattress on arrival at the camp. He adopted the same plan with regard to the boots as I did.

The next thing was to decide how we were going to break out. It was immediately obvious that through a window was the only way. Cutting through a bar was no problem for I had a hack-saw blade sewn inside the hem of the slit in the back of my greatcoat.

On Friday, 14 April Desmond, George Cook, Wee Darkie Hughes and I held a conference to finalize our plans.

Desmond was opposed to such an early break-out. He wanted to postpone things until May and could not see any need for such haste. I tried to persuade him that the earlier we went the better as the Second Front might be opened very soon which would make the Germans very jittery and probably result in a very considerable tightening-up of security measures. But it was plain to me that his heart wasn't really in it. He had been toying with the romantic idea of escaping during his two years' stay in Lamsdorf without really appreciating the danger involved. Now that the danger was imminent he shrunk from it. I could well understand it. A prisoner of war escaping puts his life in the balance. Life in Lamsdorf might have been very boring but it was not a great hardship and life at Derschau was quite bearable. The prisoners had a football pitch on which they were allowed to play on Sunday afternoons and practically every evening in summer. With a weekly issue of Red Cross parcels and the German rations people lived very well, much better than the German guards did. And as for the latter, they did their best to make life as tolerable as possible for the prisoners. Desmond was safe and comfortable where he was; escaping was full of unknown dangers. Why not postpone them a little? I knew exactly how he felt. I also know that I did not want anyone with me who was not one hundred per cent; furthermore I knew I had a far better chance of success on my own.

I said to him, 'All right Desmond. I cannot force you to come with me on Monday, but I wish to remind you that we agreed in Lamsdorf that I had the final word in all things to do with the escape and my final word is that I am going at two o'clock on Monday morning. Are you coming with me? Yes or no?'

'No,' he said. 'I'll wait until May.'

'All right. You are probably doing the right thing. You are obviously not ready for it yet. Your papers are of no use to anyone else as they have your photograph on them. You keep them. I shall go as planned.'

The Fifth Attempt

Sunday afternoon, the 16th of April. I went to see the Sergeant in charge of the prisoners and told him that I was escaping at two o'clock the following morning, that I expected his full cooperation and that of the other prisoners. To say that he was taken aback would be an understatement. Escapers were very unpopular people, nuisance and trouble-makers who caused very considerable inconvenience to others. After an escape privileges were curtailed, security measures overhauled and tightened and life became generally less plcasant. This was resented by most prisoners, particularly as ninety-nine per cent of all escapes ended in failure. There was another aspect to the matter too – an escaper was an uncomfortable reminder to the others of their duty and of their lack of enterprise. Most prisoners thought and talked of escaping, many were making continuous and elaborate plans but were waiting for the right moment to come. Needless to say, for most it never came, for which fact many were very grateful.

To begin with the Sergeant listened to me without much enthusiasm but after I had explained to him that I had identity papers and German money, that I spoke German more or less fluently and had very definite plans, he agreed to do all he could to help.

Everyone was asked to gather at one end of the room. The Sergeant then told them that I would be breaking out of camp during the night, that it was a very well-planned escape with a good chance of success and that everybody was expected to co-operate to the full. This information was received in silence. I then told them that I was going to saw through one of the iron bars on the window and asked them to form an *ad hoc* orchestra so as to drown the noise of the saw. This they did, producing a dreadful din. Men were posted at every window and at the door to give warning of the approach of any of the guards. I then got my hack-saw and started on the work. The bar was about an inch in diameter. I sawed two of them about half an inch above the window sill, but not right through. I left just enough to hold them and then filled the cut with soap which I then covered with dust. The whole operation took no more than about half an hour, George Cook and Darkie Hughes taking turns on the hack-saw blade, around one side of which I had wrapped a handkerchief to serve as a handle. All I would have to do the following morning would be to give the bars a hefty tug to complete the cut and then bend them upwards sufficiently to allow me to squeeze through feet first, face down and allow my two henchmen and Desmond to lower me to the ground some eighteen feet below, at the end of a rope made of knotted blankets. Everything passed off without a hitch and I thanked the 'orchestra' for their cooperation.

About seven-thirty or so we had to stand by our beds for the evening roll-call. That was immediately followed by the handing-in of boots and trousers. They were stowed in a room next to the one in which we slept. A guard stood at the door checking us as we went in, a pair of boots in one hand and a pair of trousers in the other. It was with a feeling of considerable trepidation that I went through the door, having waited until last in the hope that the guard would be impatient to get away. I was hoping that he would miscount and overlook me. But he didn't for he called. '*Es fehlt einer. Komm mensch, mach' schnell!*' (One is missing, come my man, get a move on.) At that I trotted past him barefooted, saying, '*Entschuldigen Sie, Herr Posten. Ich bin schon da.*' (Excuse me, Mr Guard, I'm here) I placed my faked boots on the floor at the end of the row and dropped my folded trousers over them saying, '*Ein Paar Schuhe, ein Paar Hosen.*' (One pair of boots, one pair of trousers)

I had said that every night since I had been in the camp so the guard was quite used to it and made no comment. As I went back out of the room I said, '*Gute Nacht, Herr Posten.*'

'*Gute Nacht,*,' he said and locked up.

He then went down to his quarters on the ground floor. He would not return until six o'clock the following morning. By that time I hoped to be miles away.

George Cook and Wee Darkie Hughes then made me a substantial meal, a kind of porridge made of broken Canadian biscuits and raisins mixed with the excellent Klim milk, also Canadian, followed by corned beef fried in butter and plenty of hot sweet tea. They were like a manager and trainer preparing their fighter for a world championship.

I then checked over my escape kit and went to bed. They were going to stay up to keep an eye on things and to ensure that no one interfered in any way. It took me a long time to go to sleep. Although I had already thought of everything that might happen in the event of my being caught and prepared myself to accept them I still felt uneasy. I knew that as soon as I was through that window I would feel as if I were the loneliest man in the world. Behind me would be my friends in their warm and comfortable beds, safe and secure. They would get up in the morning, have breakfast and go to work. By the time they got back there might be a letter from home. They would sit down and answer it saying, 'The war cannot last much longer and I'll be coming home. Get my room ready and my old civvy suit. We'll have such a celebration, etc, etc.' And of course they would be right – it was April, 1944, the Russians were in eastern Poland, the western Allies firmly lodged in Italy and a massive invasion of France was imminent. Germany was visibly collapsing, the signs were all around us. We knew from our conversations with the guards and with civilians at work that the Germans had long ceased to believe in victory. Yes, the friends I would be leaving behind would get home before very long. But would I – ever? If I were caught with false papers was it not more than likely that I would disappear into a concentration camp from where I would never return? Was I prepared for such an eventuality or would I break down and blubber and have to be dragged away screaming? Could I face such a fate with courage and dignity and without recriminations? I knew that I had no right to go through the window unless I was prepared to face anything, whatever it might be, without fear.

With my imagination working overtime I was so terrified at times that I was literally trembling. But gradually I overcame my fear and fell asleep, firmly believing that I was prepared for whatever might come.

I was awakened at about a quarter to two and given a steaming cup of tea. I dressed hurriedly, putting my precious wallet in the inside breast pocket of my lumber-jacket. Then I practised taking it out nonchalantly and flashing it at an imaginary policeman. My two friends had already rolled and knotted four blankets together into a strong rope sufficiently long to reach to within about four feet of the ground.

We tied one end of the rope to an uncut bar and lowered the rest down the outside wall. Grasping one of the cut bars, I gave it a tug. It didn't give. I had not cut enough. But with the help of one of my friends and an almighty tug it broke. We both nearly fell backwards on to the floor. By this time several of the other lads were taking an interest in the proceedings. We went round the beds and asked them to the perfectly quiet in case the Germans below should awaken.

The second bar broke easily. We then pulled both away from the window, bending them upwards until there was enough room for me to get through.

The Sergeant came to us. 'Everything all right?' he asked.

'Couldn't be better' I replied. 'Thanks for everything. I expect hell will break loose here tomorrow morning and you'll all have to suffer. I'm sorry about that.' 'Never mind,' he said, 'If you get through it will be worth it. Good luck.'

After shaking four pairs of hands I slid out of the window feet first. Grasping the rope firmly I climbed down it. After reaching the end I dropped lightly to the ground. Striding across the yard I climbed the barbed-wire fence and jumped clear on to the other side. I glanced back at the window and saw several hands waving. I waved back and walked quickly away. I was perfectly cool, my pulse absolutely normal and instead of fear I felt euphoric.

The Long Journey

I hurried across the fields and reached the main road. I knew in which direction Oppeln lay, having made certain of that during the twelve days I had been in the camp.

Walking along the side of the road I soon got into a good five-mile-an-hour pace which should have got me to Oppeln by about half past three. If possible I wanted to catch the first long-distance train going north and arrive in Stettin before night.

There was a moon, not full but it was quite light, a clear starry, frosty night. Couldn't be better for walking except that the frost under my feet crackled rather loudly. I tried walking on the road but that was even noisier. I returned to the grass verge and decided I would just have to be extra vigilant to ensure that if anyone was about I would see him before he saw me.

After a couple of miles I reached a forest. It was now much darker and consequently I felt considerably safer. Unfortunately, I must have felt too safe and become careless for quite unexpectedly I heard a noise behind me. Turning round, I saw a policeman on a bicycle only a few yards away. I felt that it was all over. I continued walking. The policeman stopped alongside and dismounted.

'Good morning!' I said in German.

'Good morning. Where are you going so early in the morning?'

'To Oppeln.'

'Where have you come from?'

'Derschau.'

'Are you German?'

'No, French.'

'Are you working in Derschau?'

'No, I've been visiting my friend.'

'What is he doing in Derschau?'

'Working on a farm.'

'Which farm?'

'I don't know what it is called. It's about a kilometre from the village.'

'Show me your Identity Card?'

I looked at him. I saw that he was very suspicious and that if I gave him my Identity Card that would be the last I would see of it. He would take me to the police station for further inquiries and by six o'clock all police stations in the area would be notified of my escape.

I smiled at him and pretended to take my Identity Card from my pocket but instead I struck him under the jaw. The next second he was lying on his back and I was on top of him. I pulled his pistol from the holster and cocked it. Standing over him I aimed it straight at his heart.

'*Nicht schiessen, Kamerad.*' he said. (Dont shoot, comrade)

I pulled the bike free and slung it into the wood.

'Take your belt off!' He did so and I threw that into the wood too.

'Take your boots off!' I slung them away.

He was terrified and kept saying piteously, '*Nicht schiessen, Kamerad! Nicht schiessen!* I was only doing my duty.'

I didn't know what to do. I felt nothing but pity for him and anger with myself for having been so careless. He was only a country policeman with probably a wife and children and was no more my enemy than the man on the moon.

'I shall throw your pistol into the wood,' I said. 'You'll find it and your other things when it gets light.'

I threw the pistol into the wood and ran and kept on running for a mile or more. I was soon on the outskirts of Oppeln. Finding the railway station was the next problem. I tried to keep to what I thought was the main axis, which should, I thought, lead me to the centre of the town where the station ought to be. But it was not easy for there were roads branching off in every direction. I carried on doggedly, however. There were no lights whatsoever and fortunately I saw no one. I was walking as quietly as I could on the pavement and as near to the walls of the buildings as possible, ready at the first sight of a policeman to dodge out of sight.

Oppeln is a big town and it seemed that I would never get to the town-centre. The first person I saw was an old lady who was crossing the street. I waited till she arrived on my side and addressed her: '*Guten morgen, gnaedige Frau. Wissen Sie wo der Hauptbahnhof sich befindet, bitte?*' (Good morning, gracious lady.

Do you know where the main railway station is, please?) '*Guten Morgen*,' she said. 'If you take the next turning to the left you'll see the blue light in front of you.'

'*Vielen Dank!*'

Turning left I saw the blue light. What fantastic luck! I had expected all kinds of difficulties in finding the station and *voilà* – there it was!

I walked in. The hall was dimly lit, the ticket office open for business. It was exactly a quarter past four. I walked up boldly and asked for a single to Stettin. The woman asked for my travel-permit. I took it out of my wallet and handed it to her. She barely glanced at it before handing it back to me together with my ticket for which I paid.

'*Wann Fährt der zug ab bitte?*' (When does the train leave?)

'At five o'clock.'

'*Danke*'

'It is already standing on platform two if you want to get on,' she added graciously.

'*Vielen Dank.*'

Apart from the slight difficulty with the policeman things were going like clockwork. I felt certain the policeman would not report the incident for obvious reasons.

Glancing round the hall I could see that the newspaper kiosk was already open as was also the restaurant where no doubt *ersatz* coffee and *Eintopf* (vegetable soup) could be obtained without coupons. Glancing through the window I could see several people eating. I decided, however, not to join them after my experience with the Gestapo on Sosnowiec Station, although I thought it rather early for them to be about. I made for the newspaper kiosk and bought a copy of the *Schlesische Tageblatt* and one of the *Völkische Beobachter* – Doctor Goebbels' very own propaganda sheet. I then went on to platform two and saw the train. I walked along it. It was practically empty. I boarded it and took a corner seat away from the corridor in an empty compartment. A dim blue light shone in the small bulb hanging from the ceiling.

After about a quarter of an hour a man entered the compartment and with a 'Heil Hitler!' sat down in a corner seat.

I replied and in order not to encourage him to speak opened one of my newspapers. It was only with difficulty that I managed to see the headlines. Eventually another two or three men came in, but the train was far from full. It left Oppeln dead on time. What a wonderful feeling it was!

Big X's travel-permit had enabled me to get a ticket all the way to Stettin. I didn't know whether I would have to change but I reckoned I could find out without arousing anyone's suspicions. In my neatly ironed blue trousers, my fur-collared lumber-jacket, my polished boots and my tidily combed hair and clean freshly shaven face I looked quite respectable. No doubt most of the people I spoke to took me to be a German. They may have wondered why I was not in uniform but I did not notice anyone take a particular interest in me.

It was quite light as the train picked up speed, left Oppeln behind and came into the open country. The next town of any size would be Brieg but I did not know whether the train would stop there. I opened one of the newspapers and, having read an article on the '*Terror – Flieger*' (Terror-Raids), I turned to the pages which contained the obituary notices. There were scores of them. Each one was more or less the same, as if they followed a given form. Something like this: 'At the head of his section the brave Underofficer Heinrich Schmidt fell in the heroic battle against the Bolshevik Asiatic Hordes in the defence of his Führer, Volk and Vaterland. He was faithful to the end, his name shall live forever. Heil Hitler!'

The first stop was at Breslau, a very large old town on the Oder and capital of Silesia. It is now within the frontiers of Poland and has reverted to its ancient name of Wroclaw. As we pulled into the station I heard one of the officials call: 'Passengers for Frankfurt-an-der-Oder and Stettin change here!'

I got out and looked at the departure-board. The train for Frankfurt and Stettin would leave from the platform I was on in forty minutes time. I immediately made for the lavatory. There wasn't going to be any hanging about the platform for me, particularly since it was full of people of whom a good ninety per cent were in uniform, so that every civilian stood out like a sore thumb.

Having locked myself in the lavatory, I waited, concentrating on the passage of time. I didn't want to return to the platform too early but I did not want to miss my train either. Needless to say I was in an agony of suspense. I could think of no way in which I could measure the time. I managed it somehow for when I returned to the platform the train was already in and within ten minutes of departure. What was more it was very full. All the seats were taken and even the corridor was crowded but I found room to stand. Most of the passengers were soldiers but next to me sat an elderly woman on a wooden crate. Beside her was another wooden crate on which she invited me to sit. I did so gladly. It would be no bad idea if people thought that we were together.

Soon the train moved off. The next stop, I hoped, would be Frankfurt-an-der-Oder.

The old lady had a couple of live rabbits in the crate on which she sat. I stuck my fingers between the wooden laths and fondled them. The old lady said, 'I'm taking them back to Berlin with me. I shall kill them and eat them. There's no meat to be had from the butchers in Berlin, not even the ration that one is entitled to. Aren't things terrible?'

'Yes indeed,' I said.

'Berlin is a shambles,' she said. 'Between the Amis in the daytime and the Tommies at night there isn't a moment's peace. There'll be nothing left of the town soon, nor of the people either. I've been bombed out twice already. If I could only lay my hands on them – '

'I'm sure you would give it to them,' I said.

'I would hang every one!' she said.

'Where have you been?'

'I've been staying with my daughter in the country. She gave me the rabbits to take back. I've got another two in the crate you are sitting on. They don't know there is a war on where my daughter lives. They have plenty of food and they can sleep at night without having to go to the shelters!'

She rattled on, which pleased me no end. All I had to do was to nod now and again and she was quite satisfied. All she needed was an audience and I was only too pleased to provide one; I could have asked for nothing better. A lone young man in civilian clothing would have attracted more attention than one accompanied by his mother or grandmother.

Somewhere about half-way to Frankfurt my garrulous companion opened her basket and took out a small parcel of sandwiches and a flask of coffee which she insisted I shared. I did so graciously and was very glad to.

Not long after I noticed two military policemen approaching; *Bahnhofswache* was their proper name but they were known to the German soldiers as *Kettenhunde* (Chained Dogs) because of the chains they wore around their necks from which a bar hung on which their designation was written. They were much feared as they were particularly interested in deserters and soldiers who had over-stayed their leave.

As I was a civilian I had hoped that they would take no notice of me, but as they came near I heard one say to the other '*Noch ein Drueckeberger!*' (Here's another dodger).

Then, looking at me with contempt, he said, '*Warum nicht bei Mlitar?*' (Why not in the Forces?)

'*Ich bin Franzose!*' I replied.

'*Franzose? Ausweis vorzeegen!*' (Frenchman? Show your Identity Card!)

I reached into my pocket casually and pulled out my wallet and showed him my Identity Card. He examined it carefully, particularly the photograph. With a grunt he handed it back to me and both moved on.

'Cheeky devils,' said the old woman, 'they are the biggest dodgers. They make sure they don't go to the Russian front!'

She got off at Frankfurt to catch the train to Berlin. My train was going straight to Stettin, over a hundred miles away. I helped her out with her crates of rabbits and thanked her for the sandwiches and her company. A great many passangers had got out and there was room to sit in the compartment. I didn't want to, but thought I had better do so in case my standing in the corridor might look suspicious.

Every occupant of the compartment was a soldier and naturally the corner-seats had been taken. I sat between two soldiers and opened one of my newspapers, offering the other to the soldier sitting next to me. He, however, declined it with a smile, the sort of smile that seemed to convey – What! Do you think I want to read that boring propaganda?

It was early afternoon. A brilliant sunny day and with all the windows closed and the heat full on, it was stiflingly hot. Most of the soldiers soon fell asleep. I wanted to sleep too but I was afraid of doing so in case I leant on one of the two soldiers who sat on either side of me. It was hardly thinkable that either would tolerate such a thing – a healthy looking young man who had obviously dodged the draft having the termerity to use a solder as a cushion! I would have had such a dig in the ribs, and what might my reaction have been on waking suddenly? No, I had to remain awake at all costs. But what a job it was! My eyelids felt like lead and try as I might I just could not stop them from falling. It was agonizing. I concentrated every ounce of my being on the newspaper but the letters literally danced in front of my eyes and I simply could not prevent my chin from falling on my chest. But the worse thing of all was the fact that one of the soldiers by my side was fast asleep with his head on my shoulder. I so much wanted to get up, go to the corridor and hang my head out of the window, but I was too afraid of waking the soldier.

Becoming absolutely desperate I started to pinch by backside. To begin with a light pinch was enough but after a time I had to increase the severity until I was pinching myself so hard that I was nearly screaming and shivers were running up my back and straight to the back of my head. It was the most exquisite torture. I could feel my face go hot and cold alternately and my eyes squinting with the pain. From moment to moment I kept saying to myself: I must get up and damn the soldier, damn every soldier in the compartment, damn every soldier in the German Army! But I kept answering myself: No, you must stick it. You are not going to throw everything away just because you can't keep awake! You must will yourself to keep awake!

What a relief when we reached the outskirts of Stettin! The soldiers awoke one by one and started to get their kit together. The whole train came to life and by the time we were slowing to a stop most of the passengers were already in the corridor ready to open the doors and jump out.

As soon as my feet touched the platform my sleepiness disappeared as if by magic. I was as wide awake and alert as any wolf on the prowl, watching for every sign of danger and ready to take whatever action might seem appropriate.

The passengers were streaming from the platform and through the barrier where the ticket-collector stood. I noticed two men in civilian clothes standing next to the ticket-collector. They looked very much like Gestapo to me, and sure enough that is what they were making spot-checks of people going through. Every third or fourth civilian was having his papers checked. What should I do? Retreat to the toilets and hide there till the platform was empty, or take my chance. The queue of people was moving slowly forward. In front of me walked a woman on her own. I pushed forward until I was right behind her. Just as she was handing in her ticket I caught hold of her arm, my fingers barely touching the sleeve of her coat and with my other hand gave my ticket to the collector. We both went through the barrier side by side. Anyone looking would have sworn we were together. I kept my arm on her sleeve for another few paces. The woman turned and looked at me, with a toss of her head and a baleful look she snatched her arm away. With a nod to her I bounded off, out of the station-hall and into the street. And what a sight! A long, wide, busy street and along side of it the wide estuary of the River Oder with shipping moored as far as they eye could see. Big X had told me how to recognize the ships by their flags. The first one that caught my eye was a big Swedish freighter. What a thrill! And for the first time for nearly four years I was again breathing sea air. That alone was enough to transform me. It was the smell of freedom, a smell that had been absent during the whole of my captivity.

I walked up the busy street in the direction of the centre of the town. There was considerable bomb damage from what must have been a recent air-raid with debris piled up along the pavements. I had not gone far when I saw a gang of Poles cleaning up the bomb damage. They were all wearing a purple 'P' on a yellow background on their jackets. I stopped and watched them knowing that here were people whom I could trust and who would be sure to give me what help they could. Of all the people of the various nationalities that I met in my travels the Poles were the most reliable. Never did a Pole let me down. On the contrary, there was never enough they could do. Having studied them carefully I chose two young men who were working a little apart from the main gang. I went up to them and said, '*Dzien dobry*.' (Good day.)

'*Dzien dobry,*' one of them replied.

'*Pan Polak?*' (Are you a Pole?)

'*Nie, Franzus.*' (No, Frenchman.)

'I am an escaped prisoner of war and looking for an opportunity to get on a ship.'

'Ha! Ha! Ha! That is what we would all like.'

'Is it difficult?'

'Impossible.

'If that's the case, it can't be helped. I'll have to think of something else.'

'Are you hungry?'

'Yes' I replied. I wasn't really, although I had not eaten since the previous evening. I was well used to going without food.

'Come with us then,' they said. Taking off the letter 'P' from their lapels – they had only attached it with a safety pin – they led me to a German *Eintopfrestaurant*. We had a plateful of soup and piece of bread for one mark each. Nothing to write home about but quite substantial.

While we were eating I questioned the Poles about Stettin and the possibility of finding somewhere to stay. They said, 'Come with us. We live in a camp on the outskirts and we can easily hide you there for days. There are about a thousand of us there altogether, most of whom work in various factories in the town. Some of the men work in the docks, unloading and loading the ships.'

When I heard that my heart almost leaped. That was how I could get into the docks, by taking the place of a Pole.

'I would very much like to stay with you in your camp,' I said.

We left the restaurant and took a tram to the Polish camp and got there after about half an hour. We walked in through the unguarded gates and went into one of the barrack-rooms.

'This is where we live,' they said, 'and here is a bed for you. We'll find you some blankets and you can stay here as long as you like. We'll see that you get some food and warn you of any danger.'

While we were talking another Pole came up to us. My two friends explained who I was, so he spoke to me in French, a language he spoke quite fluently. In no time I could see that he was suspicious of me so I told him in French that I was a British RAF pilot escaped from a prisoner-of-war camp but that I didn't want everybody to know. He took me apart and said that he was a Polish Army Officer who had also escaped from a prison camp. He didn't speak English but he spoke German fluently. We continued our conversation in that language.

I told him that I was looking for an opportunity of getting on a Swedish ship. He said that he was trying to do exactly the same thing but that it was very difficult. The ships were watched very closely. They were searched before they were allowed to sail, even tear-gas bombs were thrown into the holds to flush out anyone who might be hiding there. In addition the crews of the ships were terrified of the consequences which would befall them should they be caught helping anyone to stow away.

The news was not very encouraging but I still had another string to my bow – the public house 'Zur Ostsee' in the Kleine Oder-Strasse. I asked the Pole whether he knew it.

'Yes,' he said, 'it is a *Maison de Plaisir* for non-German sailors. As a Pole I am not allowed to go there but I'll show you where it is.'

We got on the tram and went to town and to the Kleine Oder-Strasse. It was about a quarter to seven in the evening and the establishment was open. The Pole said, 'You go in and see whether you can meet some of the Swedish sailors there. This is the likeliest place to find them. The trams run until midnight and the camp gates are open all night. Don't forget the number of the tram. I'll see you in the morning.'

The Girl from Moravska-Ostrava

I entered the *Maison de Plaisir* and found myself in a longish room furnished very comfortably wiht chairs and small tables and settees placed against the length of the wall on one side. On the opposite side was a long bar behind which was an impressive array of bottles of wines and spirits. At the far end of the room was a door.

There were five people in the room – four men in the uniform of the German Merchant Navy who turned out to be Ukrainians, and one young woman, a slim platinum blonde dressed in a pair of blue tight-fitting trousers, a pair of sandals on her feet and nothing else. She was being mauled and pulled about by one of the sailors.

I went about half-way into the room and sat down at a small table. There was no one behind the bar. The sailors were highly amused by the antics of their friend who was trying to force the girl to let him kiss her. She, quite clearly, was determined that he shouldn't and fought like a little tigress. That she was genuinely angry there was no doubt. I felt very uncomfortable, not wanting to show either approval or disapproval of what was going on. I was afraid of Ukrainians because they were very pro-German and had a terrible reputation in Poland where the Germans used them as members of punitive expeditions. I wanted nothing to do with them.

Fate, however, would have it otherwise. The girl tore herself free from her tormentor and came and sat on my knee, putting her arms around my neck. Her pursuer followed her and tried to prise her arms loose. He was joined by one of the other sailors who grabbed hold of one of the girl's arms and twisted it until she screamed in pain.

That was it. I jumped up and pushed the girl to one side, then turned and hit one of the sailors who measured his length on the floor. Before he knew what was happening I had sent the second one flying over chairs and tables. The others then came for me but I picked up a chair and knocked them sideways. By this time the other two were picking themselves up from the floor but, wielding the chair, I sent all four hurtling towards the door.

In the meantime the girl had disappeared through the door at the far end of the room. Almost immediately afterwards a German policeman came rushing through that door with a drawn pistol. Seeing him the Ukrainians scarpered out into the street. The policeman pursued them through the door shouting, '*Verfluchte Bande! Ich werde euch gleich was geben!*' (Cursed bandits! I'll give you something!) He was soon back and, seeing me standing there in the middle of overturned tables and chairs, he rushed at me wielding his pistol as a club and shouting, '*Du auch, du verfluchte Ausländer!*' (You too, you cursed foreigner). But the girl, who had returned, shouted, '*Nein! Nein! Der nicht! Der Nicht! Er hat mir geholfen!*' (No! No! Not him! Not him! He helped me!)

The policeman checked himself, returned his pistol to its holster and, muttering threats and imprecations, went away.

The girl put her arms around my neck and kissed me. 'Thank you,' she said.

I took a good look at her – about twenty-two or three, petite and slim, a pretty face with blue eyes, the hair obviously dyed. More or less the sort of girl one would expect to see in such a place, except that there wasn't that hardness in her face that one would normally associate with a girl who made her living in that way. She was obviously not German, although she spoke it quite well.

'Are you Swedish!' she asked.

'No,' I said, 'French.'

'French! Oh la-la. We don't get many Frenchmen here.'

'Where do you come from?' I asked.

'From Czechoslovakia.'

'And what is your name?'

'Irma. Would you like to come with me?'

'Yes,' I said, 'but where will you take me?'

'Upstairs,' she said, 'if you have twenty marks.'

'Of course, and more.'

'Come then,' and she took my hand. I then noticed that she had two keys suspended from the belt she wore around her waist. Taking the larger of the two she opened the door at the far end of the room, from where the policeman had come.

We found ourselves in a little hallway. To the left was a table behind which sat an elderly woman. Immediately alongside her was a stairway. Irma motioned me to give her the money. I gave her two ten Mark notes. She gave one of them to the woman, then led me up the stairs. At the top we turned left along a narrow corridor. Halfway along it she stopped and opened a door with the second key hanging from her belt.

'*Entrez, Monsieur!*' she said with a betwitching smile.

'*Merci, Mademoiselle*.'

The room was not much bigger than a cubicle. It contained a bed near the wall on the far side, a bedside table, a couple of chairs and a small dressing-table and wardrobe.

'Sit down,' she said. 'Have you any American cigarettes?'

'No, I haven't.'

'Would you like a Chesterfield?'

'I certainly would,' I replied.

She picked up a packet from her dressing-table and offered me one. Taking one herself she lit both with a natty cigarette lighter.

'How do you manage to get American cigarettes?'

'The seamen bring them. By the way, you have a very good leather jacket. Would you like to sell it? I could get a lot of money for that for you.'

'No, I don't want to sell it. What would I do without it?'

'I don't suppose you have any perfume or silk stockings?'

'No, my dear. All I have is what I stand in. But tell me where in Czechoslovakia you come from ?'

'Moravska-Ostrava. I dont suppose you have ever heard of it.'

'On the contrary, I've been there!'

'I dont believe you! What would a Frenchman want in Moravska-Ostrava? When were you there?'

'Just before the war. I was on a cycling tour of Czechoslovakia and I remember going through Moravska-Ostrava on the way to the mountains.'

'Really? Pity we didn't meet. I quite like you.'

'And I like you, Irma. You are a very attractive girl. Do you love your country very much?'

'Love my country? That is a funny question. What has that to do with us two? I suppose everybody loves his country! But people who come to see me don't talk about things like that. But somehow you seem to be different. You are not a German, are you?'

As she asked that question I could see the fear showing plainly in her eyes.

'Of course not! I'm French. The Germans are my enemies. They are occupying my country and ill-treating my people just the same as they are doing in Czechoslovakia.'

I got up and walked to the dressing-table on which I had noticed a framed photograph of a young man. I picked it up and examined it – a young man in Merchant Navy uniform wearing a white-topped peaked cap with anchor badge. He had a frank open face and a sunny smile and looked to me as if he might be Scandinavian.

'Who is this handsome young man?' I asked.

'Oh! That's my very special boyfriend. Isn't he nice?'

'He is a very nice looking young man,' I replied, 'and where does he come from?'

'Sweden.'

My heart nearly missed a beat when I realized the significance of what she had said.

'Oh! And how often do you see him?'

'Every time his ship comes to Stettin he comes here and brings me a lot of lovely things, – soap and perfume and silk stockings, beautiful underwear and all kinds of things.'

'When do you expect to see him next?'

'Tonight. His ship has been here four days and he's been to see me every night.'

'And what is his name?'

'Nils.'

Realizing that only this girl and a few hours separated me from this Swedish seaman I had difficulty in keeping my voice steady. Could any escaping prisoner possibly have dreamt of such good luck? It was as if Providence had intervened at every critical moment since I had broken out of camp at two o'clock that morning – the careless and unsuspecting country policeman, the old lady who had directed me to the station at Oppeln, the old lady with the rabbits on the train, the young lady who unwittingly lent me her arm to get past the barrier on Stettin Station under the very nose of the Gestapo, the two young Poles clearing the bomb damage in the street, the Polish Officer who had brought me to the Kleine Oder-Strasse, the Ukrainian ruffians who had enabled me to get into Irma's good books and now Nils the Swedish seaman. Was it going to last?

In the meantime Irma had removed her blue trousers and was sitting on the bed dressed in the briefest of briefs.

'Come and sit here with me,' she said, 'and don't bother about Nils. You are not jealous, are you?'

'Yes,' I said. 'I am; very jealous. He is very lucky. He has all kinds of things to give you and I have nothing.'

'Never mind. Come and give me a kiss and consider yourself lucky. I don't allow just anybody to give me a kiss.'

I kissed her.

'Do you allow Nils to kiss you?'

'Oh yes. Nils is someone very special. I love Nils very much.'

'And does he love you?'

'He tells me that he does, and I believe him.'

'I'm very glad, Irma. Because if you will forgive me for saying so, you are much too good to be in a place like this.'

'Don't say that. You don't know what you are talking about. This is a thousand times better than a concentration camp or a forced labour camp. I get leave from here and am able to go home to see my family. They don't know what I am doing. They think I work in a hotel.'

'Irma, I know how terrible it is in the occupied countries, in France and Poland and Czechoslovakia. Believe me I know very well although I don't come from any of those countries. I am British!'

'British! You are British? How is that? What are you doing here? Are you a spy? A British spy?'

She stood up, trembling and backing away from me, terror written all over her face. 'No, Irma. Not a spy. I am a pilot. I was shot down and I am now trying to get to Sweden from where I can return to Britain and fly again. Every pilot is needed, Irma. I must get back. Will you help me?'

'No! No!' she cried. 'Leave here at once! They would kill me if they found you here. Don't you know that this place is run by the German Police? You saw the policeman downstairs. He is in charge here. You must go at once. This moment! Don't ever come near me again! If I see you again I'll tell the policeman!'

'Irma,' I said, and put my arms around her, 'listen to me. You are a Czech. Think of what the Germans did to Lidice. You have a duty. You and I are together in this war. There are many Czech pilots flying with the RAF. Would you refuse to help one of them if he came here after being shot down over Germany? Of course you wouldn't. You couldn't. You would help him. But I don't want to endanger you at all. All I want is an introduction to Nils. Nothing else.'

She started to cry. I held her tightly in my arms. She clung to me like a lost child and sobbed and sobbed till she went limp and could cry no more. I raised her head up and kissed her again and again.

'Don't cry, Irma. Don't cry. I'll go downstairs and perhaps I'll meet another Swedish seaman in the bar. Don't cry and don't be afraid. I will not do anything to endanger you. Forget everything I have said. Here, Let me wipe the tears from your eyes.' I wiped her tears and put her to sit on the bed. Reaching for the Chesterfields I lit two cigarettes and put one between her lips.

'Here, smoke this and don't worry any more. There is no need to introduce me to Nils. I'm sure I'll be able to contact someone else.'

Gradually she calmed down. Looking at her watch she said, 'I must go downstairs. How long have we been here? I don't know what I'm doing. I'm so afraid. Wait here. I must go and wash my face.'

She dressed and went out. When she returned some five minutes later she said, 'I will introduce you to Nils but you mustn't go near him if you see him in the bar. Don't take any notice of me either. I shall bring him up here. I shall tell him about you and if he is willing I'll come and fetch you.'

'You are a very brave girl, Irma, and a real patriot.'

'No, I'm not. I'm terrified and I wish you hadn't come here.'

I kissed her again and we went down to the bar.

Nils Nilson

The place was swarming with people and the barmaids were doing a roaring trade. There must have been thirty or forty men there, seamen from the various Scandinavian countries. Some were drinking at the bar while the others were sitting at the tables with the hostesses of which there must have been about a dozen of various shapes and sizes but all young, some mere teenagers.

Having got myself a beer I sat on a sofa near the wall where I could see the whole room. Standing at the bar not far from the entrance door from the street was a group of four men, one of whom I felt pretty certain was Nils. I took a good look at him. He was fair-haired, had a fresh complexion and had an alert and intelligent face, just above medium height and strongly built; he was dressed in a neat blue civilian suit. Two of his companions were older, bigger and heavier than he, while the fourth member of the group was a young lad of about seventeen. All four were drinking spirits.

While I was watching them I saw Irma join the group and touch the man I suspected of being Nils on the arm. He turned round, smiled and said something, then clasped her in his arms and kissed her. He was my man all right, and I watched him with renewed interest. Someone bought a drink for Irma and all five clinked glasses.

It was almost incredible. I had barely been in the place an hour and there I was sitting watching the man who had it in his power to take me to freedom, to make my fifth attempt successful, and what was more I had been promised an introduction to him. I saw Irma turn round, her eyes roaming over the room until they came to rest on mine. Her eyes flashed for an instant before she turned to face her companions. It was an unmistakeable signal that she was going to keep her promise.

Conscious that I looked rather conspicuous sitting there on my own I moved over to a table near where two or three of the hostesses were standing talking to a group of men. One of them was a huge young lady, tall and big with it. She was so generously endowed, so rounded and voluptuous she would have made the celebrated Sabrina look like a consumptive! She could most certainly have stood under a shower without getting her feet wet! She had a round full-cheeked pretty face, large clear blue eyes and lips like ripe cherries. Her long well-brushed flaxen hair hung half-way down her back and shone like gold. Despite her size she was very well-proportioned and not in the least grotesque. She was the sort of woman for any man who thinks that one cannot have too much of a good thing! I looked her right in the face. She flashed me an ivory – toothed smile and walked across to my table.

'*Guten abend, Fraülein. Setzen sie sich bitte.*' (Good evening, miss. Sit down please.) She lowered herself sedately into a chair.

'*Was trinken Sie, Fraulein?*'

'*Koniak, bitte.*' (Brandy.)

I went to the bar and got her one and a beer for myself.

'*Na zdrowie!*' I said.

'*Na zdrowie!*' she said. 'You Polish?'

'*Nein.*'

'*Ukrainiec?*'

'*Nein.*'

'*Deutsch?*'

'*Nein.*'

'*Was denn?*' (What then?)

'*Finne.*'

'Oh, *Finne!* Where is your big knife? You keep your big knife away from me!'

'I've left it on the ship.'

'Good. I'll never forget when the Finns fought the Norwegians with their knives one night. There was blood everywhere.'

'Oh, we are friends again now,' I said.

'So you should be. You come here for pleasure not to fight. Go to Russia if you want to fight.'

'No more fighting,' I said.

I was very glad to have her company. Not only did it help to pass the time away but it also made me less conspicuous.

'Where do you come from?'

'*Ukraina.*'

'Oh! Is that a nice place?'

'It was. But it will never be nice again. It is finished. Everything has been destroyed. All the towns, all the villages. The people have been carted away, some by the Russians, some by the Germans. There are only wolves and bandits left there now. It's a desolation.'

'I'm sorry to hear that.'

'Never mind. Buy me another Cognac. Who cares?'

Another round of drinks.

'*Na zdrowie!*'

'Bah! *Net na zdrowie! Za vashe zdorowie!*'

'What's that?'

'Russian.'

'You speak Russian?'

'Of course, all Ukrainians speak Russian. But we are not Russian, not Polish, we are Ukrainians.'

'Very interesting. Tell me about the Ukraine.'

'No. The Ukraine is finished and soon Germany will be finished. Everywhere will be finished. Who cares? Buy me another Cognac!'

At that rate I could see her being very drunk before long.

'What have you got for me?' she asked suddenly. 'I would like some good coffee. Have you any?'

'No. I haven't been able to bring anything with me this time. But I will definitely bring you some coffee next time.'

'Next time is no good to me. Perhaps there won't be a next time. Soon we'll all be dead under the rubble. Nearly every night the bombers come over. Its no good thinking of next time. Tomorrow might be too late. Sell me that nice leather jacket you've got on.'

'I can't. I need it. I can't go about in my shirt.'

'Why not? Its not cold. Its spring. This is not Russia. I'll get you another jacket instead of it.'

'No. I'll never be able to get another one like this. We've got a war in Finland too you know.'

'Come on. Give it to me and you can come upstairs. How long are you staying here?'

'A week perhaps.'

'You can come upstairs with me every night for a week if you give me that jacket. Wouldn't you like to?'

'Certainly. There is nothing I would like more. You are the prettiest girl here.'

'I like you too. Come on, give me the jacket and we'll have a marvellous time together. Have you ever been with an Ukrainian girl?'

'No. I haven't had the pleasure yet.'

'You don't know what you are missing. No girl can love like an Ukrainian girl. Let me show you!'

She put her arms around my neck and gave me a full-blooded, resounding kiss on the lips.

'There!' she said.

My eyes were continuously wandering to where Irma and Nils stood. I saw them leave their friends and pass through the door in the back of the room. If she kept her promise Irma would soon be coming back for me. I ought to try and get rid of my voluptuous friend.

'I'm sorry I've got nothing for you tonight but I might be able to get something by tomorrow night. I know that some of my friends on board ship have managed to smuggle a few things. As we only arrived today they won't have got rid of them yet, particularly as only a few of us were allowed ashore tonight. What would you like?'

'Anything – silk stockings, silk underwear, a fur coat or cape, perfume, soap, chocolate, coffee. Anything that I can sell in the black market.'

'I'm sure to get you something tomorrow, and then you must take me upstairs and show me how they make love in the Ukraine. Is that a promise?'

'Yes,' she said, 'and when you've been with me you'll never want another woman again. Every time your ship comes to Stettin you'll come to me and you'll bring me lots of lovely things.'

'And I shall too,' I said. 'You can't imagine how much I am looking forward to lying in your arms.'

'I'll hug you like a bear and smother you with kisses. You won't be cold with me.'

'I'm sure I won't.'

'You have a very good shirt too. Let me feel it.'

She felt my good woollen British Army shirt, dyed black.

'*Prima*!' she said. 'Its wool and thick. They make shirts out of wood in Germany now, you can feel the splinters scratching your skin, and when you wash it, it goes stiff as a board. Its *ersatz*. Everything in German is *ersatz*. Sell me your shirt!'

'What! My shirt? I can't go about without a shirt.'

'Yes you can. Fasten the collar of your leather jacket and no one will notice you haven't got a shirt on.'

'No, I can't do that. I can't sell my shirt! I'll bring you something tomorrow.' 'Tomorrow! Tomorrow! Tomorrow is no good to me. I may be dead by tomorrow, We might be bombed tonight. I live for today, and to hell with tomorrow. Come on! If you give me that shirt you can come upstairs with me. It won't cost you anything. I'll give you back the twenty Marks and I'll love you so much you'll never, ever forget it. Come on darling, I like you so much.' She bent across and gave me another resounding kiss. I got up and filled our glasses.

'*Za vashe zdorowie*!'

Just then Irma appeared. She came up to me and caught hold of my arm. I got up, but so did my would-be concubine – the living proof that hell has no fury like a woman scorned. The first few oaths that she spat out must have been in Russian or Ukrainian for I did not understand them. But she followed them up with a few in Polish and German which I did understand. They were particularly blood-curdling. She wanted to know how I could possibly prefer that skinny, flat-chested little mare to her voluptuous self.

I stood between them feeling like a bone between two dogs, and terrified that Irma might withdraw and leave me to my fate as we were attracting attention. Shaking the Ukrainian fury loose, I allowed Irma to lead me through the door and up the stairs. As we went up she said, 'You managed to find a real nice girl, didn't you? You are not fit to be left on your own.'

We entered her room. Nils was sitting on the bed, a glass of liquor in his hand. He got up and came towards me.

'You Tommy?'

'Yes, I'm a Tommy' I said. 'I'm a Royal Air Force pilot. Are you from Sweden?'

'Yes. My name is Nils Nilson and I come from Stockholm. Drink?'

'Thank you very much. I would like a drink, please.'

He turned his back and poured me out a drink.

'Skol!'

'Your health, Nils!' We drank to each other.

'What is it?' He indicated the liquor in the glass.

'Whisky,' I said. 'Good Scotch whisky.'

'Right. You know Scotch whisky, eh?'

'Of course, once tasted never forgotten.'

'Where do you come from in England? London, Manchester, Liverpool?'

'From Wales, Nils.'

'Where is that?'

'You have heard of the Prince of Wales?'

'Prince of Vales? Yes, where is Vales?'

'Cardiff is in Wales. A big port in the south.'

'Oh Cardiff! Yes, I know. I have been to Cardiff. You from Cardiff?'

'No, Cardiff is in Wales and I come from Wales. I live on a farm in the mountains.'

'You are not a German?'

'No, Nils.' I showed him my false passport.

'You are French?'

'No, British. We made the passport in the camp. Better to pretend to be French than German.'

He took out a packet of Lucky Strike cigarettes.

'You know this cigarette?'

'Yes, Lucky Strike, American cigarettes.'

'Read the packet.'

I read the words on the packet.

'Good. You British. You not German. You come with me to Sweden, yes?'

'With the greatest of pleasure, Nils. And if you take me you will get a lot of money from the British Ambassador in Stockholm.'

'Yes? A lot of money? Good, I take you.'

Irma was watching and listening between tears and laughter. She must have been very relieved that my identity had been established beyond doubt and to have Nils share her dangerous secret.

'You know Vera Lynn?'

'Of course. She is an English singer. She sings songs for the soldiers.'

'Sing. Sing like Vera Lynn.'

I cleared my throat and croaked:

'There'll be Blue Birds over.
The white cliffs of Dover.
Tomorrow, just you wait and see.
There'll be joy and laughter.
And peace ever after.
Tomorrow when the world is free.

Very good! Bravo! You OK. You RAF pilot. I take you on my ship. Take you to Stockholm.'

'When?'

'Tonight. I take you on my ship tonight and maybe three or four days to Stockholm.'

'That's wonderful, Nils. Can I give Irma a kiss?'

'Yes. You give Irma a big kiss. Irma very good girl. I take Irma to Stockholm one day.' I gave Irma not one kiss but many kisses. She was crying from excitement, relief and fear.

'Irma will take you downstairs. Then she will come back. You wait for me. One hour maybe, I come down. I go out. You come out. I wait for you. OK Tommy?'

'O.K. Nils.'

'*Dowidzenia*, Irma. I shall always remember you.'

She took me downstairs, then returned to Nils. I went to the bar and bought a beer.

The incredible had happened! It was about ten o'clock, just eighteen hours since I had broken out of Derschau camp. In that time not only had I travelled some four hundred miles across Germany but I had got a firm promise that I would be on a Swedish ship that very night. It seemed that not only was I going to achieve the practically impossible, which was to escape from Germany, but I was going to do it in record time!

The room was packed with noisy, drunk seamen. Some of the girls were also very high, their faces flushed and their voices raised in an excited and inebriated babble as they were being mauled and pawed by the men, some of whom could barely stand upright.

I had to try and avoid my Ukrainian walkie-talkie doll at all costs. She must have found a client who had something other than money to offer. I retreated to one of the settees. The danger was very far from over. Was it not more than likely that such a place would be a happy hunting ground for the Gestapo? What would they be looking for? More than likely for disaffected Germans wanting to flee the country. Deserters from the Wehrmacht. Even spies moving in or out of the country or meeting their couriers. The possibilities were endless and the more I thought of them the more frightened I became. So much so in fact that I convinced myself that I looked frightened and stood out as an obviously suspicious character. Why was I on my own? Who ever heard of a seaman coming ashore on his own? Such a thing was impossible. All the others were in groups, Swedes, Norwegians, Danes, Finns, all in their own groups. I look around the room; I was the only one sitting on his own. Realizing I was doing the worst possible thing I got up and moved to the bar. Leaning sideways I pretended to be a part of a group of three or four men who were laughing and joking together. I pretended to look amused, to smile and to be following the conversation. Inside I was in an agony of impatience. But there was nearly an hour to wait before Nils came. That hour had to be got through. I did get through it, although I shall never know how. The temptation to down half-a-dozen brandies in quick succession was almost overwhelming, but I knew that would be a very silly thing to do.

Eventually I saw Nils and Irma come through the door and join two or three men at the bar a few feet away from me. They drank, they chatted, they looked around. They saw me and turned away. My heart was beating. Any moment now. I daren't look. Instead I looked towards the street door. I waited, struggling to control my impatience, a set and probably vapid smile on my face. Would Nils never leave? I stole another glance at him. He was kissing Irma! May it be his last goodnight kiss! He was saying something to his companions. He was walking towards the door. He was going through it. I glanced idly around the room, then back at the men I pretended to be with. I lifted my glass, looked at it, emptied it, pretended to look at the watch I didn't have, turned away from the bar, took a last look around the room, pretended to laugh at the antics of a couple of seamen and one of the girls in the far end, then with a last look at where Irma stood I strolled casually towards the street door and went out. Nils was standing on the pavement lighting a cigarette.

'Come,' he whispered.

It was dark. There were no street lights. There were no people about. We walked side by side at a medium pace through the empty streets. We did not speak. I was terrified at the noise of our footsteps but Nils did not seem to be aware of it. Probably he had never needed to walk quietly, to move stealthily, like a hunted animal. Sweden was a free country; Swedes were not in the habit of moving about furtively.

We hardly met a soul as we walked through the blacked-out streets, and for that I was very grateful for I did not want to be stopped and made to show my Identity Card at that critical time. What would a French electrician be doing with a Swedish sailor at that time of night? We would both have been taken to the nearest Police Station for futher inquiries.

Eventually we arrived at the riverside opposite to where Nils' ship was moored in midstream, only to find a sentry pacing up and down near the boat-jetty.

'What shall I do, Nils?'

'OK Tommy, OK. Everything all right.'

He stuck two fingers in his mouth and gave a loud whistle. It was answered from the ship.

'Boat coming,' he said.

The sentry walked up to us.

'*Hallo, Fritz!*' said Nils, '*kalt, nix gut! Nix Regen, Englische Flieger komm. Bomb! Bomb! Bomb! Stettin alles kaput!*'

'*Keine angst,*' said the sentry, who was an elderly man, obviously too old for the Russian front, '*die kommen nicht, unsere Luftwaffe sorgt dafür.*'

'*Ja, Ja,*' said Nils, '*englische Flieger kommt heute, uberall bomb, bomb, alles kaput.*'

'*Quatsch!*' said the old sentry. '*Wenn sie kommen dann fallen die Bomben auf dein Schiff, Ha! Ha! Ha!*'

'*Nix auf mein Schiff, auf Stettin. Engländer nicht bomben Schwedische Schiff. Englander bomben Deutsche Schiff, Deutsche Kriegsmarine.*'

A rowing-boat was approaching the jetty. It touched alongside. Nils whispered 'Go!' I climbed down the steps and Nils said something to the oarsman. He shoved off immediately. The old sentry shouted, '*Hallo! Du! Ich habe deinen Ausweis nicht gesehen!*' (I haven't seen your passport.)

'*Bitte?*' I shouted (I beg your pardon)

'*Dein Ausweis, du verfluchte Lump!*' (Your passport, you damned rascal.)

'*Bitte?*' I shouted again.

'*Warte bis morgen! Ich kenn dich wieder!*' (Wait till tomorrow! I'll know you again.)

'*Bitte?*' – my last word on leaving Germany!

In the meantime we were rapidly approaching the ship. The oarsmen addressed me but I did not reply. He did not persist, although he must have known that I did not belong to the ship's company.

There was a rope-ladder hanging down the side of the ship. I grabbed it and climbed up quickly and stood at the rail. The boat returned for Nils. He arrived about five minutes later and both he and the oarsman climbed on deck.

'*Komm,*' he said and took me to a deck cabin. He called the oarsman in and held a short conversation with him in Swedish. The latter looked at me curiously but gave me a welcoming and friendly smile before returning on deck where he was on watch.

'Sit, Tommy' said Nils. 'I come back in two minutes.'

When he returned he was accompanied by a tall, heavy man in his thirties.

'Ingemar,' he said. 'Donkey-man.'

'Where do you come from? asked Ingemar.

'Wales,' I replied.

'Cardiff or Barry?'

'No, from a very small country town in North Wales. You would not know it if I told you.'

'I know Cardiff and Barry. I have been there many times.'
'For coal, yes?'
'Yes. Welsh steam coal, the best coal in the world.'
'You speak very good English, Ingemar.'
'I have been to see all my life. I have been everywhere. America, Australia, Canada, New Zealand. Everywhere I have spoken English.'
Nils was fiddling with the radio dials. Suddenly he said: 'Listen Tommy! Listen! Who is that?'
I listened. It was Vera Lynn singing:- 'When they sound the last all-clear!'
'Vera Lynn!' I said.
'Yes, Tommy, yes. It's Vera Lynn!'
Nils was as pleased and as excited as a schoolboy. Any lingering doubts which he may have harboured were now totally dispelled.
'You like Vera Lynn, Tommy?'
'Yes. She's not bad.'
'Not bad! In Sweden we like Vera Lynn very much!'
'Are you hungry?' asked Ingemar.
'Well, I could eat,' I said.
Apart from the vegetable soup with the two young Poles I had not had anything since about eight o'clock the previous evening.
I had some food and a glass of *aquavit*, a particularly fiery brand of Danish schnapps. Nils and Ingemar discussed where to hide me.
Finally the latter said, 'Tonight you will sleep in my cabin where there is an empty bunk. You will be safe. Every time I go out I shall lock the door. In two days we go to the Freie Hafen to load coal; that is some ten miles down the river. One and a half days to load coal, then we go to Stockholm, OK?'
'OK. Ingemar.'
They took me down a companion-way, having first made sure that the coast was clear. Ingemar had a spacious and well-appointed cabin with two bunks, one above the other. I was given the top bunk and, despite the excitement of the day, I slept well.

The Freie Hafen

The following morning Ingemar went for his breakfast, locking the door behind him. When he returned he brought a plateful of food and a cup of coffee for me. I had already got up and dressed for I wanted to be ready for anything that might happen. I didn't fancy being caught with my pants down as the saying goes.

Before going to his duty Ingemar said, 'Don't worry; if the RAF comes and starts bombing, I shall come back to unlock the door.'

'OK Ingemar. I shall not worry.'

I laid myself down on the bunk and indulged myself in smoking Lucky Strikes and reading old copies of *Life*. Old they may have been but most of the contents were news to me after nearly four years in Germany.

Ingemar returned several times during the day to see if I was all right and to bring me food, making sure that he locked the door on going out. About six o'clock Nils came to say he was going ashore to see Irma and to reassure her that everything was all right. I asked him to thank her for me and to give her my love. Ingemar would stay on board.

That evening we sat in the cabin drinking and talking. About half past seven Ingemar went to the galley to get some food for us, forgetting to lock the door after him. Thinking that he would not be long, I didn't worry unduly. I got quite a shock, however, when the door opened and a strange seaman walked in. He stopped short on seeing me and looked in utter amazement. I got up from my chair and stared back at him, not knowing what to do. He said something in Swedish. I remained silent. He came forward a couple of steps and looked around, his eyes coming to rest on the top bunk.

I jumped towards the door, closed it and placed my back against it. I was determined that the stranger should not leave before Ingemar's return.

He turned towards me and said, '*Parlez-vous Français?*'

I made no reply, just stared at him. Then, '*You speak English?*' I still made no reply.

'*Deutsch?*' I just continued to stare at him, praying that Ingemar might come back very soon.

The seaman was undecided what to do. He stood about a couple of paces away from me looking very tense. We were like a couple of cockerels weighing each other up prior to doing battle to the death.

But suddenly I was pushed forward and sideways as Ingemar opened the door and walked in with a tray of food. He stood stock-still for a few seconds, then laughed out loud.

'It's OK Tommy!' he said. 'Don't be afraid.'

'Tommy?' said the strange seaman. 'Are you English?'

I nodded.

'Tommy is an RAF pilot,' said Ingemar, finishing his explanation in Swedish. Whereupon my unexpected visitor gave me his hand saying, 'Lars! I am Danish from the Faeroe Islands. I thought you were going to kill me!' He laughed.

'I'm sorry,' I said. 'I just didn't know what to do.'

'Everything is OK,' said Ingemar, 'but I must not leave the door unlocked again.'

The following day Nils and Ingemar told me that I would no longer be safe in the cabin as the ship was weighing anchor before proceeding to Freie Hafen and that she might be searched.

So, while most of the crew were at their midday meal I was taken to the engine-room and hidden under one of the huge boilers. There was about a foot of space between the bottom of the boiler and the floor where I lay face downwards. It was very hot but not dangerously so as the boiler was asbestos-lined.

After lying there for about an hour I heard the throb of the engines and later felt the ship moving. We were on our way. The first stage of the voyage had started and I was still undetected. It was a particularly thrilling moment and despite my ability to imagine all kinds of obstacles and dangers I had a strong conviction that with men like Nils and Ingemar I would reach Stockholm. The latter had told me that I had been particularly lucky that Lars had not reported my presence on board to the Captain. He was very anti-British because of our invasion of Iceland. He had, however, managed to persuade him to keep quiet and was confident that he could do so, if only to keep him and Nils out of trouble.

Eventually the movement of the ship ceased and the noise of the engines died out. We had reached the Freie Hafen. Confirmation of this soon came when I heard the coal dropping into the holds with a noise like thunder. I trembled with relief when I realized how lucky I was to be lying uncomfortably under the hot boiler and not crushed to death under the coal in the hole. The thought made all discomfort vanish.

I remained there without food or drink all that night and all the following day until late evening. It was pitch dark and time meant nothing. I must have slept for most of it, but at last I saw a beam of light from a torch and heard a loud whisper: 'Tommy! Tommy! Come!'

I crawled out and saw Nils and Ingemar.

'OK Tommy?'

'Yes, I'm OK.'

'The ship has finished loading coal and will be sailing early tomorrow morning. The Germans will come and search everywhere so you cannot stay here. We will take you to the water-ballast tanks in the bottom of the ship. You will be safe there. Nobody can go there, but eat this first.'

The gave me some sandwiches and coffee. Having eaten, I was taken to the very bottom of the ship where the water-ballast tanks are situated. They are a series of tanks connected by pipes and run the entire length of the ship. When the ship is empty they are flooded with sea-water to keep her down and save her bobbing about on the surface like a cork, but when the holds are full they are empty. Access to them is gained through a screwed-down water-tight steel cover. Having descended into the very bowels of the ship Nils and Ingemar loosened the nuts on the steel cover with a huge spanner. It was no light task but after much effort the cover was lifted.

'Down you go, Tommy,' said Ingemar. 'You will be perfectly safe. No one can find you there. As soon as we are in the open sea we will come for you.'

'Everything OK,' I said, 'but don't forget I'm here!'

I lowered myself down feet first and found myself in a shallow tank which allowed just enough room for me to sit with my feet stretched out but it was not high cnough for me to remain upright. I had to bend my head forward. I heard the cover being replaced and the nuts tightened. I was in total darkness, sitting in a couple of inches of water and there was a nasty dank and rusty smell. Panic almost seized me. I felt like shouting: 'Let me out! Let me out! Better anything than this! I'll take my chance under the boiler!' But I knew it was no use, no one would hear me. For better or for worse I would have to stay until my friends came for me. There was no alternative.

I took myself severely in hand, reminded myself that I had decided before breaking out of camp that I would face the consequences without a whimper whatever they might be. Nevertheless I couldn't forget Nils' words to the sentry on the quay – '*Englische Flieger komm – bomb! bomb! bomb!*' It must have been around the 20th April, Hitler's birthday! I hoped that if the RAF were bringing him a special greeting they would deliver it somewhere other than Stettin. If the ship were struck my chances of survival would have been slim indeed. But turning it over in my mind I considered that I was not much worse off than the people that were sheltering in the Underground in London who might also be the victims of a direct hit and they were civilians, women and children mostly. And what about the submariners? Weren't they in a far more dangerous place than I was?

With such thoughts did I try to comfort myself. It was extremely claustrophobic in the tank. I did not have as much room in it as I would have had in a coffin. I reckoned that should the ship sail the following morning the longest I would have to remain there would be forty-eight hours. Two whole days of complete isolation, but at the end of it a reward such as I had never dared to dream of. I concentrated on that. Freedom! Stockholm! What a celebration I would have!

I had to deal with those forty-eight hours. How? The answer – by going into suspended animation like a hibernating squirrel or an Indian fakir. Could I do it? Why not? If an Indian could do it, so could I. And I did it! I willed myself to sleep and I slept. Whenever I awoke I willed myself back to sleep. I am positive that I slept for ninety per cent of the time I spent in that tank!

As it turned out I was incarcerated for over sixty hours in that tank and Nils and Ingemar lifted off the steel cover without my hearing them. I believe that it was the light from their torch that woke me up. Then I heard them shout, 'Tommy! Tommy! Come out!'

I tried to reply but only managed a croak. The dampness had impaired my vocal chords.

'Tommy! Tommy! Come!' I struggled towards the man-hole but was so stiff that I could hardly move. Ingemar stretched down and, grabbing me by the collar, dragged me up.

'OK Tommy, OK!' said Nils. 'Goodbye Germany, Stockholm tomorrow!'

They took me to the cabin. I saw my face in the mirror. It was like the face of a ghost, so white was it.

'No need to worry any more,' said Ingemar. 'We are six hundred miles from Germany. The Gestapo will never get you now!'

'What day is it?' I asked.

'Sunday.'

'What time is it?'

'Twenty after three.'

I had been in the tank since Thursday night. But I had made it. I had escaped from Germany at the fifth attempt!

They gave me food. When it got dark they said, 'Come with us.'

I followed them. We went up on deck.

'Look! Sweden!'

We were sailing up the east coast of Sweden. I could see towns and villages all lit up. No black-out. It was like looking at fairyland.

'That is Gotland,' said Ingemar. 'As you can see, no black-out. We are in Swedish territorial waters.'

The lights more than anything convinced me that I was out of Germany where the only lights that shone at night were those of prisoner-of-war and concentration camps!

The Phantom of the Opera

The following day, Monday, 23 April, the ship docked in Stockholm, exactly one week since my break-out from Derschau camp in Upper Silesia about 1,500 miles away.

I should have been leaping with joy; instead I gazed impassively at the scene which presented itself as if it was scarcely real. The reason, most probably, was the fact that once I was on board the ship I had ceased to play an active part in the proceedings, no more than if I had been an item of freight. It was Nils and Ingemar who had taken the active role. It was a situation to which I was quite unaccustomed.

Ingemar borrowed a seaman's Identity Card and a mackintosh from a member of the crew. With the former in my breast-pocket and wearing the latter, I walked boldly through the dock-gates flanked by Nils and Ingemar. Flashing our cards at the policeman we went through unchallenged and got into a taxi. In the centre of town we got out and took another taxi to the British Legation.

We got out outside the Legation; it appeared that in those days Sweden did not measure up to an Embassy, surprisingly enough since that country, being neutral and situated so close to Germany, Finland and Russia, was a hive of diplomatic activity, intrigue and espionage.

We rang the bell on the massive door above which we could see the Royal Arms and the words: HM Legation.

It was opened by a short, elderly gentleman who looked at us with what appeared to be irritation at being disturbed after working hours and asked us curtly in English but with a pronounced Irish accent what we wanted.

'I am an escaped prisoner of war from Germany,' I replied.

'Be jabers you are!' he said. 'All three of you?'

'No, just me. These two people are Swedish seamen who brought me over in their ship.'

'Come in! Come in!' he said, 'and aren't you the lucky one! You are not English, are you? Would you be Irish now by any chance?'

'Welsh,' I replied.

'Welsh be jabers. That's what you are, you say. You may be right at that, but be jabers, you have the luck of the Irish! Sit yourselves down all of you and have a cigarette. I don't suppose you had many cigarettes in Germany and I don't suppose you had too much to eat either. Come on now, light up and I'll go and phone the Military Attaché. He'll be glad, that he will.'

He was a garrulous old gentleman. We lit up and puffed away while he disappeared into another room to telephone.

When he came back he said, 'Didn't I say you had the luck of the Irish! I just managed to catch Major Wright before he went out and he is sending a car for you. You'll sleep in a feather bed tonight my boy and you'll get a good supper. I don't suppose the Jerries gave you any supper.'

He chatted away until the car arrived. A Daimler, flying the Union Jack and driven by a uniformed chauffeur, took us to No 10 Banier Gataan, the residence of the Military Attaché who, with his wife and daughter, was waiting for us on the doorstep. When we got out of the car he came forward with outstretched arm.

'Which one is it?' he asked.

'Me, Sir,' I replied.

'And these two gentlemen? You haven't brought a couple of Germans with you, have you?'

'No. These two gentlemen are Swedish seamen who brought me over from Stettin at considerable risk to themselves.'

I presented Nils and Ingemar. Major Wright shook their hands. Turning to me, he said, 'Congratulations. A marvellous achievement! It must be a wonderful feeling for you.'

'It is,' I said, 'but I'm not sure whether it isn't all a dream.'

'Come and meet my wife and daughter,' he said. 'Then perhaps you'll realize that it isn't!'

There followed another round of handshaking.

'Let's go into the house,' said Mrs Wright, 'and we'll all have a little drink.'

After a drink of sherry I could see Mrs Wright starting to make preparations for a meal, so I said, 'Please don't go to any trouble on our account. We had our supper before leaving the ship. I happen to know that you were on the point of going out when we arrived. Don't let us interfere with your plans. We are quite capable of looking after ourselves.' I meant that too, as I was looking forward to a night on the town with my two friends.

'Good gracious!' said Mrs Wright. 'We wouldn't dream of going out now that you are here. In any case, we were only going to the pictures.'

To the pictures! I had almost forgotten that there were such things.

'An English-language film?' I asked.

'Yes. *The Phantom of the Opera* with Claude Raines, a real hair-raiser they say.'

A hair-raiser!

'You must go,' I said, 'and if I may I would like to come with you. That is, if you don't mind?'

'Mind? Not at all. But are you sure?'

'Yes,' I said. 'I can't imagine anything better than a real spine-chiller after all those boring years in a prison camp!'

For a moment they looked at me rather strangely, then Major Wright said, 'Yes, I suppose it must have been rather boring.'

Nils and Ingemar took their leave after arranging to call at ten o'clock the following morning to be presented to the Minister.

We went to the pictures in the Legation car. It was a posh cinema and we sat in the best seats.

I enjoyed the film, although I doubt whether my hair stood on end or that my spine was particularly chilled. The film was a mixture of horror and sentiment both of which seemed to affect the eighteen-year-old and very attractive Mary, who sat next to me on one side and who on occasions seemed to be rather closer than she ought to be. To avoid any temptation I folded my arms and kept my eyes on the screen. I shall always remember the theme-song of the film:

'Hear those bells ringing soft and low,
Ringing clear through the evening glow.'

It being a fine April evening I was asked whether I minded walking home. On my replying that nothing would be more pleasant, the chauffeur who had called for us was dismissed.

We walked home through a long, narrow street flanked by mediaeval buildings, Major and Mrs Wright leading, Mary and I bringing up the rear. As we went under a low archway, Mary said naively, 'It is a tradition in Stockholm that when a boy and a girl walk under this arch they kiss each other.'

Taking that to be an invitation and being a gallant Welsh Guardsman I obliged, just to please her. From her reaction it appeared that I did!

Such was my first evening of freedom, having been a prisoner, on and off, for three years and ten months.

* * *

Three weeks later I crawled out of the bomb bay of the Mosquito aircraft which ferried the diplomatic bag between London and Stockholm.

'Where are we?' I asked.

'Leuchars in Scotland,' came the answer! I had indeed made a 'home-run!'

Epilogue

In 1984 I visited Poland for the first time since the war. The purpose of my visit was to find those three brave little girls who, in 1943, at great risk to their lives, led me and my two companions over the closely guarded frontier separating the annexed western territories of Poland from the occupied territories.

Since I had never known their names or address, nor even the name of the village in which they lived and since, for reasons connected with certain duties in which I had been engaged I could not travel to Poland before 1984, I had been unable to make any enquiries concerning them. However, I had never ceased to think about them nor to hope that they had found Little Wanda where she had been left alone in the middle of the forest at dead of night and that all three had returned safely to their parents.

I did locate them. They had found Little Wanda where they had left her and had returned home safely before dawn. Not only that – they had also conducted several other parties over the frontier before the war ended in 1945. They had not received any kind of recognition for their heroism. In fact, I was the first person to contact them and to thank them.

As one can imagine our meeting was very emotional.

All three are married. Two, Krystyna Perkowska, the eldest, and Kazimiera Kaptacz are still living in the same village, the name of which I now know to be Zarki, while Little Wanda, the only name I remembered from that memorable night and whose surname is now Malinowska, lives about thirty miles away.

On my return to this country I wrote to our Ambassador in Warsaw and gave him a detailed account of the heroic action of these three ladies in 1943 when they were mere children, the eldest being only thirteen. I suggested that they should be suitably recognized for their bravery.

After the exchange of a few letters and after the Ambassador had checked my account from War Office records, I received the following letter, together with a number of photographs, one of which is reproduced in this book:

From Group Captain M. R. Jackson RAF
Office of the Defence Attaché
British Embassy
Warsaw
15.8.86

Flight Lieutenant J. Elwyn DCM RAF (Retd)
'Llidiardau'
Clawddnewydd
Rhuthun
Clwyd
North Wales

Dear Flight Lieutenant Elwyn,

I thought you might be interested in having the enclosed photographs which were taken on 23 May this year in Zarki, when my RAF serjeant and I visited Pani Perkowska, Pani Kaptacz and Pani Malinowska. We were greeted most warmly by the ladies and their husbands, and it was quite clear to us that the bravery they demonstrated during the war is still very much part of their nature.

It was a memorable day at the end of which I gave them invitations to attend my annual reception in Warsaw to commemorate the anniversary of the Battle of Britain. I very much hope they will be able to attend, and in the hope that you may also, I enclose an invitation for yourself.

Thank you for helping us to establish this connection,

Yours sincerely,
Michael Jackson

Unfortunately, I was not able to attend, but I hope that these brave Polish ladies did and above all I am glad that they have at least received some measure of recognition for their heroism.

As I am able to write Polish I correspond regularly with all three and I look forward to doing so for many years yet as my gratitude to them and my admiration for them will never cease.

August, 1986